SHOOTING STAR
THE *Amazing Life* OF *Ann Marston*

BY ALANA PALUSZEWSKI

To Judy,

Best regards,

Alana

2007

Published by Momentum Books, L.L.C.

2145 Crooks Road, Suite 208
Troy, Michigan 48084
www.momentumbooks.com

ISBN-10: 1-879094-78-9
ISBN-13: 978-1-879094-78-9
LCCN: 2006939983

Cover image courtesy of *Sports Illustrated*. Photograph of Ann Marston by
Courneye Tourcotte, courtesy Miss Michigan Organization.

Table of Contents

Introduction

EVEN THOUGH WE LIVED IN THE SAME CITY, I never met Ann Marston. I remember watching her on television in *The Story Princess*. It is quite possible that I went to one of her archery demonstrations in the Detroit area. I attended many local dances in the '60s which featured bands that she managed. We shared a mutual friend, who told me that she was helping a blind woman, who turned out to be Ann, and I remember when the newspapers reported Ann's death in 1971. She was so young.

Ann Marston floated back into my awareness while I was compiling *The Pride of Wyandotte: The History of Roosevelt High School 1923-2003*. She was an obvious choice for a chapter on distinguished graduates. Around the same time, Ann's mother Florence died. I introduced myself to Pamela Wood at Wyandotte's Nixon's Funeral Home. She was the only relative who was present. While Florence Marston lay in her casket the night before her burial, Pam and I decided Ann's remarkable story should be told.

Pam generously shared the family's artifacts, memorabilia, and documents, which took a full year to sort and catalog. The items included archery records, home movies, costumes, photographs, audio recordings, newspaper and magazine stories, and public relations material. The quality of the data varied. Ann's mother saved a massive amount of clippings and articles, but many items did not have dates or recognizable sources to credit. Florence was guilty of perpetuating myths to enhance

Ann's publicity, so it was often challenging to uncover the truth. Every effort was made to identify the facts and cite resources in this text.

The reality is indisputable—Ann had beauty, skill, and intelligence. She was competitive, charming, and was a very successful female athlete at a time when women were still somewhat inhibited. Ann was more famous than her friends and neighbors realized, even when they were watching her perform on the top television shows of the era or compete in the Miss America Pageant. She was a hometown girl, and enjoyed living in a small, middle-class community.

Ann was the sole support of her family from the time she was a young teenager until her mid-twenties. As much as she loved her parents, she deeply resented her mother's domination. As a result, Ann did not have the opportunity to have a life and family of her own. In her career, she knew many of the world's most famous celebrities, including Ed Sullivan, Johnny Carson, Joe DiMaggio, and The Beatles. Ultimately, she died a lonely woman.

The chronicle of Ann's life history is complete. She will continue to be an inspiration and positive role model to young people. She was a gifted athlete, celebrity performer, beauty queen, and businesswoman. Her lifelong struggle with diabetes highlighted her tremendous strength of character. Courage was Ann's most outstanding trait. She proved it even though the disease took her sight, her independence, and her life.

Love and gratitude is extended to my supportive family, especially my husband, Richard, for allowing Ann's life to become such a big part of ours. Inspiration came from friends who are sight impaired, particularly Hope Springstead, Dan Henderson, and Tammy Grimes. They each demonstrate that a person's greatest vision comes from within, as Ann learned. Young Emily McGrath's future as a diabetic will be brighter than Ann's because of continued medical research and the support of the Juvenile Diabetes Foundation.

The staff at Momentum Books has generously offered advice and encouragement. My professional and personal thanks are extended to Edward Peabody, Steve Wilke, Kelly Gehart, and Leah Clark. It would be impossible to list all of the people who assisted with research. I appreciate everyone who responded to the query, "Did you know Ann Marston?" Ann would be pleased to know that many of her friends are now my friends, too.

Most important to this project were Ann's personal journals dated from 1955 to 1966. The diaries provided more than an accurate timeline. They enabled Ann to tell much of this story in her own words.

Alana Paluszewski
February 2007

PROLOGUE

ANN MARSTON spent the morning of Tuesday, March 3, 1971, working in the basement apartment of her parent's suburban Detroit home. The previous night, one of the rock bands she managed auditioned for Punch Andrews—the same music producer who promoted Bob Seger, and she had high hopes that her group would be considered for a recording contract. At age thirty-two, Ann was a successful agent for several young musical groups, such as Tea and Julia. There was always paperwork waiting to be completed for her business, but she was legally blind—a tragic side-effect of diabetes. If the light was very bright, she could see well enough with her binocular-strength glasses to use the typewriter.

Music was an important part of Ann's life—she had a piano, a tape recorder, stereo system, and a diverse collection of record albums in her bedroom. The Beatles were still her favorite group, even though they had disbanded in 1970. George Harrison and Paul McCartney telephoned her occasionally after she met them at Olympia Stadium in 1964.

Shelves over the built-in bar area were reserved for the archery trophies that Ann and her parents, Frank and Florence, had earned. She garnered eleven national titles herself, including the first one in her native England when she was only nine years old. By the time she was fifteen, Ann was the United States Women's champion in Field Archery. (The minimum age was supposed to be eighteen, but she broke every record in the Junior division and was allowed to compete with the adults.) For several years she dominated the field and was featured on the cover of *Sports Illustrated* magazine.

A baseball signed by her friend Joe DiMaggio was on display, along with other personal treasures collected over the years. More awards and commendations filled the walls of the living room upstairs. Ann's photo albums and journals documented her life as a competitor and highlighted her show business career. She appeared frequently on television, including Ed Sullivan's *Toast of the Town* show. She made three movies and a television pilot, and performed her archery act at hundreds of sports shows, fairs, and rodeos. Ann had also worked with most of America's entertainment legends including Dick Van Dyke, Johnny Carson, Captain Kangaroo, Roy Rogers, and Andy Griffith.

The closets in the dormer storage rooms on the upper floor were filled with dozens of glittery costumes and the props and tackle that Ann had used in her archery act. A wardrobe cabinet encased the white lace dress that she wore in the Miss America Pageant and a large wooden box that held the Miss Michigan crown.

Ann loved poodles, and wall shelves in the knotty pine-paneled room held her large collection of china poodle figurines. Her own dog, a black miniature named Charlie Brown, stayed close to her, as always.

Ann's father had already left for work that morning when her mother heard Charlie Brown whimpering in the basement. She went downstairs to investigate, and found Ann collapsed on the floor. Florence frantically called a neighbor, an ambulance, and her husband. Ann had suffered a massive cerebral hemorrhage and was rushed to Detroit's Henry Ford Hospital.

Four days later, Ann was still in a coma and connected to a ventilator. Florence held Ann's hand and talked to her softly. Frank sat quietly and watched as the life slowly faded from his only child. The Marstons' world revolved around their talented daughter, and now the doctors said there was no hope for her recovery. When Ann had said goodbye to her father on Tuesday morning, it was the last time he would hear her speak.

1

BORN IN THE SHADOW OF SHERWOOD FOREST

ANN PENELOPE MARSTON was born on August 7, 1938, in London on Priory Park Road, Kilburn. Ann was an attractive baby with a full head of hair, bright eyes, and a sunny disposition. Her mother, Florence, entered Ann in a beauty contest at ten months old. She won the competition for Class "A" girls aged nine to twelve months, and was launched into a modeling career. Baby Ann posed for a wide variety of advertisements—from children's clothing to medications. In an ad for Potter's Asthma Remedy, she posed contentedly with a stuffed animal. Florence doted on Ann, and was fiercely protective of her baby daughter.

Ann's father, Francis (Frank) Reubin Victor Marston, was born in London on April 23, 1912, eight days after the *HMS Titanic* sank. His father, Francis John, was retired from the British Navy and augmented his small military pension by working as a chauffeur for a prominent furrier company in London. He drove the owners around town in a big LaSalle automobile and transported them on holidays to the exclusive vacation resort of Biarritz, France. Frank had four siblings, and although the Marstons weren't considered well-off, they never went hungry. Meat was often scarce, but their mother, Rose, purchased offal from the local butcher. Offal consisted of the more undesirable parts of cattle including tripe, kidneys, liver, and tongue. It was an inexpensive way to feed a large family.

Young Frank inherited a sense of humor and natural musical ability. He played the banjo, ukulele, and harmonica, and he sang in the Holy Trinity Church choir.

He was a good-looking, slender young man who wore stylish suits and argyle socks. Frank grew up happy and secure, and at age sixteen he trained to be a plumber.

What little is known about Florence Elizabeth Penning's personal history is dismal. She was born in London in 1910, but she and her sister Agnes were removed from their mother's custody and placed in foster care when they were quite young. Their mother was in a common law marriage, which was illegal in England, but their two brothers were allowed to remain with their mother. "Florrie" had a difficult time while growing up in the miserable conditions of foster homes, and she struggled to overcome the social stigma of her mother's indiscretion. Nevertheless, Florence developed into an intelligent, strong-minded young woman who was determined to rise above her depressed background. She polished her speech pattern to soften her Cockney accent and to emulate the "Queen's English." Florence lived on her own and successfully sold Electrolux vacuum cleaners door-to-door to earn her keep. She was an excellent seamstress and purchased used clothing to make over in updated styles.

Details of how Frank and Florence met are lost, but they enjoyed bustling around town in a Morgan three-wheeler, a peculiar vehicle with two wheels in the front and one in the back. During their courtship they played tennis and danced at local ballrooms. Frank was twenty-three and Florence was twenty-five when they married on April 12, 1935.

World War II began in Europe when Ann was two years old. Frank and Florence moved next door to Frank's parents in Edgeware, Middlesex, on the outskirts of London. Ann's grandfather Marston reenlisted as a gunnery instructor, and all of her aunts and uncles enlisted in the service. Even Frank's younger sister, Doris, joined the British Air Force at age twenty-one and was a staff car driver for military officials.

Frank joined the Fleet Air Arm of the Royal Navy and went to Australia during the war. Florence sent Frank a photo of Ann wearing a gas mask and holding a teddy bear. While he was gone, he often wrote directly to little Ann, and Florence would read his letters aloud to her. " … I told you a long time ago, that if you did everything your Mummy told you to, you would become a clever girl and better than other boys and girls … Look after Mummy till I come marching home. Daddy."

Florence scrimped, rationed, and scrambled with Ann to the bomb shelters at the sound of air raid warnings. Neighbors occasionally returned home to find glass windowpanes shattered and debris in the streets. Local children played in the destroyed buildings nearby, using the bricks as toy blocks. They rummaged in the orchards and fields to glean apples and corn for the chickens. In spite of the war, Ann Penelope was growing up to be the image of a perfectly dressed English girl, properly decked out in ribbons and curls. She was not permitted to play rough with the other children or to get dirty. On Sundays, the entire family went to visit Grandma Rose. Ann and her cousin Pamela were out walking with one of their uncles, and somehow Ann stepped into some wet cement. The poor man tried as hard as he could to clean her shoes with his handkerchief because he was terrified of facing Florence's wrath.

Florence supplemented the family income by making clothing for affluent women, such as Mrs. Janet Dufore Cole of Marble Arch, London. Correspondence indicates Mrs. Cole invited Ann and her mother for tea in 1944 with the notation, "… the white bear [rug] would like to remind you that he doesn't mind being trodden on if you are wearing indoor shoes, so please don't forget to bring them."

Ann became a successful child model under her mother's aggressive management and appeared in numerous advertisements and catalogs. By age six she was enrolled at Aida Foster's prestigious School of Dramatics and Dancing. Jean Simmons was a student at the school and starred in a 1944 London stage presentation of *Cinderella*. Ann portrayed one of six ballerina ponies in the production. (Simmons went on to Hollywood, appearing in *Spartacus* and *Guys and Dolls*. She received an Academy Award Nomination for Best Supporting Actress as Ophelia in *Hamlet* in 1948.)

By the time Frank was discharged from the British Navy, Florence had arranged for the family to relocate. Her friend, a Mrs. Staines, was commissioned to renovate a ruined building in Albion Mews at the Royal Toxopholite Society's elite archery club. Florence was employed as a stewardess, or caterer, and Frank was hired as a steward. Ann was enrolled in a private school nearby, and the family moved into their new living quarters on the grounds. For Christmas that year, Mrs. Staines, known to Ann as Auntie, presented her with the gift of riding lessons in Rotten Row, Hyde Park, "where the Princesses rode." Ann enjoyed riding tremendously. This new life at "the Tox" was refreshing.

In spring of 1947, the archery season commenced at the Royal Tox. Frank wasn't much interested in the sport until a member gave him a damaged bow to discard. Instead, Frank repaired the bow and decided to try it on the range after regular club hours. When he returned home he told his wife, "This is not kid's stuff." Ann watched her father shooting the bow, and asked him to make one for her. He manufactured a miniature bow and some arrows, and Ann enjoyed the activity immediately. She and Frank possessed natural talent, and devoted their free time to developing their archery skills. A wealthy member of the club, Skip Weston-Matre, took notice of Frank and persuaded him to enter the British Southern County Archery Championships in Oxford. At age nine, Ann was entered in the National Junior division. After only a few months of experience with their cast-off bows and arrows, both father and daughter won their events. Frank was nicknamed "the freak archer" and Ann was proclaimed a prodigy.

J. Arthur Rank was an innovative movie maker in England, and responsible for the establishment of Europe's largest studio empire. In 1947, one of his subsidiaries began production of a movie titled *Colonel Bogey*. The movie starred Jane Barrett and Heidi Anderson, and was directed by Terrence Fisher, who later became a prolific director of horror films in Hollywood. The title was a play on words: *Colonel Bogey* is the name of a famous piece of music later used as in the 1957 film, *The Bridge on the River Kwai.* In British folklore, a bogey is a mischievous spirit or poltergeist.

Colonel Bogey was set in the late 1890s. The plot featured a bogey who didn't want to give up his house to the new family, and the screenplay required an archery scene. The production company elected to film the sequence at the Royal Tox. Frank Marston was called in as archery technical consultant and to serve as a stand-in for the actors. Ann was recruited for a bit part. The wardrobe department dressed her in a Victorian white lace pinafore and button-top shoes, and her hair was arranged in long curls. A producer remarked that Ann was a likely candidate for Rank's prestigious Film School of Charm when she was old enough. Florence was thrilled.

After filming was completed on *Colonel Bogey,* Ann was busy with school, modeling, and lessons in dance, ice skating, piano, archery, and riding. She was invited to the Children's Ball, an offshoot of the Annual Film Star's Ball. Her young escort was the son of Major G.L. Webb, and Frank and Florence struck up a friendship with the family. The wealthy Major Webb owned a dilapidated building in the country that he intended to turn into a hotel and archery club. He asked the Marstons to oversee the restoration of the building and to manage the club.

In 1948 Frank, Florence, and Ann moved to High Road, Byfleet, Surrey, and began renovating the old Royston Chase Hotel. Ann was delighted to find that she had a stable of horses to ride. Frank designed the archery range and hired a bulldozer to level a portion of the property in front of the estate. Meanwhile, the exquisite old manor house was remodeled to include a dance floor and bar in the clubroom, and canvas awnings for the outdoor lounge areas. The new complex was only thirty minutes by train from London, and it wasn't long before the clientele of lawyers, doctors, and archery enthusiasts discovered the resort. Many of the Marstons' friends from the Tox began to stay at the hotel to enjoy the amenities of the fancy new club.

Frank and Ann were quickly becoming a sports phenomenon, and they appeared in a Pathe newsreel in 1948 that was filmed on the grounds of the Royston Chase. The one-minute, nine-second long featurette titled *Junior Toxopholist* opened with Ann aiming at the target while dressed in a Robin Hood-style outfit. Frank demonstrated a technique and she confidently hit the bull's-eye and flashed a wink and a smile. The narration follows:

> *Meet a young lady who, without a word of a lie, draws the longbow better than anyone of her age in the world. Daughter of archer Frank Marston of Byfleet, Surrey, Ann Penelope at 10 is the Junior Champion of the difficult science of Toxophology.*

A century ago, archery was practiced by every well-bred Victorian miss. Today the ancient and graceful sport is rapidly finding favor again with lovers of the outdoor life.

Here is a modern William Tell to demonstrate the correct aim and stance for a bull's-eye. Anything Dad can do, little archer Annie can do just as well. Yes, it's a bull for the belle of the archery buffs. So popular is the sport with local residents that a bowman's club has been formed. A bit of Olde England in the countryside.

England hosted the World Archery Target Championships in 1948, and Frank Marston entered the contest. The newcomer took the existing champions by surprise when he won fourth place in the Short Round. At the meet, he was befriended by several Americans, including Carl Strang, who was planning to open an archery shop in the Detroit area. Strang offered to sponsor the family's entry into the country, with the understanding that Frank would work in the new store. Florence and Frank were very excited at the prospect, and Frank sailed to the United States on the ship *American Scientist* on February 20, 1949.

Ann and Florence left England to join Frank on May 13, 1949. A London newspaper photo showed Ann, smartly dressed in coat and matching hat, holding her miniature bow case. The caption read:

All dressed up in button and bows—and arrows, Little Miss Ann Penelope Marston, junior archery champion, left London today on the boat train. Her target is the United States. She arrived at Waterloo carrying a box of her best arrows with which she hopes to startle young America. She is 10, the daughter of Mr. Frank Marston of Paddington who has gone to Detroit to open an archery shop.

Her father, steward of the Royal Toxopholite Society (highbrow name for the bowmen of England), met many Americans last year when they were here for the world championships. Miss Marston has still some way to go before she can equal the sort of shooting her father puts up. Last June he scored "an impossible" [score].

Florence announced the news of their immigration in a press release typed on stationery from the United States Line. It said:

S.S. Washington (Capt. Harold Milde) is due to sail for New York from Southampton (Berth 105, Western Dock) on Friday May 13th. Amongst those embarking at Southampton are Mrs. Florence Marston and her daughter Ann Penelope, aged 10, who is Junior Archery Champion of Great Britain for under 14s, and a winner of a silver cup from the Royal Toxopholite Society. The bow she used has a 21 lb pull, with a 21" arrow, and she shoots on a 30-40-60 range.

This exceedingly photogenic youngster has taken part in the J. Arthur Rank film Colonel Bogey, and in a Pathe Pictorial Short on Archery, and was destined for the Rank School of Charm. She has also done a considerable amount of commercial modeling.

On board the ship, Florence and Ann were invited to join Captain Milde for dinner. Florence often repeated an anecdote about Ann's behavior. "During dinner Ann was eating a pear to the very last pip, and the captain smiled and said, 'Ann, no more rationing, dear, you're on your way to America, the land of plenty.' "

After arriving in New York, they boarded a train to Detroit. Frank rented a modest home with a small flower garden in the yard in River Rouge, Michigan, a few miles south of Detroit. They purchased a used 1938 Chrysler.

Florence and Ann arrived on a Saturday and by the following Thursday, the family traveled with the Strangs to the Brown County Open in Indiana. Ann won her division and was on her way to a successful archery career in America. The week of Ann's eleventh birthday they attended the National Target Championships in Fond du Lac, Wisconsin. Ann won the first-place trophy and as a result, appeared on American television for the first time:

Miss Ann Penelope Marston, 11-year-old daughter of Mr. and Mrs. Frank Marston, 99 Pine, recently won the title of National Champion archer of Cadet Girls at the tournament held at Fond du Lac, Wisconsin. Ann, who shot 286 of a possible 288, had a total score of 1886. Her closest rival took second place with a total score of 908, making 191 hits out of a possible 288. ... Ann will be televised tomorrow on a CBS program at 7:45 p.m. Miss Marston now holds two titles, the Junior Championette of Great Britain and the title won last week.

The talented Marstons now included Florence as a competitor. The family joined the well-known Lincoln Bowmen Archery Club and provided serious opposition for established U.S. champions. Accounts of the 1950 season indicate that Ann broke records regularly. At the Maumee Valley Bowmen Invitational Tournament in Toledo, Ohio, she took first place in the Junior American round. Frank was a very strong contender in the men's division and just missed tying for second place. Florence also shot reasonably well at the meet and took third.

The National Target Tournament was held at Franklin Marshall College in Lancaster, Pennsylvania, that year. Frank won second place in the long international competition and Ann placed first in the girls' intermediate round, using a nineteen-pound bow and aluminum arrows. The Marston photo album featured pictures of the royalty of the archery world at the time, including Mr. and Mrs. Harold "Uncle Hat" Titcomb, Fred Bear, Earl Hoyt, Marvin Schmidt, and "Doc" Elmer.

Frank's job working at the archery shop fell through. An experienced industrial plumber by trade, Frank submitted the necessary paperwork to become qualified for a commercial plumber's license in the United States. He reported to the union office on the days he needed a job assignment. The arrangement allowed him to take off the days and weekends required to attend shooting competitions.

Archery was definitely a family experience in those days, and the Marstons were adapting well to the Midwestern American lifestyle. They celebrated holidays and went on Sunday drives and picnics. They upgraded their old '38 Chrysler and purchased a maroon 1949 Hudson with wide whitewall tires. Frank was invited to go bow hunting for whitetail deer in Tawas, Michigan. The women stayed at a cabin nearby while the men roughed it in tents in the woods at deer camp. There was a horse available, and Ann brought her jodhpurs so she could spend the holiday riding.

Florence was an exceptional seamstress, but she was forced to leave her sewing machine in England when they immigrated to Michigan. Archer and friend Gay Kaufman owned a leather shop in Wyandotte and gave her a spare sewing machine. She made her own clothing and designed most of Ann's wardrobe, including archery outfits with matching hats. When Ann outgrew clothes, Florence packed them up and shipped them to relatives in England, or shared them with other little girls in their circle of friends in the United States.

Ann participated in the service squad in the sixth grade at River Rouge's Visger Elementary School and received a certificate of recognition. She continued modeling and appeared in ads for educational movies and slide presentations. When the family moved a few miles away to Allen Park, she enrolled in a new school for the 1950-1951 academic year. Some of Ann's new junior high school classmates made fun of her British accent, childish clothing, and old-fashioned curls. But little Miss Marston was an expert at shooting a lethal weapon and garnered respect across the country.

Around that time, Ann was diagnosed with what is now known as Type 1, or juvenile diabetes. She was hospitalized for a week in July 1951 and was insulin dependent for the rest of her life. Before the discovery of insulin, diabetic patients faced a grim future. Complications of the disease resulted in blindness, poor blood circulation, stroke, amputation, and a very painful death. Diabetes had been recognized by physicians as early as 1500 B.C. It wasn't until the 1860s that doctors discovered the part of the pancreas that produced, stored, and released the essential hormone.

At the time Ann was diagnosed, insulin had been in use for a relatively short time but it was hailed as a miracle drug. In the 1950s the general medical consensus was that diabetes was not considered a serious health issue. Insulin controlled diabetes with a minimum of effort, and most patients usually took just one injection every morning. Diabetics didn't monitor their own glucose levels daily, but visited their doctors every few months to be tested. Medical professionals now understand that diet and physical activity are significant factors in influencing blood sugar levels, and diabetics must consistently maintain a safe balance.

In spite of her diagnosis, Ann achieved the first-place rank in the Junior Girls' division at the Metropolitan Field Shoot in Port Huron, Michigan. But the accomplishment was not Ann's biggest thrill in the summer of 1951. She auditioned and won a spot on *The Paul Whiteman TV Teen Club*. The show featured talented youngsters, and she was one of nine Detroit-area children selected from a field of 450 applicants. The nationally televised show was broadcast live from Philadelphia and was sponsored by the Nash-Kelvinator Company to celebrate Detroit's 250th birthday. The youngsters were sent a three-page instruction packet describing the itinerary. They were told: "to be worthy of this honor, be certain to conduct yourself on this trip so that Detroit, Mr. Whiteman and your parents will be proud of you." They were required to obey the fasten seatbelt signs on the plane, to remain with the group and chaperones, and to sit in their seats during rehearsals.

After rehearsal they had dinner at a seafood restaurant, and the kids were treated to baseball game; their home team Detroit Tigers played the Philadelphia Athletics at Shibe Park. Ann had her picture taken with Tiger Manager Red Rolfe and third baseman, George Kell, and it made the Detroit papers the next day. The children were sent back to the hotel for the evening. "Turn in right away so you'll be fresh as a daisy." The next day, there was another rehearsal for the 8 p.m. live telecast.

Once on the air, Paul Whiteman used the occasion to editorialize about television's negative influence on American teens, and then he introduced the talented participants. Ann performed her archery exhibition, while back home her friends and family proudly watched on tiny black-and-white TV sets. Over the next few years, Ann appeared on the Whiteman program twice more.

The following week in Saginaw, Ann won the Junior Girls' division trophy at the Michigan Archers Association's annual state tournament with a score of 1,250 points. Although a newspaper mistakenly reported her name to be Ann March, a *Detroit News* photo caption dubbed her "Little Miss Robin Hood."

Once again the Marstons moved, settling in nearby Wyandotte in a rented home at 517½ Elm Street. Ann entered Lincoln Junior High School that fall and made the Honor Roll with A's and B's. Principal Bessie Davis noted, "Ann, this is a nice report," even though from September 1951 to January 1952, Ann missed thirty-three half days of school because of her travel and competition schedule. The second semester report reflected similar good grades with only fifteen half days absent. She earned a certificate of honor for "regular attendance, good deportment and commendable progress in the studies of the eighth grade."

The summer archery competition season was conquered by the Marston family in 1952. As members of both the Lincoln Bowmen and Wyandotte Chemicals teams, Frank, Florence, and Ann enjoyed stellar scores at meets all over the state. In June alone, Ann captured first place in three state tournaments. In Lincoln Park she won the target junior championship, breaking her own record by 130 points. At Adrian she won the junior field trophy and took first place in Western Wayne's field tournament. When they cleaned up in Jackson at the Ken Hager shoot, it made the papers:

> The Marston family, archery experts from Wyandotte, is continuing to annex titles to an already impressive list of wins in archery meets. In five events entered this year, Ann Marston has finished with a clean sweep five. Her latest wins came July 13 at Ypsilanti while entered in the Metropolitan Field Archery Tournament, where she captured the Junior Girls' Class. A week prior to this, at the Ken Hager Day in Jackson July 6, Ann won the Junior Girls' Guest place, and during the meet she earned her 6th gold pin award for getting 6 successive arrows through the center of the target. Ann's parents also took competition honors at the Jackson meet. Mrs. Marston taking first in the Women's Guest shot, and Ann's father winning first place in the York Shoot for Men's Guest.

While competing at Eaton's Ranch in Minneapolis, Minnesota, at the National Field Archery championships, Ann broke all records in the Junior Girls' Instinctive Division, topping her opponents by 240 points. She won first-place trophies for all four divisions—Field, Hunters, Broadhead, and Small Game—all by wide margins.

In Toledo at the Recreational Festival, Ann earned the Junior title; Florence competed in the Senior division and took third place. The family went back to Jackson, and Ann dominated the Junior division again by breaking ten records at the National Target Championship competition. Florence came in second in the Women's Wand Shoot and the family earned the title of National Family Target Champs. They traveled to Saginaw where Ann defended her title in the state meet. She broke the Hunter's Round record of 368 with a score of 441, making her the Junior Girls' Free Style champion of Michigan once again.

That busy summer, Ann and Frank modeled for a big *Detroit Free Press* photo story on recreational activities in the area. In addition to her competition schedule, some of Ann's archery exhibitions were booked by famed Detroit talent agency

Gail & Rice. On WXYZ-TV, she gave a demonstration for a Torch Drive broadcast. Ann staged a performance for disadvantaged kids at *The Detroit News* Day Camp at Island Lake in Michigan, and shot at balloons and apples. In late summer she and her mother flew to remote Negaunee, Michigan, in the Upper Peninsula to perform at halftime during a basketball game.

Ann was a regular on local television sports shows such as *Michigan Outdoors* with Mort Neff and Jerry Chiappetta. WWJ-TV featured her on *Sports Closeups* with athletes including boxer Johnny Bratton, golfer Ray Maguire, and Detroit Tigers Manager Fred Hutchinson. Detroit sportscaster Budd Lynch enjoyed a long friendship with the Marston family. After being wounded and losing an arm in World War II, Budd worked at the BBC in London. He brought his wife and three small daughters to Dearborn, Michigan, in 1949 and was hired as announcer for the Red Wings hockey club, the year they won the Stanley Cup.

WWJ was the first television station in Michigan and hit the airwaves in 1947. Beginning in 1950, Lynch and the late Paul Williams hosted a show on WWJ-TV titled *Sports Profile* and later named *Meet the Sports*. They interviewed local athletes, members of the Michigan Sports Hall of Fame, and pros like Detroit boxing legend Joe Louis. For variety they searched out talented athletes in sports that were unique at the time, like Sunday wrestling, girl's basketball, or synchronized swimming. The bow and arrow was historically considered an adult hunting weapon, so it was a novelty for a young girl to be proficient at archery. Ann Marston was a frequent guest on the show beginning in 1950 at age twelve. Her parents drove her to the television station in Detroit and Florence was a typical backstage mother, Lynch recalls: "Momma was always there in the background, practically telling Ann what to say. She was a dominating Brit, but truly encouraged her daughter's career." Lynch has fond memories of Ann. "She was truly charming, poised, and talented, and was helpful with many friends and students who took up archery."

Ann and her parents regularly practiced at the Wyandotte Chemicals Club building on Biddle Avenue. Students at nearby St. Stanislaus Elementary School also used the facility for their weekly gym class. The boys weren't allowed in the gymnasium until Ann was finished with her session. Resident Paul Balog used to peek around the corner of the locker room to watch Ann shoot her bow. He was fascinated by her talent and said, "She never missed!" Ann often provided archery lessons to students in Wyandotte and helped local Boy and Girl Scout troops earn merit badges. She had other instructional duties, too. The Department of Physical Education and Recreation for Women at Michigan State College in East Lansing invited Ann to "tutor archery, to give exhibitions and share whatever information she can about the bow-and-arrow sport." She was fourteen years old and about to enter high school.

2

LITTLE MISS SURE SHOT

ANN'S TEEN YEARS were hectic as she balanced the demands of school work with coast-to-coast travel with her parents. The gifted young athlete attended local and national competitive archery contests, and in spite of her youth she was permitted to successfully compete in the women's events. At the same time, Ann began a new performance career. She achieved national recognition and was featured in many of America's top magazines and major television shows.

The family moved to a rented house on the south side of Wyandotte. By the time Ann entered Theodore Roosevelt High School as a freshman in the fall of 1952, she was already a nationally recognized sports figure. The student body had a bona fide celebrity in its midst. The school newspaper, *The Wy-News*, did a long article on Ann's background and archery accomplishments. Somehow the student reporter had the mistaken impression that her father had been "the official instructor to the English Royal Family."

Ann had an average class load and maintained high grades in most classes, in spite of numerous absences. Roosevelt High School junior Steve Arnest first saw fourteen-year-old Ann on stage in the school auditorium performing an archery demonstration in the school's talent show, *Spotlights on Parade*, in early 1953:

> She came on and I was immediately smitten, so I tried to get to know her and would catch her at the lockers. I taught her how to bowl and we

played canasta at her house. I finally asked her to my junior prom, the J Hop. She was so young that I had to convince her parents it would be all right for me to take her. There was a little battle with her mom; she was stern. She gave me the third degree and set a very early curfew. My parents were chaperones at the dance; so I think that won the day. After the dance we went to dinner at Joey's Stables and I took her home too late. Every light was on in that house on 7th Street. I escorted her up to the steps, said goodbye and that was it. She was so busy that we never went out again.

Life magazine sent a writer and photographer to do a story on Ann in May 1953. Detroit-based photographer Joe Clark was assigned to take unique photos of Ann shooting. Clark called himself the "Hill Billy Snap Shooter," and used the initials H.B.S.S. after his name. He was a low-key Southern character and wore a trademark straw hat. He was already a veteran photographer for distinguished publications such as *National Geographic, Sports Illustrated, Time,* and *Look.* Clark prided himself on capturing seemingly impossible live action shots. He set up the photo shoot at a local outdoor archery range, and devised a way to photograph Ann's arrow in mid-air. A Plexiglas panel with a built-in target area was constructed to allow the camera to view the action. Electric lights were strategically arranged and plugged into a very large battery power unit. After many hours of posing and practicing, Clark finally got a spectacular shot of Ann with her bow in the background and the arrow piercing an egg in the foreground, splattering it to smithereens. The article appeared in the August 31, 1953, issue of *Life*:

Archery Expert Aims at an Egg
Girl champion tries out a new type of target
The pretty blonde disciple of William Tell is the best young archer in the U.S. As an 11-year-old, Ann Marston of Detroit won the national cadet target championship and a year later added the intermediate target championship. Now a seasoned competitor of 15, she has a room full of assorted cups and medals. When she is bored with shooting regulation archery targets, Ann likes to use odd objects like beer cans and bottle tops. Last month, with Photographer Joe Clark on hand to picture the results, she took dead aim at some eggs.

Clark later displayed the photos in an exhibit at the Detroit Institute of Arts. Florence estimated that they received thousands of dollars worth of publicity for the one-paragraph story and the accompanying three photographs. With the archery competition season in full swing, Ann barely had time to think about the impending *Life* magazine release. She won the girls' title at the Maumee Valley Ohio target shoot, and shattered the record for junior girls at Ypsilanti at the Michigan State field archery meet. On a soggy course in Two Rivers, Wisconsin, she competed in the National Field Archery tournament, breaking two of her own world records in Junior Girls' Free Style. The minimum age requirement to compete in the Women's division was eighteen, and she had four more years before she reached that milestone. Although she was too young to officially participate in that category, her score became the new world's record. In Pontiac she was awarded the Michigan state trophy for Girls' Intermediate Free Style. While shooting at Western Wayne, Ann unofficially broke another world record in the Women's field competition. At the National Target Championship in Amhurst, Massachusetts, she gained four more first-place honors in the Junior Division.

Camaraderie was a highlight of these long-distance trips to Nationals, and a large contingent of Wyandotte friends traveled together. Gay Kaufman, who owned Wyandotte Leather, designed and manufactured a canvas tent camper for his entire family to sleep in for the duration of the meets. Participants may have spent the day as rivals on the archery range, but after hours the party began. The adults socialized and hashed over the events of the tournament while the kids played games or sang songs around the campfire. The fun was evident in photos placed in the Marston family album from that summer. They featured legendary archer-friends Ann Corby, Babe Bitzenburger, Bob Rhode, Earl Hoyt, Nubby Pate, Roy Hoff, Rube Powell—and the legendary Fred Bear.

Fred Bear hand-made his first bow in 1927 and eventually designed a technique to mass-produce bows that revolutionized the industry. He opened a factory in Detroit and continued to refine his product by integrating Fiberglas to strengthen and add flexibility to the bows. "Papa" Bear was an unassuming person but a true outdoorsman and unrelenting proponent of archery. He was a champion target archer from 1933-1945, and while exhibiting his wares at sports shows, he frequently gave demonstrations of his trick-shooting ability. His passions included fly-fishing, but he was renowned for hunting exotic animals in every corner of the globe. Bear earned world trophy records for African elephants, lions, grizzly and polar bears, and also collected alligators, lions, tigers, pythons, wildcats, antelope, and moose. According to Dick Lattimer, author of *I Remember Papa Bear*, many of Fred's adventures were filmed and shown on *The American Sportsman* television show or featured in *Outdoor Life* magazine. Bear also wrote numerous articles and made guest appearances on *The Tonight Show*, *The Mike Douglas Show*, and *To Tell the Truth*. He eventually moved his factory to Grayling, Michigan, and later to Florida. Bear was a very special friend to the

Marstons from their early days in United States and maintained a business relationship and lifelong friendship with Ann, Frank, and Florence.

The word was out regarding Ann's astonishing natural talent, and after the story in *Life* magazine hit the racks in August, she was invited to go to New York City for performance negotiations. With Florence as her mediator, Ann landed a contract to appear on Joe DiMaggio's radio sports show for the month of September. She was also scheduled to be interviewed on Arthur Godfrey's show.

Ann then scored the biggest triumph a performer could hope for in the 1950s. It was the Holy Grail of the show business world: Ed Sullivan invited her to appear on his *Toast of the Town* television show.

In days past, vaudeville fulfilled the public's entertainment needs by offering an assortment of live acts. Sullivan brought that variety to early American television broadcasting. He possessed an uncanny ability to locate and introduce a diversity of international talent to the airwaves. His program was the showcase for hundreds of performers who knew they finally made it big in show business when they landed a spot on Ed Sullivan's show. The program was incredibly popular, and seen by millions of viewers every Sunday night from 1948-1971.

Although the Sullivan show archives are incomplete, they do include at least one of Ann's performances from December 13, 1953. She appeared quite modest and charming, and she was on the stage for about two minutes. After Sullivan introduced her, she did trick shots with balloons and shot an apple off a wooden dummy's head. Her father, Frank, assisted onstage with the props and targets. Other guests on the show included singers Jimmy Boyd and Frankie Laine. Florence was backstage as usual, serving as Ann's manager. Ed Sullivan was impressed with Ann's talent, and her diaries indicate that she may have appeared on the show two more times. When the family visited New York they often attended the tapings as members of the audience and sometimes Sullivan introduced Ann on the air. Ann kept an autographed a picture of herself and Sullivan: "Ann - It was swell to have you on the show. Ed Sullivan." She later reflected on her experience and the effect that the Sullivan show had on performers' success: "I had to cut my act to two minutes, but I don't think there's an act in show business that wouldn't appear on *The Ed Sullivan Show*. It's a great showcase and in America this is what you have to do; either appear on a major TV show or have a hit record or the like. In the days of the old vaudevillians, going from cities here and there, they just couldn't get the exposure like we can on television."

Frank and Ann began to travel throughout Michigan to perform exhibitions including a banquet for coaches and athletic directors of Michigan high schools and colleges. They also appeared at the annual gathering of Wyandotte Federation of Indian Guides, and again at the Michigan State Fair.

The Marston family headed "up north" in Michigan that fall for an outdoor adventure: bow hunting for deer. They were guests at Val Fallu's Green Gables Lodge near East Tawas. All three Marstons bagged whitetails during their two-week stint. Ann claimed a five-point buck, Frank got a doe and Florence downed a button-buck. Florence planned to use the tanned deer hides to make costumes for Ann. Their hunting exploits were well documented in the newspapers in Tawas and Detroit, as well as in *The British Archer* magazine:

> *Archers in this country who knew Frank Marston before he and his family emigrated to America will be interested in this photograph of the family with deer bagged by each of them. Accurate shooting may be expected of a man who once shot a Hereford [score] of 144/991, still a Club Record, but here we have a situation where daughter tends to outstrip father. Ann Marston is now American Junior Girl Target and Field Target Champion, and Michigan State Junior Girl Champion.*

Ann's first formal performance booking was in October at the Memphis Mid-South Fair sports show in Tennessee. She had been compensated for exhibitions in the past, but this booking was the first arranged by a new agent, Alan Corelly. With a contract for professional representation and a paycheck, she was no longer considered an amateur. She would be disqualified from competing in the Olympics if archery were ever reinstated in the Games. But since the sport had not been included in the Olympics since the 1920s, the decision was made for Ann to pursue a career and earn her living as the first female professional archer.

Ann was maturing as a performer and as a public figure, although her mother still accompanied her to interviews. *Memphis Press* reporter Eldon Roark asked if she was nervous before a performance. "Oh, no," she replied, "The bigger the audience, the better I like it. I guess I'm just a big ham." Ann also explained to Roark that she had to bring her school books to keep up with assignments during the ten days that she was appearing at the fair. When Roark asked about Ann's boyfriends, Florence made it clear that her young daughter didn't usually date. "She's so busy that Ann doesn't really have time for that kind of social life." Florence's position was also firm regarding Ann's finances. "Her allowance is still $1 a week. The money she is earning goes into a trust fund."

Florence was encouraged by Ann's potential and signed a three-year contract with William Shilling Theatrical Productions for appearances at several sports shows. Ann was booked in Boston and New York for the following spring 1954, as well as several engagements in the Detroit area. Driven by her mother's aggressive ambitions, Ann's professional performance career was officially launched.

Florence Marston proved to be a promotional genius. She was very organized, and managed competition and appearance schedules and made all the travel arrangements. She was Ann's wardrobe mistress and selected the music used in the act. Florence's strong point was public relations, and she knew how to spin the media machine. She loved to talk, and she particularly enjoyed talking about Ann. Her press releases read like literature, with drama and humor—and more than a little fabrication. Florence embellished the family's history and dramatized their war experience. In press releases she often stated that the Marstons had been bombed out of either four or five homes in London, which simply wasn't true. She also maintained that Ann "took her first steps in Sherwood Forest."

Florence vicariously enjoyed Ann's rising star and took great personal pleasure in the attention her daughter received. In the tradition of George Palmer Putnam, who used every means available to promote his wife, Amelia Earhart, in the 1920s and 1930s, Florence set out to make Ann Marston's name a household word. Soft-spoken Frank rarely voiced a dissenting opinion—and it probably wouldn't have done any good anyway. Florence intended for Ann to go all the way to the top. Ann continued to do what she always had done—follow her mother's directed course without question.

At fifteen years old, Ann was evolving into an attractive young adult. Her skin was tan and her hair was a medium blonde that gradually lightened when she spent time outdoors. She was graceful because of her physical disciplines, never experiencing the gangly clumsiness that most adolescents wait to outgrow. She administered daily insulin injections to control her diabetes. As she reached her mid-teens, she developed a well-formed, athletic figure. Florence took care to outfit Ann in feminine, modest clothes, and the teenager was still forbidden to wear makeup to school, although she was allowed to wear a little lipstick for performances onstage.

School became a compulsory interruption to Ann's career, and going on to college was certainly not a part of the plan. Ann had the pressure of finishing high school coursework, whether she was present for the classroom lectures or not. Classmates often shared their notes, and her locker partner rarely had to make room for Ann's possessions. She was limited regarding the extra-curricular activities she could join because of her numerous obligations outside of school. She didn't have any lifelong childhood friends since she didn't grow up in the area. After arriving in the United States in 1949, the family moved several times, and this was only her second year in the Wyandotte Public School system. Although she was reasonably popular at Roosevelt High, maintaining normal "girl friendships" was difficult when she was out of town so often. Dating was nearly impossible—especially since most of the adolescent boys were apprehensive about Ann's celebrity, not to mention the presence of her overprotective, intimidating mother. And this girl spent more time with her parents than most American teenagers would tolerate.

It was early 1954 when the family went on a tour that included an eight-day stint at Boston's New England Sportsmen and Boat Show, with appearances at two shows a day. Then they traveled to New York City's Madison Square Garden for a week. The stage was so large that Ann required two targets, one at each end, so the large audience could see her shoot. A New York sports writer anticipated her performance, based on favorable reviews from Boston:

> *Ann Marsten [sic] should be an interesting addition to the list of outdoor celebs. Ann's archery exhibit is said to be on the breathtaking side. Seems the little miss shoots an apple off a bumpkin's head at 75 feet. That's a thrill for our dough.*

There was nothing like *People* magazine or *Entertainment Tonight* around in those days, but Ann managed to keep a high media profile. Stookie Allen had a syndicated newspaper feature called *Keen Teens*. He drew a sketch of Ann shooting the bow, and wrote about her accomplishments:

> *Pretty 15-year-old Ann, of Detroit, has a room full of medals won at archery. She was national champion. Recently she put on an exhibition at Madison Square Garden that amazed 13,000 customers twice daily at the national sports show. Soon she will make a movie short. The beautiful little blonde has been written up in some of the nation's finest magazines. Ann gets a nice fee for appearances at shows all over the country.*

Ann was in demand with other publications, and that spring she modeled with various household cleansers for the cover of the *Wyandotte Wigwam*, a newsletter printed by the Wyandotte Chemicals Company. She also was cover girl for *Scholastic Magazine's Practical English*. The May 12, 1954, issue included an account of her achievements. She was listed as an outstanding personality in *Information Please Almanac*. *Seventeen* magazine had an estimated audience of more than 2½ million readers and featured Ann as one of five "Teens in the News" for its May installment. A *Wyandotte News Herald* article in April listed her many talents:

> *A very accomplished teen, this Roosevelt High sophomore is also proficient at tennis, tap and ballet dancing, roller skating, swimming and horseback riding, plays clarinet in the school band, and models for TV and movie shorts. Attributing her success in these varied endeavors to a "mad*

passion for each," Ann states, "I love each of those things. I've done them well and I've stuck to them consistently."

The Building Tradesmen, a trade journal for plumbers, wrote a story on the Marston family and mentioned Frank as "a member in good standing of Local 98." Florence, too, was quoted and referred to Ann's success. She said: "Certainly we are proud of her achievements and we have great hopes for her future. But we are trying to rear her in true American fashion and hope to keep her unspoiled despite her numerous successes." The patriotic tie-in referred to the fact that the family earned American citizenship in 1954, as soon as they were eligible after the mandatory five-year waiting period. *The Detroit News* ran a photo of Ann, Frank, and Florence beaming with pride at the Federal Examiner's office in Detroit when they received their citizenship papers.

The schedule for early 1954 included sports shows in Flint, Michigan; Ottawa, Canada; and a trip to the nation's capital. While in Washington, D.C., Ann was invited to appear on Dave Garroway's *This is Today* show. For her debut on color television, she and her target were positioned in front of the Jefferson Memorial under the blooming cherry trees.

At fifteen, Ann's record-breaking scores in Junior and Intermediate divisions the previous year qualified her to compete in the Women's division of the National Field Archery competition in 1954. The minimum age requirement of 18 was waived based on her remarkable accomplishments as a Junior champion. The tournament was held at a ski resort in Mt. Sunapee, New Hampshire. Ann won the Free Style event and easily swept the trophy away from the other women contenders, breaking the existing record by 106 points. In Bay City, Michigan, Ann won the Women's State Field shoot by a margin of seventy points, surpassing her closest contender, Betty Lifford. Sports columnists were beginning to compare her in print to male sports icons Ted Williams and Joe Louis.

Back in Wyandotte, the Fourth of July was the setting of a week-long centennial celebration for the Marstons' adopted home town. Wyandotte boasted a long history, dating back to the Native American Wyandot tribe. The community hosted a multitude of events to commemorate its 100th anniversary. By then Ann was an accomplished equestrienne and proudly led the Youth Parade on a palomino horse outfitted with a silver and gold saddle valued at more than $5,000. She gave archery demonstrations at the Wyandotte Theater every afternoon and played clarinet in parades with the Roosevelt High School Marching Chiefs. She also appeared in the Centurama Pageant, a historical drama performed nightly by a cast of hundreds of citizens at the high school's stadium.

Later that summer the family journeyed to California and spent several months on the West Coast. In Los Angeles, Ann performed on *The Art Linkletter Show*, country western singer Spade Cooley's show, and visited Knott's Berry Farm with archery friends, the Doug Easton family. On a side trip to Palm Springs, the Marstons spent time visiting with the Roy Hoff family. Hoff was the owner, editor, and publisher of *The Archery Magazine (TAM)*, the official publication of the National Field Archery Association. Ann competed in the National Target Championship and came in fifth place in the Women's division. First place went to another young contender, Laurette Young, the 1951 National Junior Girls champ.

You Asked for It was a popular television show hosted by Art Baker, and viewers wrote to the program requesting proof of unusual feats or talents. Ann was asked to perform a sequence for the show. The crew shot one of Ann's scenes at Lake Arrowhead, but the location was so windy that dozens of arrows were destroyed when a target blew over. The next day they filmed at cowboy movie star Tom Mix's ranch. Ann rode Little Beaver's horse, Pete, who appeared in the *Red Ryder* film adventure series. While attempting to shoot from horseback during rehearsal, the horse went out of control. Ann hit a tree branch and was badly bruised. After production was completed she remarked: "We spent a lot of hard hours making this movie and took a lot of risks, as Pete wasn't a trained horse. I couldn't shoot and rein him, too. After we'd seen the film, we felt it was worth it."

Ann turned sixteen in August 1954 and began her junior year of high school. She joined the Trenton chapter of Rainbow Girls, a youth club affiliated with the Masonic Service Association. Apparently the young men were no longer bashful about noticing Miss Ann Marston. In November she was selected District Sweetheart in a beauty contest sponsored by the local teen boys' DeMolay chapter.

She was presented with a five-year diary at Christmas 1954 and Ann began a habit of journaling that continued for most of her adult life. Early entries from her teen years were very brief accounts of mundane daily activities and typical teenage experiences. She chronicled the family's travel adventures and revealed snap-shot glimpses of her rise to fame. In the process of recording her daily life, she always referred to her own professional performances as group activities with her parents: "We've appeared on *Ed Sullivan* ..." or "Our act seems to fit into nearly all kinds of shows." Ann identified Florence as "Mummy" then later as "Mother," but Frank was always "Daddy."

That winter, Ann appeared in the Theodore Roosevelt High School talent show, played clarinet in the band, took drama and singing lessons, earned her driver's license, and auditioned for a part in a school play. "Got the lead in the play," she wrote, "but I can't do it. I already have a contract." She was a very busy girl, answering fan mail, studying to maintain her honor roll status, and practicing with her father to refine the archery act. Even though she saw her doctor regularly to monitor her blood sugar levels, she suffered from several bad colds that season, likely brought on as a result of her demanding schedule. "I dragged myself to school this morning," she complained in her diary, "I was pretty tired after coming in at 1 a.m."

Ann and her family were regular visitors to the Big Apple—a minimum twelve-hour drive. In February 1955 they checked into the Belvedere Hotel for four days while she was appearing at the RKO Palace in New York City. She earned $250 for the engagement and good reviews in *Variety* and *Billboard*. Her advocate in New York was Mark Leddy, who was also Ed Sullivan's manager. Leddy was a great promoter and arranged several jobs for Ann, and Western Union telegrams from him arrived frequently at the Marston home. During their trips to New York, Ann and her parents fielded many other proposals. Over the course of that year there were discussions of a modeling career, a movie screen test, and a tour with the USO in Korea. They also considered marketing an Ann Marston signature scarf, an entertainment cruise to Havana, Cuba, a regular television show, and the prospect of a European tour. None of these ideas materialized.

Philadelphia's Convention Hall hosted a large sports show at which she appeared for eight days in March, and it landed her a cover photo on the *Philadelphia Enquirer* magazine. The audiences were huge: One night more than 20,000 people were in the arena grandstand. Ann said, "I can't understand where all these people are coming from. The place is packed every day!" After the Philadelphia engagement, the family returned directly to New York City for another audition. While visiting they met performers Harry Ames and Perry Como, who "sure is a nice guy and spoke with us quite a while." They once again attended a taping of *The Ed Sullivan Show*.

Ann missed quite a bit of school that winter because of her busy agenda and ran into trouble with her social studies teacher, Miss Pansy Blake. It took an intervention by the principal to smooth things out. "Today I went back to school," she wrote. "Everybody was nice except Miss Blake. Mummy called Mr. Whitney and he was very nice."

Florence was admitted to the hospital for an undisclosed operation and it was up to Ann to cook, clean, and manage the house. Both Ann and Frank visited the hospital daily, and Ann frequently stayed until bedtime. Florence's medical complications required several blood transfusions and she spent the entire month of April in the hospital. Florence checked herself out of the hospital when she felt well enough, and she arranged her own transportation in an ambulance. Ann took a few more days off school to stay with her mother at home.

Florence recovered and Ann picked up the pace by appearing with TV comedian Soupy Sales at a Junior Achievement fundraiser and performing at several other local engagements. While she was at home her social life improved, and she went to movies and school dances and played tennis with her friends. Now that she was allowed to date she casually went out with friends Dave Bailey, Earl Figby, Jim Farkas, and Tom McConnell. She practiced shooting to prepare for the summer archery competition season and to defend her National Field Free Style Championship in Ludington, Michigan. She was aiming to win dual championships by capturing the National Target honors that summer in Oxford, Ohio.

Sports Illustrated magazine contacted Ann for a photo shoot in June. The only comment in her diary was: "I went out and got pictures taken for *Sports Illustrated* and almost missed my history exam." The magazine sent John G. Zimmerman, a former news photographer who was assigned to shoot his first cover for the periodical. It was the first of more than 100 *Sports Illustrated* covers that Zimmerman would produce in the next fifty years. He also worked for *Life*, the *Saturday Evening Post*, and *Time* magazines. Zimmerman was an innovator in the field of sports action photography, and the Ann Marston cover shot was splendid. The color photograph depicted Ann in a close, waist-up shot nearly facing the camera. She drew back the bowstring and aimed just off the top right corner of the cover. The sun illuminated her blonde curls against a dark green background and she wore a confident smile. The liner notes on the index page introduced Ann to *Sports Illustrated* readers:

> *Sixteen-year-old Ann Marston, who won the National Women's Free Style Archery Championship last week, is an old hand at winning competitions (she has held at least one national archery title at every year for 5 years). When she was 10½ months old, Ann won a baby contest held on the surprising criteria of looks and build. The ensuing 16 years have admirably borne out the judges' early hopes and predictions. So much so, in fact, that Ann has now set her sights for Hollywood and a dramatic career. But her first love, she confesses, is archery—just as it is for the millions of other U.S. bowmen about whom SI reports in an article on page 48.*

A smaller close-up photo of Ann graced the opening of the article, titled "Pulling the Longbow" by Reginald Wells:

> *Four million Americans are doing it as archery becomes the nation's fastest growing family sport. With effortless ease, blue-eyed, 16-year-old Ann Penelope Marston, a blonde, 115-pound senior from Roosevelt High School in Wyandotte, Mich., arched her bow against its 23-pound pull, slowly took aim over the slim metal shaft of her broadhead arrow and, with breath held, sent it twanging toward a simulated rabbit target.*

21

The moment the shaft left her hand she knew it was over. After three days of tough national competition in which she shot 462 arrows at 168 different targets in the field, hunter and broadhead divisions, Ann had racked up a total point score of 2,080—200 more than her closest competitor—and retained her National Women's Free Style Field Archery Championship crown. For a national champion who first won this imposing title at the precocious age of 15, pert and pretty Ann takes a casual approach to her sport. Prior to joining 800 other field archers last week at Ludington State Park, Mich., in the largest national championships ever held, Ann had put in only about a week of concentrated practice ...

The news report continued with the customary PR tale of the family's British origins, the made-up ordeal of being bombed out of several homes, and it listed Ann's previous archery accomplishments. Young Ann's story was a natural lead-in for the article that went on to describe the sport's phenomenal rise in America. The week following the *Sports Illustrated* magazine release, Ann shot poorly in Oxford, Ohio, and missed the National Target trophy.

Before Ann began her senior year of high school in the fall of 1955 she was in New York City again. She was a guest on an episode of *I've Got a Secret*, heralding her accomplishment as the U.S. Women's Field Archery Champion. She also auditioned for a television talent show hosted by Dennis James called *Chance of a Lifetime*. She spent a week with the marching band at camp in Interlochen, Michigan. Back at Roosevelt High, Ann was named Girl's Sports Editor for the school newspaper, the *Wy-News*. Her fall academic classes included chemistry, world history, English, and typewriting. "I thought I had an easy schedule, but extra-curriculars are keeping me busy," she wrote. "The semester is well on its way. I'll be glad to graduate." She tried out for the Senior Class play, *January Thaw*, and won the part of Marge Gage in the comedy. "The play went off wonderfully well; I ad-libbed quite a lot."

When she had time, Ann attended home football games and went to movies and pajama parties with her friends. She was very active in the Trenton Rainbow Girls organization. Ann loved poodles and the family adopted a white puppy named Beau. Ann tried out for another school play, *The Silver Whistle*, and wrote: "Found out I'd made the part of Mrs. Hammer for the Thespian play and was happy. It's the part of an old grouch."

In early December, she took a call from CBS in New York. She elatedly wrote in her diary: "They want me on *The Morning Show* all next week. Hot dog!" Ann quickly assembled her school homework assignments, and the next day the Marston family flew to New York City to rehearse. "Today was the first show. Dick

Van Dyke interviewed me. I shot balloons with the weather report under them." On December 6, she was asked to stay on for a second week, with a slightly revised weathergirl routine:

> I'm happy to think they asked me as soon as they did. The producers devised a unique way of giving the weather report. The weatherman gave the report on various parts of the country, and I would shoot an arrow into the map pointing it out. The day I learned that I'd made National Honor Society, I was so excited that I nearly changed the whole weather pattern by shooting snow into Florida!

During the second week of *The Morning Show*, the director allowed Ann more close-ups. She shot streamers attached to the arrows and helped with a dog act that was on the show.

The Marston family enjoyed the exciting two weeks in New York. After Ann finished working at the studio, they attended shows and dined with associates. Ann went for an interview with famed television producer, Boris Kaplan, who was the film supervisor for the popular *Omnibus* television series. Another important contact was Buddy Basch, a prominent writer and talent agent who befriended the Marstons. He took them to an exclusive press showing of the movie *Miracle in the Rain*, a wartime love story starring Jane Wyman and Van Johnson. One evening Ann was featured on camera several times while they were in the audience at *The Ed Sullivan Show*.

The teacher/director of the school play replaced her with another actress while Ann was out of town on that trip. She approached him on her return and wrote, "I finally saw Mr. B.; He gave me back my part. Kathy was upset, but I think he made the right decision." She was occasionally frustrated with the casual attitude of other cast mates. "We waste so much time," she wrote. "If we could just get down to business …" Her performances on both nights of the show were good and she was pleased with the result. Ann was named Most Talented Actress at the awards ceremony for the National Thespian Society Troupe 50.

Ann was elected to the leadership position of Worthy Advisor within the Order of Rainbow for Girls organization. She bought a formal dress for the induction ceremony and hosted a party at her home following the ritual. As Worthy Advisor she was responsible for selecting a board of directors and presiding over membership meetings and initiations for the upcoming year. She planned to attend the four-day-long Grand Assembly state convention in Traverse City in April 1956 with her group and other advisory board members.

The family attempted to buy a tree on Christmas Eve, but the lots were all sold out, so they simply did without one that year. It was just as well, because on December 29, they packed up the car and the poodle and drove to New York City. Ann had a one-week engagement at the Apollo Theater, doing three or four shows a day. She shared the bill with the Detones, Arnett Cobb and his band, and the Tap A Teers. On a previous trip to New York, the car had been vandalized, so this time Frank stored it in a garage and they took the subway to the theater in Harlem. In her free time, Ann went ice skating at Rockefeller Center and horseback riding in Central Park.

In February she spent a busy week performing at a sports show in the Chicago Amphitheater and as usual, she was the subject of several television, newspaper, and magazine interviews. The hectic pace was beginning to take its toll: "Another big day with huge crowds. Tonight I was on the Howard Miller TV show. I have a dreadful cold and I'm so tired from late nights."

She apparently wasn't too sick and exhausted to try something new: She had the opportunity to scuba dive in a pool, and to shoot her bow and arrow underwater. A staff member with an underwater movie camera recorded the event. A large photograph of Ann, outfitted with a mask, tank and target was published in the March 1, 1956, edition of the *Chicago Daily News*.

Swimming Pool Sport? Underwater archer
Anne Marsten [sic] 15, women's national archery open field champion, tries her skill with a bow underwater in what is believed to be the first attempt at this sport anywhere. She gave the demonstration in an aqualung class in the Playdium, a recreation center in Glenview, and scored repeated bull's-eyes. Al Sindell, an aqualung instructor, is with her.

Ann enjoyed another unique experience while in Chicago. She was genuinely thrilled to be named an Indian princess and wrote an article for her school newspaper *The Wy-News* on March 13, 1956:

Archery Champion is Shuta-Wan-Cha (Win)
After reading this, if you see me whooping through the halls, you will know the reason why. Recently, while in Chicago, at a Sportsman's Show, I had the honor to be made an Indian Princess. It was quite a thrill and I have since discovered that in order to make this official, it will have to go through Washington, the Department of the Interior and the Commission of Indian Affairs.

Warrior Black Elk bestowed this honor on me, making me a member of the Ogalala branch of the Sioux Nation. He named me "Shuta-Wan-Cha (win)" meaning "The One Who Never Misses." The "win" is to designate a girl. In any Indian name you see this, it if is a boy's name it is just left off. The ceremony was a very impressive one, with Black Elk speaking in Indian to the four directions, the Great Spirit and the Earth. Then, of course, the traditional pipe of peace. After this he placed the headdress on my head and I became a full-fledged princess, to my delight.

Black Elk was telling me of his home in South Dakota and of the All-American Indian Days, a colorful Indian pageant held annually. Something he said was of special interest to me, for he mentioned that most Indians like to be American and most Americans like to be Indian.

Ben Black Elk was one of the nation's most visible Native Americans. He appeared in five movies and was the official greeter at Mt. Rushmore National Park for twenty-seven years until his death at age seventy-three. Florence's press release described Ann's induction ceremony with a typically dramatic touch. "The young archer's blonde beauty was a sharp contrast to the bronzed sinewy Sioux 'Black Elk' officiating before the campfire."

After a week-long engagement in Cleveland, Ann went to a photographer and had her senior portrait taken, was measured for a cap and gown, and worked on her final term paper, *How to Improve Traffic Safety*. "Went back to school and things are beginning to buzz. A month from today exams will be through. Thank goodness!" Homework was a priority, and Ann worked hard to keep current. She occasionally mailed assignments to her teachers when she was on the road, but her stress was evident in her diary entries. "Went back to school and studied like mad," she wrote. "I spent nine hours on homework this evening … That's all I do these days. My chemistry is the most difficult to make up." Her final report card reflected a B in English, A in world history, C in chemistry, A in civics, with a total of forty-four half days absent. She received recognition from the National Honor Society, the Quill and Scroll journalistic honor society, earned a Thespian pin, and a Band letter.

Financially, the family was comfortable between Frank's regular plumbing job and Ann's supplemental income. When they were in New York City, the Marstons dined frequently with other celebrities in Manhattan at Toots Shor's restaurant. They stayed in New York's nicer hotels and enjoyed shopping at Macy's, Klein's, and other fine stores. Ann purchased a small, white, fur cape to wear to formal events, and her parents shopped for a new car. Frank and Florence eventually bought a coral and white 1956 Hudson, and later the same week they bought a used 1950 Plymouth for Ann's graduation gift.

Ann could finally catch her breath that summer after being relieved of the demands of school and homework. She enjoyed beach parties at Sugar Island, casual dates with boys, and cottage visits with friends up north. Florence and Ann spent time shopping and going to the movies. She appeared at shows in Detroit and Windsor and practiced in the evenings with her father for the competition season. Ann participated in local archery contests and had several performance engagements, including the Ohio State Fair in Columbus, where she was on the bill with canine TV star, Lassie. She took great pleasure in outdoor activities and took over the yard and gardening chores. Florence and Ann designed an English-style garden, complete with hedges, in their small backyard.

Ann was named Carp Queen at a local carnival, and when she was asked to preside as queen for a charity event at Flat Rock Speedway, she had her poodle Beau tinted pink for the occasion. Although she was only seventeen and weighed 115 pounds, the young beauty was concerned about her weight. She consulted a doctor, but apparently her diabetes wasn't considered detrimental to the treatment. "He gave me a shot and some pills in order to curb my hunger."

After the usual round of graduation activities and parties, the Marstons packed up the Hudson and headed for the 11th Annual Field Archery Nationals in Colorado Springs, Colorado. The family drove cross-country for two solid days and slept in the car both nights. The contest itself was quite an adventure, according to Robert Rhode's account in the book, *Archery Champions*:

> *An outstanding feature of this tournament was a hail storm that came in off Pike's Peak, dropping the temperature 25 degrees and catching the archers out on the courses. Lightning struck two trees on the courses and archers rapidly departed. The hail piled up in drifts. Water rushed down through the camping area, and many had wet bedding that night.*

Using two bows that Fred Bear sent for her graduation gift, Ann came in second in the National Free Style round, an event she had won in 1954 and 1955. A month later in Pontiac, Michigan, she garnered the Women's Free Style championship for the state of Michigan.

Back in New York, Ann was a guest with funnyman Ernie Kovacs on his variety TV show that was geared for family audiences. She also appeared in *The Kiddie Spectacular; The Story Princess*, a show produced by Lee Cooley. It was a huge production that required costume fittings, elaborate sets, and five full days of rehearsal. Both Ann and her father were featured on camera, and everyone was pleased with the result. She was now ready to explore the world of children's television entertainment. Much of children's programming in the early 1950s consisted of three essential elements: puppets, cartoons, and noise. Even Detroit had goofy local hosts like Soupy Sales, Johnny Ginger, and Jerry Booth to pump up the volume for the young audience.

Paul Winchell was a ventriloquist who fronted the *Winchell-Mahoney Time* show that was enjoyed every Saturday morning by kids across the nation. The raucous format featured an assortment of silliness hosted by dummies Jerry Mahoney and Knucklehead Smif. Mahoney was a wise-talking character who flirted shamelessly with the female guests. Ann was no exception, even though she shot an apple off Mahoney's head. She later said, "Paul was real nice and we had a lot of laughs." Back at home Florence took pictures of Ann and Mahoney from the television screen. Ann was a return guest on Winchell's *Circus Time* show the following year.

The popular *Howdy Doody Show* with host Buffalo Bob also had all three wacky fundamentals, but the clown, Clarabell, was a soft-spoken ex-Marine named Bob Keeshan. In 1955, Keeshan was offered a spot on CBS to develop his own show and he had a better idea. *Captain Kangaroo* also had puppets, but the basic concept for the new program was original. On his show children were treated with loving concern and reverence. Instead of slapstick routines and violent cartoons like *Popeye*, in the Treasure House, the children were introduced to a gentler realm of imagination, literature, music, and science. Commercials were screened personally by Keeshan, who approved ads for creative toys such as Play-Doh and Etch A Sketch to be aired during his program. He and his production team carefully planned every aspect of the show with an innovative philosophy. Keeshan explained the concept in his autobiography, *Good Morning Captain, 50 Wonderful Years with Bob Keeshan, TV's Captain Kangaroo*, published by Fairview Press:

> *Everyone involved with the show believed that our audience was composed of intelligent human beings worthy of our respect and with potentially good taste. The show was not a lesson but entertainment of the highest quality. The finest teacher is an entertainer. Some teachers find that a demeaning concept, but to teach is to pass on knowledge, and being a scholar is not enough. A teacher must engage the mind of the student for knowledge to pass from one to another. If that is best done with a tap dance or a funny hat, so be it.*

Resident characters were puppet, animal or human—such as Mr. Moose, Bunny Rabbit, Grandfather Clock, and Mr. Greenjeans. Part of the fun was when the Captain introduced new friends from the outside world. Many stars from show business were guests, including Dolly Parton, Pearl Bailey, Milton Berle, Phyllis Diller, and even Mister Rogers. Athletes were invited, too, and Olympic gold medalist Bruce Jenner, baseball player Lou Brock, and football player Rosey Grier all showed up to play at the Treasure House. Keeshan held that "… our famous guests from so many fields were invited for one reason. It is my belief that children

deserve the best performance possible, and these artists were supreme in performing their art. Simple as that: give children the very best."

Ann Marston first appeared on the *Captain Kangaroo* show on September 15,
1956, and was invited back on December 1 of the same year. Since she frequently
traveled to New York City, it wasn't difficult to schedule guest spots on the show,
which required only one day of rehearsal and a second day for the live broadcast.
After her first appearance she wrote: "They seem very pleased and the director
said he'd like me to return again soon." By her sixth appearance in 1958, Ann was
invited to join the cast. "On *Captain Kangaroo*, I did something different; a dance,
etc.," she wrote. "They might want me as a regular." The role was tempting but was
too confining to accommodate her tour plans, and she declined the offer. Ann was a
guest on the show eight times in three years, from 1956-1958. Unfortunately, CBS
didn't begin videotaping *Captain Kangaroo* until 1959, so her performances were
never recorded.

3

Sweetheart of the Bow and Arrow

Now that Ann was out of high school, her dual career of competitive archery and show business moved into high gear. She was still a well respected competitor on the archery circuit, and she joined *Sports Illustrated*'s annual Tour of Champions. The archery act was very popular and her skills were at their peak. Both of her parents were indispensable to Ann's success, with her father assisting on stage and her mother orchestrating the business details.

Multi-talented Ann joined a performers' union, filmed a television pilot, and competed in several beauty pageants. The Marston family traveled to their native England in 1958 for an acclaimed appearance at the London Palladium.

Preparation for Ann's performances required a tremendous amount of effort. As business manager, Florence arranged accommodations, handled contract and financial issues, and helped Frank chart driving routes. When they traveled, the car was packed with all the equipment for the act as well as maps, contracts, sheet music, and itineraries, as well as clothing and personal necessities for all three adults. Ann's supply of insulin had to be bought and kept at a controlled temperature, so they carried a small cooler. Of course, their dog Beau came along and required food and rest stops. Florence did not have a driver's license, so Frank did most of the driving. Ann occasionally relieved her father behind the wheel, but her mother was extremely nervous whenever Ann drove.

Florence was also responsible for maintaining Ann's wardrobe, including head-dresses, undergarments, tights, footwear, and accessories. She repaired the garments, replaced lost sequins, beads or feathers, and polished Ann's boots. On long trips she did an amazing amount of laundry in tiny motel sinks and then completed the necessary ironing. Florence also attended to Frank's stage outfits and kept track of supplies. Eggs, apples, paper cups, candles, and balloons were needed for the act, and she used a small electric compressor to inflate about fifty multicolored balloons before each performance. When all was ready, she watched intently from backstage or from the audience and offered detailed critiques after the show.

Ann was nineteen by now and had developed her own persona. She was comfortable taking over most of the interview duties from her mother. She possessed a dazzling charm and her father's sense of humor, and she truly enjoyed the media attention. She endorsed her fellow performers and tried to provide intelligent, interesting comments to interviewers. For example, Ann described her performance philosophy to a reporter from the *Tampa Tribune*: "The act isn't a demonstration as such. We try to keep it as entertaining as possible. In show business the primary purpose of your act is to entertain the crowds; you must be fast and daring. But in competition you become slow and methodical—aiming only for the mark." Ann went on to express her joy at having children attending the shows:

> We've had some terrific audiences. Even though you shouldn't, you do work much better to a receptive audience. It's always fun, but it is something that sort of keeps you humble, because when you miss [the target] it's there for everybody to see.
>
> It's wonderful to play for the young people in the audience, because let's face it, they are our future athletes. The kids are marvelous because you can do a show for adults and they see you and forget you. But children remember what you were wearing and what you were doing and in what sequence.

Frank was Ann's prop master and onstage assistant. He was a good-looking man at forty-five years old, and he wore a small but dignified mustache. He had an archer's upper body strength with powerful arms and biceps. His costumes ranged from neat slacks and polo shirts to a complete Robin Hood-style outfit. His foremost job was to ensure that the equipment was in place and functional. Balloons, cups, and candles were attached to the target with long iron pins and specially fabricated brackets. Before the show, Frank paced off the long shot with Ann and checked the bows, several dozen aluminum arrows, and all props and targets. He perfectly complemented her routine with efficiency, energy, and his subtle sense of humor.

Safety was a vital issue in the act, and they were both vigilant about position-ing the targets carefully. Ann refused to shoot an apple off a person's head or a cigarette out of someone's hand. She joked: "We have a little dummy called Oscar that travels with us, and he doesn't have any holes in his head." In an interview she described her responsibility to the audience:

> Of course anything can be dangerous if the right precautions aren't tak-en. That's the reason, with our show, we never shoot apples off people's heads or do things such as that. Children might get the idea that "Gee, I can do that, or maybe I'll be good enough to do it." We try to stress the safety. It's perfectly safe, if there is the right backing and children aren't [permitted] to shoot at each other.

Ann often came into an auditorium behind the audience, and shot an arrow over their heads to hit a target on the stage. Today's safety standards would most likely prohibit that kind of dramatic entrance.

Before each performance, Ann dressed in costume, fixed her hair and applied her own makeup. Then she worked with the orchestra and the emcee to ensure functional microphones, correct musical cues and accompaniment, and a proper in-troductory speech. If there was an announcer for her act, he was provided with scripted comments. If Ann announced for herself, she used the remarks as ad-libs. Following is a sample synopsis of a performance with song cues:

- *Loud opening with heavy drums and timpani—Indian music.*
- *Cymbal crash-Piano—"The Indian Love Call." Ann ran onto the stage.*
- *After opening applause, Ann bowed. Then the Trick Shots; Six Balloons, Cross Balloon, and Dropping Balloon.*
- *Apple shot—"William Tell Overture" in F.*
- *Egg Trick with "Turkey in the Straw." (Her usual comment after breaking the egg was "That's no yolk!")*
- *The Magic Balloon trick—reprise the "Indian Love Call" followed by the Liberace (shoot out candles) and the "Nocturne" Waltz.*
- *Long Shot music background—"A Hunting We Will Go."*
- *Bow Music Trick—"Cherokee" in E flat.*

She took her job seriously and didn't want to be known as merely a novelty act. There were definite scientific principles that applied to the logistics of archery, and she frequently referred to the *Life* magazine photo. "We discovered that it was taken with a high-speed camera and found out that the arrow had gone completely through the egg before the egg broke." She also had to factor in the entertainment value to keep audiences engaged. She explained the concept to a reporter:

> *... They really aren't tricks. We found a long time ago, that in all of the thousands of people in an audience there are very few archers. So you have to do things to entertain the audience. I've got a whole car full of eggs that I shoot and apples and magic balloons and candles ... The long shot distance from the top of the grandstand balcony is hard to judge because you are shooting downhill and trajectory is different and so it's probably between 150 and 200 feet.*

Sports Illustrated invited Ann to join their tour of champions that summer. She appeared with many sports figures, including one-armed golfer Jimmy Nichols, Olympic two-time decathlon winner Bob Mathias, tennis star Tony Trabert, and New York Giants star halfback Frank Gifford. They garnered much publicity as they traveled the sports show circuit through Chicago, Philadelphia, and Pittsburgh, and finished in Detroit at the Northland Center shopping mall.

Ann acknowledged the meager number of female athlete role models in the 1950s, and took it upon herself to endorse archery as an important women's sport. At that time in America, a woman's personal identity was primarily characterized through her husband. A married woman routinely didn't use her own first name, and was normally merged into a minor extension of her man, i.e. *Mrs. Henry Vale*. Ann was determined to make her own impact on this inequity by words and deeds. She was quoted in *The Detroit News* as saying: "I'm all for more women in archery. Women have the idea in their heads that they shouldn't be on a par with men in sports. I think it's just a mental thing." But she, too, inadvertently deferred to the quirks of America's male-dominated society. She made a contradictory comment in a magazine interview when she coyly revealed another good reason for women to take up archery. "Here is a scoop for your [male] readers. Tell them to have their wives, sweethearts, daughters, and secretaries practice with bow and arrow every day. Take it from me, it will—how shall I say it?—do 'wonders' for them!"

When asked how she remained so feminine in spite of her vigorous activity level, she replied, "Well, I don't overexert myself with a big bow." For performances she generally used a light bow with a twenty- or twenty-three-pound pull. Much heavier bows were used for target practice or game hunting. During the course of another interview she predicted an expansion in the sport by women: "Of course, with archery, women are becoming interested, too, because you don't have to be strong anymore. At one time you pictured an archer as a huge man with a 100-

pound bow with his foot on a line. Now it really is a family sport and like with bowling, women are going to be responsible for the growth of archery."

Ann lived the majority of her life in the archery world, and enthusiastically promoted it as a family activity. In an interview with a reporter from the *Minneapolis Tribune*, Ann explained the positive aspects of the sport: "A good archer doesn't have to be big and muscle bound. In fact, there is no age or size limit to the sport. With modern, lightweight bows, anyone can take part. And more and more people are finding it to be an ideal family sport." She went on to say, "Archery is not only fine recreation, but it's a good basic sport for coordination. Other sports—tennis, golf, skiing—are much simpler once you've mastered archery."

She spent much of her free time enlightening fans about archery, and often held instructional clinics to help enthusiasts improve shooting techniques. She especially loved working with kids and used her own childhood experiences as an example:

> We all travel together; my mother and father and my little poodle called Beau. We used to do a trio, my mother also shoots and we held the American family championship. My father was Fourth world champion and British champion. We used to go on tour and we would all shoot. I was a little bitty thing shooting, you know how children are, and pretty soon I stole the show.
>
> ... I started when I was 10, which is a good time for children to start archery in particular, because it's a wonderful sport for coordination. Kids are a little different than adults because they have wonderful concentration, and don't care if they win or lose. They're just having a lot of fun. With adults they have more things mentally to worry about. I'm all for starting children as young as possible.

Ann also shared her expertise regarding archery history, and often took the opportunity to educate the public with the truth about the Robin Hood legend:

> I don't want to disillusion all the tykes who watch television and read books about the glamorous bandit of Sherwood Forest, but some of the feats attributed to the archers of the Middle Ages are sheer malarkey. For example, in a big tournament at Nottingham the villain sends an arrow zipping into the center of the target. Robin Hood steps up and nonchalantly splits the arrow. The chances of that happening are one in a million. It's impossible to do it intentionally ... Old-time bows were crude implements made of yew trees and the arrows also were rough wooden things with a heavy head. Today bows are made of glass [Fiberglas], our strings

of nylon [Dacron] and our arrows of aluminum. Anything they could do with the bow and arrow then, we can do 20 times better today.

Ann had an informed opinion about Native American bowmen. "They were tremendous stalkers, but their accuracy with a bow and arrow from a distance was horrible. Their hunting success lay in sneaking up on animals and killing them from a short range . . . Now we are more concerned about coordination and skill than those early hunters, whose only thought was to obtain food or kill enemies."

She took a short break from the *Sports Illustrated* tour and flew to Watkins Glen, New York, to compete in the 1957 National Field Archery Championship. In front of more than 1,000 archers, Ann attempted to win back the title in Women's Free Style that she held in 1954 and 1955, but had lost in Colorado Springs in 1956. She not only took first place, but in the process broke the standing world record by an exceptional 287 points. Ann herself set that record in 1954 when she was seventeen years old. Cleo Roberson came in second, ten points behind Ann.

Ann accepted a new challenge by entering local beauty contests in early 1957. She won Miss Amvet for the city of Wyandotte's Post 99, but failed to succeed at a higher level. "Had the Miss Michigan Amvet contest on the Bob-Lo boat; I was third, but politics were involved . . ." She also was one of the top ten finalists for Miss Photoflash, sponsored and judged by the Detroit Press Photographers association.

Ann joined the American Guild of Variety Artists, a union that represented a wide range of performers. Alan Sherwood Enterprises in Houghton Lake, Michigan, adopted Ann for professional management in late 1957. Florence was skeptical, but Ann had faith in him. "Mummy doesn't like Sherwood—the way he works—but I think he'll do us good." Sherwood was negotiating a television series for Ann in conjunction with Jack Goldstein of New York. The pilot was to be filmed in Blanchard Springs, Arkansas, and had a working title of *Land of the Bow and Arrow*.

Ann was partnered in the pilot with The Fabulous Kelly, the Wonder Dog, and the producers were hoping to cash in on the success of television's *Lassie* series. Kelly was a white German Shepherd that already had several Hollywood movie credits on its resume. He had recently costarred in a 1957 movie with Van Johnson titled *Kelly and Me*. In an advertisement in the *Billboard Cavalcade of Fairs*, Ann received only slightly higher billing over the dog:

> *Now! For the first time! Two Great Champions Together!*
> *In the Smash Box-Office Hit of the New Season*
> *Ann Marston National Women's Archery Champion*
> *Cover Girl "Life" & "Sports Illustrated"*
> *America's No. 1 Sports Queen*

The Fabulous Kelly
Hollywood's Greatest Wonder Dog
Featured in Universal-International's production
"Kelly and Me" starring Van Johnson
Raves! "Ann is really great." Ed Sullivan
"Ann Marston breaks archery world record." N.Y. Times
"To the short list of Hollywood's Canine Stars,
add a new name, 'Kelly.' " London Picturegoer
"Kelly is just wonderful." Los Angeles Times Philip K. Scheuer

In similar ad published in *Variety* a month later, a supplemental comment was added about Kelly the Dog: "He does everything but talk." The title of the series was initially announced to be *The Amazing Adventures of My Dog Kelly*.

Florence was the queen of spin, and along with the legends of the family being bombed out multiple times during the war there were many other exaggerations about Ann that appeared in the press. There was an enormous discrepancy in the media campaign for the upcoming TV series that stated Ann was "Cover girl for *Life* and *Sports Illustrated*." The fact was that Ann was on the cover of *Sports Illustrated* in 1955, but she was not the first woman featured on the magazine's cover as her mother often claimed. Additionally, she never appeared on the cover of *Life*, although she was highlighted in a brief photo story in 1953. Florence perpetuated the myth and invented a cover by cutting out a *Life* logo and pasting it over a picture that featured Ann. Florence re-photographed the phony cover and passed it off as an original in Ann's press kit for a while.

Florence released press statements regarding Ann's new film role, and set up interviews wherever they traveled. When asked by a New York paper about her future success in the movies, Ann speculated, "I don't know if I'll like Hollywood so much. They say they try to change you. But we'll see what happens."

Still excited about the prospect of the television series, the family drove to New Rochelle, New York, for an appearance with singer/actor Rudy Vallee that was arranged by Mark Leddy. Ann committed to several engagements in the spring and summer including a trip to Montreal and visits to New York for return appearances on the *Dave Garroway Show*, *Ed Sullivan*, and *Captain Kangaroo*. She made the cover of the March issue of *The Eastern Bowhunter* magazine. Ann signed to tour again with *Sports Illustrated* and a new cast of champions, including fitness expert Bonnie Prudden, Wimbledon tennis star Vic Seixas, and golfer Arnold Palmer.

Ben Pearson approached Ann about the production of a signature archery set, and she was equally delighted when Bear Archery offered her an annual commission of $5,000 for her personal endorsement. After agent fees and taxes were deducted, the first Bear check came to $1,685. To celebrate, she went shopping and purchased a full-length, brown seal fur coat.

The new television series contract was taken to Detroit to be assessed by the Marstons' business lawyer. The family then traveled to New York to meet Kelly's trainer, Ernie Smith, and series promoters Harold Sherman, Al Pollard, and Jack Goldstein. Pollard was an advertising executive based in Little Rock who co-scripted the story with Sherman, who was respected in Hollywood for writing the screen-play for the successful 1944 movie biography, *The Adventures of Mark Twain*, which starred Fredric March as Samuel Langhorne Clemens.

Mountain View Productions was a company created and funded by the citizens of the Ozark Mountain-area towns of Mountain View and Batesville, Arkansas. Ben Pearson's marketing director, Jack Witt, was also involved in the project. The group's mission was to promote tourism with film projects. The expectation was to shoot the pilot and then attract national sponsors to finance the first twelve installments. The ultimate hope was to obtain funding for thirty-nine half-hour episodes.

Sherman and Pollard hired Dan Milner of Milner Brothers Productions Inc., to direct and film the pilot. Milner edited dozens of insignificant films in Hollywood as far back as 1931. In early 1957 he directed two cheesy science fiction pictures, *From Hell It Came* and *The Phantom from 10,000 Leagues*.

The formal publicity announcement for the film was made in the Little Rock office of Arkansas Governor Orville Faubus. Faubus and Harold Sherman were friends and business associates, and the governor arranged for state funding for the pilot film. On January 29, 1958, Ann and Kelly applied signature and paw print to their respective contracts. Following the signing, Ann changed from heels and a black afternoon dress into a red-sequined costume to perform an archery exhibition for the press. Along with her usual trick shots she popped a balloon that was held by the governor. The *Arkansas Gazette* reported that, "She took a stance about 30 feet from a well-padded target and started firing away. Of course, not once did she split the fine paneling of the reception room." The *Gazette* ran a front-page photo of Ann and Kelly posed in front of the state capitol building and provided a long article describing the series concept. The newspaper quoted information garnered from a publicity brochure provided by the promoters:

> *The story revolves around an Ozark character called Bo King, a game warden in the Ozark National Forest. The romantic interest is supplied by Marianne, a young lady who loves the outdoors and is quite a competitor with Bo King. But she always ends up with a warm feeling in her heart for the game warden.*
>
> *The German Shepherd called Kelly is a dramatic dog who has worked*

*in many movies and is quite capable of adding a broad animal interest to
all episodes. In short, the idea is to create sequences packed with adventure, thrills and conflict and resolved at the climatic moment through the
use of the bow and arrow by the hero, Bo King.*

The director and producers searched for the perfect leading man and decided
upon handsome Robert Roark. His Hollywood background included bit parts in
several forgettable sci-fi movies such as *Killers from Space, Princess of the Nile*, and
Target Earth. He appeared in minor supporting roles for several 1950s television
series including *Sergeant Preston of the Yukon, The Lone Ranger, Wagon Train*,
and *Sky King*. His most identifiable movie part was in 1955, when he played a sailor
named "Insignia" in *Mister Roberts*. Roark was several years older than Ann but
was cast in the lead role as Bo King: game warden, hero, and Ann's antagonistic love
interest. Her character's name was changed from Marianne to Ann Mason. The
pilot also was renamed once again to *The Amazing Adventures of My Dog Sheppy*.
The dog still got top billing.

Ann and her parents drove to Blanchard Springs, Arkansas, in late April 1958
to prepare for the filming. As usual, the car was full of costumes, luggage, and archery equipment. Kelly the dog and his understudy, Timber, were already in town
with owner/trainer Ernie Smith. Dan Milner was also in the Mountain View area
to scout locations and make necessary preparations. Ann met with him to select her
wardrobe and to style her makeup. She was impressed with the positive reaction of
the locals, saying, "The residents treat us like royalty."

The cast included minor juvenile players Billie Conners and Meredith Ross, who
were the winners of a talent search that was sponsored by a local newspaper. Jimmy
Driftwood, a local folk singer, was given a small part. When Roark arrived he made
a good first impression with Ann. She reported in her diary: "Robert Roark is my
leading man. He's very nice and a riot." Ann and Roark got to know each other better
after shooting the first few scenes. "We got off at five o'clock and then I played gin
rummy in the evening with Bob." Publicity photos from the set indicate they were
comfortable together and seemed to enjoy their new partnership.

The first two days of production brought great results according to Ann: "A
beautiful day and they got some dandy shots. We have a good crew and they seem
very pleased with me." The nice weather didn't hold for long, and since most of the
scenes were outdoors they lost valuable filming time. The crew was forced to wait
for short breaks in the rain to continue the shooting schedule. The hot, wet weather
and the multitude of mosquitoes and other biting insects added to the uncomfort-
able conditions. "Miserable day," she said. "It rained but we shot anyway." The
script required Ann to kill a bobcat on the last day, and she was not happy about

it. "I shot the bobcat and I felt awful, but it had to be done. The conservation men [assigned to the movie] were very impressed."

The film company completed the project after sixteen days and Ann was sad to have it end. "It was rather depressing saying goodbye. We had dinner and then we danced. Later Bob and I went for a drive, came home and we all talked 'til late." Roark and Ann exchanged letters that summer, and she made several appearances with Kelly the dog at fairs. In correspondence to a friend she said: "We have completed the pilot film, and the latest word from Hollywood is that the rushes are good, so now we just have to wait."

In late June, Ann prepared for the Miss Universe preliminaries. She bought a new gown and had photos taken by Joe Clark in Detroit. At the Miss Michigan portion of the contest at Northland Shopping Center, Ann was chosen as one of the top eight finalists. A few days later she competed in the Miss Universe Pageant at Detroit's Fox Theatre. She didn't earn the crown and was disappointed. "The audience picked me, but the judges didn't."

The previous year, in 1957, Ann planned to qualify for the World Archery Tournament that was scheduled to be held behind the Iron Curtain in Prague, Czechoslovakia. It was the first time that the United States planned to send a complete team to the World Championships. The Bear Archery Company and *Sports Illustrated* agreed to sponsor Ann, so she and her father received polio and smallpox vaccinations and completed their passport applications. She was ready to go including "… having the U.S. Team official uniform and willing to pay my own expenses." She soon learned that she didn't meet the criteria as an amateur according to the Federation Internationale de Tir a' l'Arc (F.I.T.A.) standards, and she was disqualified from the team. That year in Prague, both the U.S. Men's and Women's teams conquered the competition by winning first, second, and third places. The Women's team was headed by Carol Meinhart, who earned first place, and Ann Clark, who took second.

In 1958, Ann submitted her request to participate in the N.A.A.-F.I.T.A. meet in St. Louis. She hoped to earn a spot on the U.S. team at the World Target Tournament in Brussels, Belgium. Clearly she wasn't an amateur, but Frank hoped the rules could be re-interpreted to allow her eligibility. He wrote a letter of appeal to J. Robert Kest, secretary-treasurer of the National Archery Association. In his response to Frank, Kest quoted new policies that strictly prohibited professional archers. Kest said the rules were intended "to exclude anyone who has received more than $40.00 for money and to exclude those who have capitalized on their athletic fame in any way by profiting commercially therefrom, or by accepting special inducements to participate."

Archery was included in the Olympics in 1900 and women were allowed to compete in 1904 and 1908. The sport was eliminated from the Olympic lineup after the 1920 games, mostly because of a lack of standardized international rules. In his letter to the Marstons, Kest had warned that strict compliance to the F.I.T.A. rules was essential to protect the possibility of the sport's future inclusion in the Olympics. "It will be evident to you how all of this would bear upon—and quite possibly prevent—our country's participation in any future Olympic Games where, it is proposed, archery will once again be introduced." However, archery wasn't reinstated into the Olympics until 1972.

Based on her existing contracts with Pearson Archery, Bear Archery, and *Sports Illustrated*, and the fact that she had a talent agent, the truth was that Ann earned several thousand dollars a year with her archery skill. But the Marstons took issue with Ann being singled out from all the other "amateurs" who had lucrative affiliations with commercial archery enterprises. The amateur/professional debate raged for years and seemed to be far from resolution. Ann held bitter feelings about her exclusion and wrote a letter to Bill Stump of *The Eastern Bowhunter Magazine*:

> I wanted to do my part to represent the women field archers, and I sent in an application that was <u>rejected,</u> in no uncertain terms. The reason given was that they felt I was no longer considered an amateur. It seems a little odd to me that of 5 million archers in the United States, I, at 19 years of age, should be considered the only professional. I don't have to tell you that I am very hurt …
>
> According to the rules as set up by the N.A.A., it only excluded archers who receive pay for demonstrations, but not tutors of archery or salesmen of archery equipment, etc. It's common knowledge that nearly all our top archers are associated with archery manufacturers in some way or another, and several have also appeared in paid archery demonstrations, which incidentally, does not contribute to one's archery skill. The point is this, why have I been selected the guinea pig?

In a letter to Stump she recounted Kest's insistence that archers would jeopardize their amateur status if they competed for prize money in an upcoming contest:

> Mr. Kest went on to tell me that anybody winning any prize money in the Fred Bear Money Shoot to be held in Grayling would automatically be excluded from the F.I.T.A. competition. If this shoot was to be affiliated with the Olympics, I could whole-heartedly agree. But this, of course, would be an entirely different story because an Olympic competitor could not even receive so much as a neck of an arrow from an archery manufacturer or dealer, as you well know.

The St. Louis N.A.A.-F.I.T.A shoot-off was held in June and Ann Marston stayed home. The following month in Brussels, Ann Weber Corby of the U.S. Team won an individual second place rating. Corby, from Boonton, New Jersey, was a well-established champion with a successful competitive career. Her score helped the United States women's team take first place in the World Tournament.

Meanwhile, Ann worked hard practicing to defend her archery Free Style championship at the upcoming Nationals scheduled at Grayling, Michigan. Most often she went to the Lincoln Bowmen range and spent the day shooting. Sometimes she packed a picnic lunch and returned home late and exhausted.

The National Guard Camp in Grayling was the site of the 1958 National Field Archery Association Tournament. The weather was beautiful that week, and Ann wore a modest white bustier top and cuffed white shorts. She was featured in newspaper photos several times during the four-day event. Once again Ann cinched the National Free Style individual title—with a high score of 2463—followed closely by Cleo Roberson for the second year in a row.

Roberson was a young mother, and she and her husband, Pete, shared his Bear bow for competitions. "I went into archery even though I had four kids. After carrying them around my arms were very strong, so my bow was heavier than all the other ladies' bows." There were, naturally, personal rivalries in the competitions, but Cleo Roberson had an opinion of what is the most important attribute for building a champion. "It is knowing how to hold your tongue and keep cool," she said. "I always went up and shook hands with my competitors before shooting. Whoever shoots the highest score is the winner. You don't have to put someone down to put yourself on top. But Ann Marston wasn't like that; she was a very nice gal."

In the book *Archery Champions*, author Robert J. Rhode commented about Ann's outstanding performance at the N.F.A.A tournament that year:

> The 1958 National Field Archery Tournament at Grayling, Michigan, drew the largest number of archers in the history of the event. It was at Grayling that Ann probably had her greatest triumph, setting new records in the Hunters and Animal rounds, and carrying the aggregate score to 2463, which brought her 4th National Field Championship ... Few, if any, archery champions have done more to present archery to the general public than Ann Marston. This combination of a fine competitor, an excellent showman, and a beautiful young lady makes Ann truly one of our great Archery Champions.

Other female champions at the contest included Jo McCubbins of Santa Ana, California, who won the Instinctive Women's Round. Ann Weber Corby, recently returned from the World Championships in Brussels, took second in Instinctive with an aggregate score of 2197.

The N.F.A.A. tournament was followed the next day by the very first Fred Bear Archery Money Shoot that offered generous cash prizes totaling $5,000. There was tremendous excitement in the field about the new contest. Ann Marston, America's first female professional archer, registered for the Women's event along with seven talented rivals. In an interview published in the April 15–May 15, 1961, issue of *The Archers' Magazine (TAM)*, Ann Weber Corby described her motivation for entering that competition in 1958—she wanted to beat Ann Marston:

> *My archery avocation dates back to my first championships in 1939-1940. Had there been Olympic competition for archery at that time, I would have been eligible and without a doubt a Gold Medal winner. I doggedly shot in this "dream" world, not accepting bows, expenses or help of any kind until the summer of '58. Against my better judgment, I was persuaded by Clayton Shenk (who incidentally paid my entry fee and assured me it would not affect my F.I.T.A. standing) to enter the first Bear money shoot. Now mark this—I have always shot field instinctively [without a sight] and had won the N.F.A.A. Championship in 1955.*
>
> *There was always a question among the "students" of archery as to whether I could beat Ann Marston if I shot Free Style [with a sight on her bow]. Ann had won the Free Style division of N.F.A.A. several times. This was a chance to meet her and decide the issue. So I allowed myself to be induced to accept the challenge!*

Ann Marston's dignified rebuttal to Corby's comments was published in the June 15–July 15, 1961, issue of *The Archers' Magazine (TAM):* "I happen to love archery, and it's my fond desire to see it in the ranks of our other great American sports. For many years now I have been promoting archery to the best of my ability." She continued, "To me it is a great privilege to be a professional archer, for it is the professional in any sport that makes it great; and it is through the professional that archery will gain the recognition it so richly deserves."

On that hot August day in 1958, Ann Corby won the Women's first prize purse of $1,000. Cleo Roberson earned $400 with second, and Ann Marston came in third, collecting $200. Unfortunately for Corby, the consequence of winning the money meant she immediately lost her amateur standing under the N.A.A.-F.I.T.A. ruling, and was therefore disqualified from competing in the next World Target Championship.

However, the N.A.A.-F.I.T.A. professional/amateur regulations were later re-interpreted, enabling to Corby to compete at the 1959 World Target Tournament in Stockholm, Sweden. She earned the individual gold medal and led the Women's team to another first-place victory.

The following year the universal policies were altered again, and Corby was formally declared a professional and ineligible to compete again at the international level. The ruling changed the course of her future. Corby described her disappointment in the November 1975 issue of *Pro Archer* magazine: "With all competitive incentive gone, no chance to defend my world title, and being an 'outcast' at the tournaments, I hung up my Hoyt, closed my tackle box, crawled into my shell and put my nose to the grindstone managing Robin Hood Archery Company." After withdrawing from competition, Corby continued to be an avid bow hunter and successful businesswoman. Her immense talent was formally recognized in 1972, when she was enshrined in the Archery Hall of Fame along with her husband, Earl Hoyt.

Back on the show circuit, Ann did exhibitions at fairs in Bay City and Escanaba. At the Michigan State Fair in Detroit, she arrived in a helicopter for her performance. In Canada, she had shows in Dresden and in Aylmer, Ontario, where she shared the bill with Pinky Lee. Mark Leddy offered an appearance for Ann at the Maid of the Mist Festival in Niagara Falls for no salary, just expenses, and she accepted. It was a tremendous opportunity for publicity, and she once again was invited to be an honorary Native American. Members of the Tuscarora Nation held a ceremony and named her "Yeh-Tah-Rah-Qwes," meaning "She Chooses the Arrow."

In New York, Ann scored an appearance on Jack Paar's *Tonight Show*, which was hosted that night by Johnny Carson. According to Ann, she "had a lot of time on it," and Carson posed for a photograph with Ann and Frank. Ann performed on *Captain Kangaroo* once again. Later that fall, she and her father took a short deer hunting trip, this time to Ivan James' lodge in Curran, Michigan. They both bagged whitetail deer at the ranch and took home movies of Ann and Frank sitting in the blinds and shooting at targets.

When asked during interviews about her British heritage, Ann often replied that she was "half and half. Half of me was born in England and the other half resides in the United States." The Marston family always wanted to tour Europe, and through Mark Leddy they got the opportunity to go to London in December 1958. He arranged a contract through respected London producers Lew and Leslie Grade to co-represent Ann for the engagement. The 15 percent agent commission was to be split between Leddy and the Grade brothers. Ann agreed to accept $1,500 for two televised performances.

The Marstons left Detroit, switched to a Pan Am jet in New York, and had a layover in Labrador. The London airport was fogged in and they landed in Paris to wait for clearance. After waiting several hours in Paris, they took off again and landed in Scotland. From there they boarded a train for a ten-hour trip to London.

They finally arrived in London and checked into the Cumberland Hotel in Marble Arch at 6 a.m. Ann was treated like a major celebrity, and newspaper reporters from the *London Star, The Evening News* and the *London Daily Herald* conducted interviews with her in the morning. Later in the day some of their British relatives came to the hotel to visit. Frank's brothers Victor and Charles lived in the area with their families, as did Florence's sister, Agnes. They all were invited to see the show.

The London Palladium had a reputation as being one of the world's most desirable venues for performers. *Sunday Night at the London Palladium* was televised every week—with a variety show concept similar to Ed Sullivan's show. Ann was also contracted to appear on television later in the week for a companion show, the *Saturday Spectacular*. The newspapers made a big fuss about Ann that week; *The Star* headline read: "Miss Robin Hood Comes to Town." *The Evening News* referred to her as "The Most Dangerous Blonde in Town." *News* Reporter Kendall McDonald wrote an article about Ann's upcoming performance:

> There is a beautiful blonde in town whom I rate the most dangerous woman I have met. And tomorrow on the Sunday Night at the London Palladium show, that 20-year-old American will provide one of the most unusual acts seen on television here.
>
> For young Ann Marston is the world's champion woman archer. She holds 11 American national championships. On the Palladium show, she will be shooting aluminum arrows (from a bow with a pull of 24 lbs.) at candles, balloons, apples and other targets.

On Sunday, December 7, 1958, Ann and her parents arrived at the famed London Palladium. Ann shared the stage with an interesting mix of co-stars including "American Dance Stylists" Harrison and Fisher, comedian Georgie Kaye, tenor Thomas Hayward, and show host Bruce Forsyth. Another featured performer was sultry Sallie Blair, who cut an album on Bethlehem Records in 1957, and dramatized the part of Serena on a recording of *Porgie and Bess* earlier in 1958. A newspaper article described Blair's unique talents:

> … Other big names will be Harrison and Fisher in a dancing act, and Sallie Blair, a coloured singer who has been in the news in the U.S. for the past two years. Sallie has been hailed by U.S. critics as "the most exciting young singer in years." She has a frenetic uninhabited style which can leave you almost breathless as she kicks off her show and "Hots Up." Sallie's best known songs are "That Old Black Magic," "It's almost like Being in Love," and "Hold 'Em Joe."

43

Britain's top TV show aired at 8 p.m. The next day Ann received a favorable review from newspaper critic Hilton West. "I admired attractive Ann Marston's archery display, though. She at least was on target. And on what was very much a routine night on Channel 9, that was certainly something to be grateful for."

Another London paper picked up the story and complimented Ann's performance that Sunday night:

> *Robin Hood had developed some unexpected curves, the children must have thought if they stayed up watching Channel 9 last night. English born Ann Marston, America's champion girl archer, neatly snuffed out three candle flames with her arrows in Sunday Night at the Palladium. In a bill which was all American except for compere [master-of-ceremonies] Bruce Forsyth, Ann provided the only note of originality—again excepting Bruce Forsyth.*

The news of her talent reached as far as Amsterdam, and she was featured in a Dutch newspaper story. The office clerks of Lew and Leslie Grade Ltd. were already forwarding fan mail to Ann. She was invited to the studio of London's *Sunday Pictorial* newspaper, where she was featured in a large photo spread:

> *Watch out Robin Hood! For when lovely Ann Marston takes aim with her bow and arrow, she scrambles eggs at 340 m.p.h. That's the speed of the arrow flashing through the shell in these amazing Sunday Pictorial pictures. On the right you can see the egg shattering after the arrow has passed through it. Ann—20 and born in Britain—is an American archery champion. Now she is in London with her trick-shooting act.*

During their visit to their native London, Ann, Frank, and Florence went sightseeing and visited friends and relatives during the Christmas holiday. Home movies recorded events such as when Ann fed the birds in Trafalgar Square and posed with her bow and arrow in front of Buckingham Palace and Big Ben. The British relatives threw a farewell party and saw them off at the airport. The Marstons flew home to the United States in early January 1959, never to return to England.

4

Michigan's Monarch

Ann's diverse talents took a new direction in 1959 when she was named Miss Detroit. She was later crowned Miss Michigan and enjoyed the prestige of participating in the Miss America Pageant. All three of the pageants were held in 1959 in preparation for the 1960 reigning year. Ann continued touring as an archery attraction, but her duties as Miss Michigan often conflicted with her contracted performance schedule. Her stint as beauty queen was full of stress and controversy, which affected her health.

Her 1959 appointment calendar was fully booked, and along with the usual sports shows in the New York area, Ann made several television appearances on *Captain Kangaroo*. She was a guest on the daytime quiz show *Who Do You Trust?*, with host Johnny Carson and announcer Ed McMahon. She answered a sufficient number of trivia questions to win $100. On the road she often got top billing, earning up to $500 per day with "The Ann Marston Show," and the family toured Minneapolis, Omaha, Akron, and Nashville. Financially, it looked like another prosperous year, so Ann purchased a mink stole for her mother's birthday in April.

An exclusive preview of *My Dog Sheppy* was held at the Wyandotte Theater on May 17-19, 1959. The pilot film for the proposed television series was on the bill with *Intent to Kill*, starring Richard Todd and Betsy Drake, and a second feature, *The Remarkable Mr. Pennypacker*, with Clifton Webb. The local newspaper ads touted: "Ann Marston in person! On the screen in her first movie, *My Dog Sheppy*."

Most Downriver residents were very impressed with Ann's celebrity, and her archery demonstrations in the Detroit area were always well-attended. One local woman kept a scrapbook of Ann's accomplishments, and there was a fan club forming in Ohio. Ann often had her dog Beau's fur tinted in pastel shades and his toenails painted for their personal appearances. She sometimes decorated each of her own fingernails with a different shade of polish and wore majorette-type boots jazzed up with glitter and tassels. Ann Marston was an idol to little girls who fantasized about a glamorous lifestyle in those days before high-fashion Barbie dolls hit the market. She was the closest thing to a fairy princess that daughters of Detroit steelworkers and assembly line men would ever see. When Wyandotte resident Mary Ellen Caruso was a child, she was awed by Ann's fame. She said, "My world stopped so I could watch her every time she was on television."

Despite the Marstons' hopes, *My Dog Sheppy* never was chosen. The producers determined that the public and animal rights activists would not be tolerant of the scene where the bobcat was killed. They sent Ann a copy of the 35mm print, and the original shipping box containing three lead film cans was eventually stored away. Ann must have been disappointed but she had other plans: Her entry was the very first that was received for the Miss Detroit contest. Initially, she was reluctant and told an interviewer: "I was invited to enter the Miss Detroit Pageant. Of course I immediately refused, because I wasn't too interested in beauty contests. I had a career, which was shooting bow and arrow, but finally I was sort of talked into it."

According to a newspaper report, the pageant's rules stated: "Any young woman between the ages of 18 and 28 who is a high school graduate, and who has never been married is eligible to compete. In addition the entrant should have some talent and can be either professional or amateur." With her years of performance experience, Ann was more than ready with the talent portion. Although she had been modeling since she was ten months old, Ann felt she needed some expert guidance to polish her skills for the beauty pageant. She enrolled in a local finishing school and contacted the best photographer she knew to shoot her publicity photos. The day after she was selected as one of ten semifinalists in the Miss Detroit contest, she got serious. She wrote: "I had my first two lessons at Patricia Stevens—Visual Poise & Figure Control. Also went to Joe Clark for pictures."

On June 11, Ann arrived at the Detroit Women's Club for the Miss Detroit Pageant. The five judges were former U.S. Ambassador Frederick M. Alger, local television personality Mary Morgan, dance performer Joseph Easton, dress designer and shop owner Madeline Sinasac, and Joe Clark, who photographed Ann for her beauty pageant portrait and did the *Life* magazine layout six years earlier in 1953.

Ann performed the archery act, winning the talent element of the competition. She came in second in the swimsuit category. The newspapers recorded her official height as 5'7", weight of 118 pounds and figure measurements of 35-22½ -35½. Thanks to time spent researching at Wyandotte's Bacon Memorial Public Library, she answered appropriately when asked the three qualifying questions:

> *"What is the significance of the St. Lawrence Seaway opening to Michi-gan and Detroit?" "In what area has Michigan made the greatest progress in the last five years?" "As a young lady, what is the greatest contribution you can make?"*

She was poised, talented, and beautiful, and earned the rhinestone crown while her parents proudly took home movies of the event. That night Ann modestly wrote in her journal: "Tonight I was selected as Miss Detroit by five judges at the Women's city club."

Detroit Times reporter George E. Van was entranced with Ann. In an article, he enthusiastically reported his impressions: "She could be called a typical American beauty but she was born in England. Wholesome doesn't fit either. It implies being healthy but dull. Ann's healthy and rosy-cheeked but she's bright-eyed, animated and poised … it's a wonder that Hollywood hasn't taken her over."

As the new reigning Miss Detroit, Ann was awarded a ball gown and several other gifts donated by local merchants. One of the prizes was a $500 scholarship to the prestigious Patricia Stevens Finishing School operated by Doris Wood, unofficially known as the "Queen Maker." The previous year Doris guided Patience Pierce to victory as Miss Michigan 1959. Ann aimed to achieve that honor on July 10.

The month leading up to the Miss Michigan Pageant was filled with many appearances, including interviews on Budd Lynch's and Lou Gordon's radio programs, both based in Detroit. She was honored to be named Miss C.F., representing the National Cystic Fibrosis Society. Detroit Mayor Louis C. Miriani invited Ann to appear at the first International Freedom Festival, which celebrated the friendship between the United States and Canada. The July 4 event also highlighted the recent opening of the St. Lawrence Seaway. Ann stood on a barge in Windsor with the Ambassador Bridge in the background, and shot an arrow across the Detroit River toward the United States, symbolizing the partnership of the two nations.

Ann visited Madeline Sinasac's shop in Detroit to inspect the dressmaker's design for a unique gown to wear at the pageant. It was sleeveless, and made of white lace with blue accents to symbolize an automobile wheel, in tribute to the Motor City. The "Wheel of Detroit" dress was described in *The Detroit News*: "The dress was designed like a wheel with inserts of blue lace connecting the spokes. The under-skirts were blue, representing the water of the Detroit River and Lake St. Clair."

Ann had many preparations for the competition besides fittings for gowns and attending lessons at the finishing school, so she elected not to compete in the Field Archery Nationals held that summer in Bend, Oregon. Cleo Roberson was the Free Style champion that year. "I didn't beat Ann Marston," Roberson said. "The only reason I won that year was because she wasn't there."

The entry contract for the Miss Michigan competition incorporated sections regarding the judging process, scholarship awards, and the management of Ann's personal appearances as Miss Michigan for the next year if she won. Ann signed the contract on June 17, witnessed by her father and Doris Wood.

The Michigan Theater in Muskegon was the site for the state's largest beauty pageant. The sponsor was the Greater Muskegon Junior Chamber of Commerce, under the direction of their manager, Leonard Van Bogelen. The incentive package for the debutantes was impressive. Pepsi Cola offered a $500 scholarship to the queen, and a wide range of Michigan sponsors stepped up to donate a nine-outfit wardrobe, prizes, and services totaling $2,250. The winner of the talent portion would be awarded an additional $250 scholarship, and the girl selected by the other contestants as Miss Congeniality could adopt a cocker spaniel puppy donated from a local breeder. The title-holder would participate as Miss Michigan in the ultimate beauty contest of the 20th Century, the Miss America Pageant.

Ann faced a field of twenty-four state competitors for the Miss Michigan crown. The pageant stretched over a three-day period and included photo sessions and banquets. It began with a parade on Wednesday headed by Michigan Gov. G. Mennen "Soapy" Williams. The beauty queens traveled in open convertibles and were accompanied by floats, majorettes, and marching bands. Ann's white 1960 Oldsmobile 98 convertible and driver Robert Kish were provided by Dave Menhart, owner of one of Wyandotte's automobile dealerships. Several dignitaries attended the festivities, including a business representative from the Miss America Organization, and incumbent 1959 Miss Michigan, Patience Pierce, who was standing by to pass the crown to the next lucky girl.

Rehearsals for the contest were conducted all day on Thursday, with the girls separated into two units for judging purposes. The groups rotated in the two different segments of the competition on Thursday and Friday evenings, alternating the talent exhibition and the combined evening gown/bathing suit division. According to *The Detroit News*, there apparently were some negotiations required to allow Ann's participation in the talent contest:

> *Contestants are not allowed to use professional skills in this phase of the competition. Although Miss Marston is paid for performances with the bow and arrow at sports shows, she was allowed to demonstrate these talents here in the theory that archery is not a "professional sport." In the*

talent division of the Miss Michigan contest, Miss Marston displayed her skill as an archer, shooting at moving targets, putting out lighted candles with an arrow and bursting swinging balloons.

The Miss Michigan Pageant master of ceremonies was Chicago-based entertainer Jack Herbert, and piano accompaniment was provided by a local musician. In the televised program, and in front of a sold-out house of more than 1,800 people, Ann Marston lost the talent award to violinist Barbara Anne Youngdahl, Miss Kalamazoo. She scored high in the evening gown competition and tied for first place in the swimsuit event. Ann was ultimately selected as one of four finalists. An important question was posed to the contestants: "If you were chosen Miss Michigan, how would you sell the state to the world?" According to *The Detroit News*, Ann replied: "While Michigan is known as a great industrial center, the world should also know it as a delightful place in which to live; a place blessed with all that God can offer."

It must have been an acceptable response, because Ann won the competition and was selected as Michigan's next representative in the Miss America Pageant. A photo caption from the *Muskegon Chronicle* described the final dramatic moments of Ann's victory:

> *Comes the Dawn ... Second runner-up is identified; first runner-up is called on stage ... eeeee! I'm IT!! With a squeal of delight Ann Marston of Detroit, archer, "got the message." By process of elimination, she realized Miss Michigan of 1960 was her title. Pamela Anderson, Miss Muskegon, a finalist, stood ready to congratulate Ann as soon as she could come down to earth.*

With her proud parents in attendance and her eyes shining with delight, Ann Marston was proclaimed Miss Michigan for 1960. She was immediately crowned by Patience Pierce. Ann sat on a throne that was flanked by the two runners-up, and accepted a bouquet of red roses and a trophy. The *Detroit Times* reported, "After her victory, Miss Marston said: 'I am very proud and humble. I can't find the words to thank each and every one of you who made this honor possible. All I can say is thanks from the bottom of my heart.'" Ann was later asked if she cried when she won, and she jokingly said: "I cry when I lose! Actually it was very funny because I didn't cry, and I thought how ridiculous it is for everybody to cry when this great honor is bestowed upon them."

For the next eight weeks the path to Atlantic City promised to be full of duties and obligations. The Marstons stayed in Muskegon for several days following the

Miss Michigan contest to attend the official Coronation Ball. Ann was fitted for her complimentary wardrobe and made the initial round of personal appearances for the Greater Muskegon Junior Chamber of Commerce. She presided over parades in Grand Rapids and Kalamazoo. Back in Wyandotte, officials were preparing a royal welcome for their own girl next door. The local papers had a field day, and one of them confirmed the community's giddy delight:

> … Now, heads are held high over the tremendous honor accorded our fair young lady, Ann Marston, voted last Friday night as being the queen of the state in her new title of "Miss Michigan." Of course, we can't say in mere printer's ink how proud we are of Ann, who has for many years been one of the greatest, proudest possession this 105-year-old city owns. Statuesque, beautiful, poised, talented, friendly, unspoiled, and genuine are only a few of the adjectives that come readily to our typewriter. Not only has the press of the nation acclaimed our world's champion archer for all her qualities, but her home town next Monday is going to show her how much they appreciate entering the magic circle of "Miss Michigan" cities for the first time in history.
>
> Miss Marston has had a tremendous week with parades, shows, and appearances all over the state; she is accustomed to the ooh's and aah's of tens of thousands of spectators. But we'll bet that no welcome has ever been more heartfelt that the one she will get from her happy, proud, misty-eyed townsfolk … who see in one of their girls the future Miss America!

Upon her triumphant return to Michigan via Detroit Metropolitan Airport, Ann was accompanied by state police to the city's border, where she was then escorted by a sixteen-vehicle motorcade of Wyandotte's police officers. The official parade began at the Menhart automobile dealership on Eureka and proceeded down Biddle Avenue, the city's main street. The procession stopped at City Hall, where Ann was greeted by city dignitaries and Mayor John McCauley. He presented her with a formal resolution from the City Council:

> This body is proud and happy to take official note of the fact that Miss Ann Marston, a Wyandotte citizen, has been chosen Miss Michigan in statewide competition held in Muskegon, thus adding fresh laurels to her crown as National Champion Archer and bringing credit to herself and favorable publicity to Wyandotte.

Led by director Ken Hauer, the Roosevelt High School Marching Chiefs performed for their former clarinet player, who wept with delight. The *Wyandotte News Herald* followed the story. " 'My heart is indeed full,' said Ann Marston. While Roosevelt High School band members two-stepped in tempo to their rendition of 'Oh, You Beautiful Doll,' Miss Marston choked up and was unable to answer questions put to her by several local and Detroit reporters." The festivities were televised by Detroit's WXYZ-TV station. Ann wrote in her diary that "it was the thrill of my life."

In the days that followed her Wyandotte homecoming, Ann traveled to the Michigan capitol in Lansing. After a photo session with Gov. Williams, she was invited to address the Michigan House of Representatives. Rep. William Copeland offered a resolution congratulating Ann on her accomplishments.

Her schedule was immediately filled to capacity with appearances as Miss Michigan and performances as Ann Marston. Most of her personal diary entries during this time were hurried and concise, as she made speeches, attended autograph sessions, banquets, press conferences, and several professional archery engagements. Her Oldsmobile dealership sponsor received credit at many events because "In My Merry Oldsmobile" was the theme music for Ann's arrival and departure. She presided over a well-attended charity event at Flat Rock Speedway with the proceeds designated for handicapped children. Ann arrived in the white convertible formally dressed in high heels, strapless gown, and crown. She looked a bit comical as she shot her bow while wearing the regalia, but the crowd loved every minute of her performance.

After a busy week traveling from New York to Muskegon and Chicago, she returned home and was violently ill for two days. She was anxious about the episode and wrote: "… guess it's all the pressure." She continued to suffer from frequent colds, and her glucose levels ran high, averaging between 215 and 230. By current standards, diabetics test themselves frequently every day, striving to maintain blood sugar levels between 80 and 120. That was not the case for diabetes patients in the late 1950s, who were tested only during doctor visits every month or so.

Miss America 1999, Nicole Johnson, experienced similar symptoms during intense pageant competitions. Her book, *Living with Diabetes*, vividly describes Johnson's personal experiences as a modern Miss America and an insulin-dependent diabetic. In an e-mail interview she reiterated the effects of pressure on a diabetic: "Stress amplifies the crazy sugars and plays a huge role in diabetes control. It is common for people with diabetes to feel more run down; the autoimmune aspect of the disease causes that. Colds can also be linked to high glucose. Traveling is not easy … I wear an insulin pump. I don't know how I could have performed as Miss America without it."

Ann kept her diabetes a closely guarded secret. Only her family and closest friends knew of her illness. Johnson's opinion is: "It has almost always been ta-boo to mention diabetes or any other chronic conditions. There are many reasons; people assume you are fat or lack self-control. There may be assumptions that you are unable to participate or live like others with restrictions in lifestyle. There was ignorance and fear of catching the condition."

Although she weighed only 118 pounds, Ann attempted to lose weight during the two months between the Miss Michigan and Miss America pageants. A physician put Ann on diet pills once again. According to Johnson, "Weight gain is common and a struggle. Insulin is a hormone, so it is similar to hormone therapy when women gain weight. There is a constant balancing act between glucose levels and caloric absorption."

Ann was quite accustomed to a hectic lifestyle and wouldn't allow concerns about her physical health slow her down now that she was also Miss Michigan.

William (Willie) Heston was a football player from University of Michigan who was named All-American in 1903 and 1904. He later became a Detroit judge and founded Michigan Memorial Park in Flat Rock, Michigan, in 1927. In 1955, his son, John, established the Willie Heston Sports Hall of Fame, which inducted several Michigan athletes to the roster each year and included Joe Louis, Ted Lindsay, and Ty Cobb. Ann's accomplishments in 1959 caused waves in the sports world and prompted Hall of Fame Director Heston to take unusual action by nominating an additional candidate. He made the following proposal in a letter to the twenty-eight voting members:

> *The Willie Heston Sports Hall of Fame is now in its fourth year. We take pride in the manner in which we conduct our selections, never having swayed from our original purpose which was to have those already in the Hall of Fame vote for the seven to be added each year. However, we have recently had an event occur in Michigan of which we are justly proud. In our midst is a girl who has won top honors in the sports world of archery. She has now been selected Miss Michigan and will be entered in the coming Miss America contest. We should like to nominate Miss Ann Marston, now Miss Michigan, as a candidate for our 1959 selection.*

The existing members of the Heston Sports Hall of Fame overwhelmingly approved Ann's addition to their ranks, and she became the twenty-ninth inductee. It was remarkable that in 1959, Ann became the youngest member and only the second Michigan female athlete to earn the honor. Jean Hoxie was the first and was known as "The Queen of Tennis" for her championship record and accomplishments as a high school tennis coach.

Ann and her parents attended the induction ceremony in Detroit, and afterward she sat for the official portrait rendered by artist John Coppin. Her framed portrait hung with the twenty-eight other honorees in the Sports Hall of Fame building located in Michigan Memorial Park in Flat Rock.

A technical question remained regarding Ann's eligibility as a contestant in the Miss America Pageant: Was she an American citizen? Ann was born in England, but she received American citizenship as soon as she and her parents were eligible, so she definitely qualified for the pageant. Wyandotte Councilman Richard Kelly commented in the *News Herald*, "International relations might note that a girl born in England can become Miss Michigan, and even Miss America. This is especially significant for an international border city such as ours."

"Queen Maker" Doris Wood of the Patricia Stevens School took Ann under her wing and scrutinized everything from her eyebrows to her posture. Ann was assigned a detailed exercise regimen: her makeup was refined, mannerisms critiqued, and hair restyled. In a letter Ann said:

> … I enrolled in a finishing school and started extensive preparation for the Miss America contest. I lost weight, learned to walk all over again, etc., etc. The director of the school insisted that everything be letter perfect, for she said, in Atlantic City they know their business. I learned that certain points of your legs must touch while others must not. I studied the correct position of the spine. Everything matters, even down to the exact earrings to wear and gloves. All summer we looked for <u>the</u> bathing suit and dozens of other items, both large and small.

Seemingly insignificant details held great importance for the beauty queen. According to resident Mary Thorson, Ann was in a local shop searching for a new pair of gloves to wear for the pageant festivities. Ann was frustrated because the only gloves in the store had stitched ribs on the back of the hand. Thorson overheard her remark that the style was old-fashioned and not suitable for her pageant ensemble.

The big day was approaching fast and Ann posed for the local newspapers. The *Detroit Sunday Times* on August 30 provided an up-close look at Ann's preparations for the pageant:

> *Michigan Beauty Goes Into Training for Title*
> *"I never realized I was such a total wreck before." One of the best-looking "total wrecks" around was talking. Her hair is honey blonde, her skin is tanned, her eyes are blue and they smile a lot. It all adds up to Miss Michigan and/or Ann Marston. She sat with legs gracefully crossed at*

*the ankles, hands folded in her lap, looking as if she is a finishing school's
finished product. She is.*

*... Ann's been getting around very well on two legs for years, but
she found out there are tricks to standing, walking, sitting. Hers was a
healthy walk—the long strides of an athlete who walked 4 miles a day
during archery tournaments ... Ann figures she's spent 50 hours studying
make-up, posture, exercises, and diets.*

Both *The Detroit News* and *Free Press* ran extensive stories about Ann during
the week before the Miss America Pageant. *The Detroit News Sunday Roto* article,
themed "How a Beauty Gets Started," included childhood pictures of Ann. There
was a contemporary photo of her in a white bathing suit, with her mother looking
on. *The Detroit Sunday Pictorial* topped it all with a sensational three-page spread,
including a stunning full-color cover shot of Ann in the "Wheel of Detroit" gown.
By this time, the newspapers in the Detroit area and in Muskegon had full confidence in Ann's name recognition, and often used only her first name in headlines.
Reporter Georgia Hughes informed her readers of some of the pageant's basic facts:

*The best wishes and hopes of all Wyandotte will go with Ann Marston as
she leaves this Sunday for Atlantic City to compete in the Miss America
contest. Currently "Miss Michigan," Ann is the first Wyandotte girl to
enter the Miss America event, which has been staged 32 times since 1921,
and halted for a few times during the Depression.*

*The national finals in Atlantic City this year will have 54 contestants,
including for the first time a representative from every state in the union,
a Miss Canada, a Miss New York City, a Miss Chicago, and a Miss District
of Columbia.*

*A lot is at stake in this dazzling pageant. The winner receives over
$150,000 in prizes, engagements and personal appearances throughout
the United States, Europe and South America.*

Ann and Florence boarded an airplane to Atlantic City on the Sunday before
the pageant, escorted by Ann's official state traveling companion, Doris Wood. The
Wyandotte News Herald and *Wyandotte Tribune* newspapers combined funds to
hire photojournalist Ron Tocco to document Ann's adventures in Atlantic City and
to call the papers daily with his report. Tocco was a Wyandotte native and had
recently photographed Ann for the cover of *Photo Topics* magazine. True to her
overprotective nature, Florence was uneasy about young Ron's influence on her
daughter. She wanted to ensure that he was a gentleman and could be trusted to

be alone with Ann, so she telephoned his mother. Eileen Tocco was annoyed, and assured Florence that Ron was indeed responsible enough to be affiliated with Ann in Atlantic City, as well as in Wyandotte. So, Tocco accompanied Frank Marston on the long drive from southeastern Michigan to the Jersey Shore. In the trunk was luggage, camera equipment and all of the bulky paraphernalia required for Ann's archery performance in the talent competition.

An optional talent competition was first scheduled in 1935 to enhance the traditional bathing suit and evening gown events. The compulsory talent segment of the Miss America Pageant was mandated in 1938 by Executive Director Lenora Slaughter. With her formidable presence, Slaughter's efforts resulted in a new, improved Miss America realm. At first, talent category was designed to be worth a third of the judges scoring, and it immediately improved the entire production. Slaughter ruled the roost and her management style was sometimes referred to as "the iron fist in a velvet glove." She was recognized in the official program as celebrating her 25th anniversary with the Miss America Organization.

Ann Marston fit Slaughter's pattern for the ideal American female with her wholesome looks, ladylike demeanor, and natural charisma. For the 1960 pageant, there were four equally valuable scoring elements of the upcoming contest: Swimsuit, Talent, Evening Gown, and Personality. Ann's petite body was tanned and nicely proportioned because of her athletic lifestyle, and she was encouraged when she tied for first place in the swimsuit category during the Miss Michigan contest. Based on past television broadcasts of Miss America performances, there was absolutely no doubt that Ann could shine in the talent division. The evening gown competition for Miss America was probably going to be the toughest part of the contest, but thanks to Doris Wood's tutoring, Ann was comfortable wearing tiaras, Cinderella gowns, and dyed-to-match shoes. As a longtime veteran of show business, she wasn't concerned about suffering stage fright while being spotlighted on national television. Ann had made dozens of appearances on all the biggest shows since she was a child; she undoubtedly had more TV experience than all of the other contestants combined. She was certainly well-prepared to win over the judges with her self confidence, wit, skill, and charm.

Win or lose, the opportunity was guaranteed to generate a substantial amount of fame and fortune for Ann Penelope Marston. The publicity alone was worth the effort. It had potentially better press exposure than her appearance on Ed Sullivan's show. The incentive of winning one of the $30,000 scholarships and awards was another factor that she considered. Pepsi Cola sponsored $1,000 each for the winners of various talent segments, and she certainly had a decent shot at that. The young woman who would be crowned Miss America stood to win a $10,000 scholarship and additional rewards. The scheduled speaking engagements were worth additional thousands of dollars over the course of the one-year reign. Runners-up got $1,000 to $3,000, and the girl elected by her peers as Miss Congeniality would receive $1,000 toward her education.

A long list of entry requirements and regulations existed for the entrants. Ann complied with all of them—even the defunct "Rule Seven," eliminated in the mid-1950s, which stated that the contestants be "in good health and of the white race." Ann did not consider her diabetes to be a medical hindrance to holding the office of Miss America, and she most likely did not even mention it to pageant officials. She could easily administer insulin injections without any fuss. She was aware that stress of any kind was a factor in the management of the disease, and the week promised to be chaotic. Florence would be on hand to ensure that Ann rested whenever possible and controlled her diet.

Ann, Doris Wood, Ron Tocco, and her parents checked into their assigned hotels for the duration of the pageant. After registering at the Claridge Hotel, Ann received her identification credentials and was introduced to her chaperone/hostess. Members of the Atlantic City National Hostess Committee were carefully trained. They were responsible for keeping the girls on schedule for rehearsals, meals, and press events, and to offer protection, guidance, and support. Ann attended an orientation meeting regarding conduct during the week and was briefed on the rules of the competition.

Vivacious Ann arrived in town earlier than most contestants. She was immediately popular with the press, and was featured in several papers the week of the pageant with photos provided by UPI and AP newswire services. There were prominent mentions in *TV Guide, The Philadelphia Enquirer* and *The Philadelphia Evening Bulletin.* The *Atlantic City Press* ran a front page photo of Ann and several other beauties posed on the railing of the boardwalk. "Ann Penelope Marston, Miss Michigan, another of the first 6, who specialized in archery and whose hobby is collecting china poodles, also flew here from her hometown, Wyandotte. She brought a rabbit's foot for good luck." The *Detroit Free Press* ran the same photo, with a different caption: "… Ann Marston, from Wyandotte, our own Miss Michigan, is the only Yankee in sight. A champion archer, she carries State hopes in the contest this week."

All of the girls received pins signifying their membership in Mu Alpha Sigma, the Miss America Sorority, and Ann got acquainted with some of her new sisters/rivals. One contestant was the entrant from Reno, Nevada—Dawn Elberta Wells. A drama student and performer, Wells later gained celebrity as an actress in 1964 when she played the part of castaway "Mary Ann" in the *Gilligan's Island* television show. It was a casual custom for the girls to exchange small offerings, and Ann brought archery sets donated by the Bear, Pearson, and Fleetwood archery companies. Ann received a campaign-style pin from Miss Nevada with Wells' photograph and a metal token mounted on a red ribbon that said: "A Bit of Silver from the Silver State."

Miss Mississippi, Lynda Lee Mead, enjoyed the days before the pageant. "I was thrilled," she said. "I hadn't really done a lot of traveling at that period in my life. We [her family] had gone to New York before the pageant week and seen shows, and that was so much fun. Going on to Atlantic City was worlds of fun. I was dazzled by it all … I found the girls wonderfully nice. There wasn't any backstabbing; everybody was courteous and polite. There's sort of a cliché about girls in competition, but it was not like that … I remember Ann quite well although I never saw her again after." Marston and Mead posed for a publicity photograph together that week. Ann aimed her bow and arrow at Lynda, who crossed her fingers for luck.

With a format similar to the Miss Michigan proceedings, the fifty-four young women were delegated to one of three groups to be initially judged in rotation over the course of three evenings. The finale was scheduled to be televised nationally on CBS Saturday night. Ann's schedule for the week consisted of the preliminary evening gown competition on Wednesday night, the swimsuit category on Thursday, and the talent event on Friday.

Sandwiched in between the preliminary competitions were press and photo sessions, rehearsals, fittings, beauty treatments, and formal interviews with the judges. Ann said: "… This is a very good idea. They can learn so much from this; it's very, very important. The girl that finally represents her city or state goes on to do interviews, and she has to know how to talk and meet people—lots of people."

The contestants were officially presented to the press corps at a poolside photograph session at the Blenheim Hotel. Each girl was photographed individually and in groups. Ann wore a demure white swimsuit with wide straps and a squared neckline and white high heels. She posed for pictures at various locations on the beach, the boardwalk, and on a military vessel while four sailors admired her strolling past. The girls dressed to impress each other as well as the media. Since she was not a starving college student, Ann could afford a wardrobe that was fashionable and versatile. One of her most stylish outfits was a chic, fitted black sheath with double shoulder straps. She wore short black lace gloves, carried a leather box purse, and donned a mink stole to ward off chilly ocean breezes.

The *Sports Illustrated* editors formally recognized Ann as a bona fide athlete-participant in the competition. A sidebar notation and an accompanying article complimented her and contained information about "Athletes at Atlantic City:"

> *Ann Marston, shapely* Sports Illustrated *cover girl (August 8, 1955), who has shot arrows into bull's-eyes for three world records and 11 U.S. titles, quivered the judges' eyes with a 35-22-35, to be voted Miss Michigan.*
>
> *In their annual rummage for the well-rounded girl, the Miss America people introduced in the 1930s what their euphemistical press agentry*

optimistically call the "talent judging." Since then the pageant has come a far piece from ukulele renditions of "That's where my money goes/To buy my baby clothes."

This week in Atlantic City, for instance, Miss Michigan will give an archery demonstration. This is not the first time that a Miss has done a sports turn on the Convention Hall stage. In 1949 Miss Kansas rode a misbehaving horse. In 1957, Miss Tennessee fretfully bounced on her trampoline. In 1958 Miss Georgia flubbed an archery exhibition. But it will undoubtedly be the finest sports bit in contest history, for Miss Michigan is Ann Marston (35-22-35), the 1958 National Field Archery champion.

Although Miss Michigan is the pageant's most celebrated sportswoman, the Miss America vital statisticians have done some earnest and momentous tabulating and discovered that their fifty-four contestants participate, more or less, in 19 sports. These are: fencing, tumbling, badminton, field hockey, rifle shooting, golf, tennis, swimming, water and snow skiing, skating, boating, fishing, basketball, archery, volleyball, bowling, horseback riding and sports car rallying.

Journalists in the 1950s had no qualms about publishing a girl's "vital statistics," so personal figure measurements were a predictable part of the media's pageant reports. The numbers were also up for review in the pageant program, including a listing of all past Miss America winners. Ann's official recorded height was 5'7", weight 118 lbs., bust 35", waist 23", hips 35" and aged 21 years, with blonde hair, blue eyes and fair complexion. Her training included tap and ballet, piano, clarinet, and modeling, and her hobbies were collecting china poodles, gardening, and doing crossword puzzles. Her listed talent was an archery demonstration.

A major highlight of the pageantry in Atlantic City included an illuminated boardwalk parade of the contestants. The evening event was an opportunity for the media and local enthusiasts to have an up-close glimpse of the contenders. The parade was televised live nationally for the first time that year on Tuesday night and was hosted by CBS correspondent Douglas Edwards.

In the 1920s, vehicles used to exhibit the contestants were human-powered wicker rolling chairs that were normally hired by tourists. Eventually the queens rode in automobiles. A new option for the 1960 contestants was the opportunity to ride on a small float. Some twenty-two contestants acquired sponsorships for floats contracted from a company in New York City. The floats were generally designed to represent regional affiliation, but unfortunately no one volunteered to subsidize the $500 necessary to commission a float for Miss Michigan. Photojournalist Tocco personally ordered a float the week before leaving for Atlantic City and paid for it with his own money. He visited members of the Wyandotte Merchants Association and chastised them for not contributing to the cause. He was already in New Jersey when he learned that the Association finally committed to fund the project. He ordered a plaque with the organization's name to be placed on the float at the last minute. After all his efforts, Tocco said: "It was on television for about five seconds."

For the 1960 pageant, the Parade Grand Marshall and pageant judge was Cliff Arquette, who was known to television audiences as "Charley Weaver." Arquette frequently appeared on *The Tennessee Ernie Ford Show* and Jack Paar's *Tonight Show* with a low-key comedy routine that revolved around homespun "Letters from Mamma." In later years he was a regular on *Hollywood Squares.*

Tocco was unfamiliar with Tuesday's parade route and judged that his best opportunity to take pictures of Ann would be at the end of the procession. He guessed wrong, so he began to lug his bulky camera equipment to the other end of the boardwalk. Luckily, Arquette spotted him trudging along and said, "Come here, buddy, get in the car." Arquette gave Tocco a ride in his convertible and transported him several miles to the starting line-up of the parade.

The parade route followed the boardwalk and advanced in alphabetical order by state. The royal procession began at 8:30 p.m. and included corporate-sponsored floats, drum majorettes, marching bands, motorcycle escorts, and the Philadelphia Mummer's String Band. Oldsmobile convertibles were the official transport of the queens who were not gracing a float. It took about ninety minutes for the entire procession to pass the reviewing platform at the Convention Center. The parade was attended by an estimated 250,000 people.

The result of Tocco's crusade with the Wyandotte Merchants Association was an impressive float that represented Michigan's Mackinac Bridge. It had a platform designed for Ann to stand on, and a small post to hold while she was smiling and waving to the crowd. Ann was elegant in a white gown with lace accents, three-tier drop earrings, rabbit-fur cape, and full-length gloves. Unfortunately, Ann lost a part of her regal demeanor in front of thousands of people when the vehicle hit a bump and she nearly fell off the float. She quickly recovered her composure, and Tocco got some wonderful photographs of Michigan's queen in the parade to show the folks back home.

The regulation forbidding contestants from speaking to men privately during the week of competition no longer existed, but it was still firmly enforced by Ann's mother. Tocco ran several errands for the Marstons the week of the pageant, and occasionally her mother asked him to bring fresh fruit to their hotel on Ann's behalf. After purchasing the items, he was required to knock lightly on Ann's hotel door and leave the shopping bag in the hall. In a radio interview, Ann jokingly commented on the limitations: "You aren't allowed to speak to any men. I had to speak through an interpreter. In my act, my father helped me, so it was very difficult to tell my chaperone's chaperone: 'Would you mind telling my father that I need those arrows pulled out of the target' … but there's a good reason behind it because there could be quite a few people there that might be agents or so forth, and they could bother the girls."

Her account was an exaggeration, according to 1960 Miss Mississippi Lynda Lee Mead's recollections: "I was with my dad and my brother the whole time. I never had to ask permission to talk to anyone." Ann recanted her statement in an interview at a later date by saying: "Another misconception was that of being chaperoned at all times. This was true, but only to a point. When we were in public we had a chaperone, but at night we were left off at the hotel and permitted to walk unescorted to the elevator, up the elevator alone, and to walk through the hotel to our room alone."

Ann's father Frank served as her performance assistant as usual, and on Friday night Ann competed in the talent portion of the Miss America Pageant. They set up the targets on the Convention Center's stage. Costumed as a female Robin Hood, she wore a short, black sequined dress and matching hat. "I shot at balloons, apples and eggs, and it was basically my regular routine that I do on stage. Of course, I had to cut my act, which normally runs 15 minutes or longer, down to three minutes, which was rather tight." Employing the best parts of her show, she snuffed out three flaming candles and shot an apple off the head of her wooden dummy, while making her usual commentary to the crowd. She aimed at the balloons, hit two and missed the third. The audience forgave her as she quipped: "During Michigan's hunting season you're only allowed to shoot two deer." She later said in an interview: "When you make a mistake alone you're on your own, but when you represent a whole state you've got to be real careful." Nevertheless, Ann won the preliminary talent competition and the Pepsi Cola scholarship award of $1,000. The next night was Saturday's official pageant competition.

American interest in monarchs was fanned by the popular Fred Astaire and Jane Powell movie *Royal Wedding* in 1951. The musical was loosely based on Britain's Princess Elizabeth's marriage to the Duke of Edinburgh in 1947. The royal obsession was unquestionably influenced by the 1953 coronation of Queen Elizabeth II that was shown repeatedly in color newsreels in theaters and on television. By the time the Miss America Pageant first hit the airwaves in September 1954, thousands of young girls dreamed about being crowned, robed, and throned on TV. It was the ultimate fairy-tale dream of the day, brilliantly perpetuated by mass media.

When an estimated 27 million people turned on their black-and-white television sets for the 1954 pageant, the occasion immediately became a national institution. The live broadcast broke every record for television viewership as the population watched weepy Lee Meriwether become the latest member of the majestic sisterhood. One of the judges was stately Hollywood beauty Grace Kelly. For the telecast the following year, pageant officials added personable game show host Bert Parks as the master of ceremonies. For the first time he serenaded a Miss America during her promenade with "There She Is—Miss America" composed by Bernie Wayne. Grace Kelly married Monaco's Prince Rainier in early 1956, becoming known to the world forevermore as Princess Grace. Their glamorous wedding perpetuated the royal fantasy, and the Miss America Pageant became a hot commodity. Television networks competed energetically for the rights to broadcast, and corporations waited in line for the opportunity to sponsor scholarships. For the 1960 pageant there were eight CBS television cameras set up in Convention Hall, and officials predicted another record-breaking audience. Philco was the sole commercial sponsor for the televised event.

Backstage there were racks holding swimsuits and talent costumes. A storage area was designated for the talent props, and long tables were set up with mirrors for last-minute primping. No parents were allowed—only the hostess chaperones—and security was extremely tight. Frank must have been issued a special pass in case Ann was selected as a semi-finalist and was required to perform the archery act with his assistance.

Lynda Mead recalls her final moments before the televised broadcast: "You didn't have much time backstage because you were waiting to be cued to go on. I think all of the preparation that I did, like my hair and whatever little makeup we wore when we were 19, was done in my room before I came. It was much, much less sophisticated than it is now. Girls wore a little lipstick or maybe a little eyeliner, but none of us really did a whole lot to ourselves."

The officials presented the scholarships and trophies for the preliminary winners before air time. Ann Marston accepted her trophy and $1,000 scholarship certificate for winning the talent portion. It was an encouraging sign, and she must have felt there was a good chance of being selected one of the top ten finalists in the pageant that night. She later commented: "I think what they are looking for is basically a clean-cut, all-American girl with good ideals. She has to be pretty well-rounded, and talent is very important. I don't think they have to be the most professional talent in the world."

Statistically, she really didn't have much of an advantage with her special ability. Up to 1960, only seven preliminary talent winners in the pageant's twenty four-year history went on to become Miss America. The swimsuit champions had the edge, with nineteen queens taking preliminary awards. Three Miss America winners had not won either preliminary swimsuit or talent. Only one Miss Michigan had become the nation's winner up to that point in time. Detroit's Patricia Mary

Donnelly did not win the preliminary talent when she played her bass fiddle, but she became Miss America 1939.

The pageant to crown Miss America for the year 1960 opened with a glorious wide shot of the audience, stage, and runway at the Atlantic City Convention Center. A bevy of girls in creampuff gowns and equally poufy hair were congregating on the stage. CBS hired Miss America 1958, Marilyn Van Derbur, to co-host the telecast with newsman Douglas Edwards. An estimated 60 million television viewers saw Van Derbur win her crown, and she was just as photogenic serving as the current year's Philco hostess. Van Derbur used binoculars to get a better view of the stage from the anchor desk positioned high in the balcony. The camera image showed both the stage in the background and the announcer in the foreground. He wore a white tuxedo and held a headset to one ear.

> Good evening everybody coast to coast. Douglas Edwards reporting from Atlantic City, where once again, that Cinderella hour is approaching. Before this night is over we'll have the answer to that big, that momentous question, who will be Miss America for 1960?
>
> Some 25,000 people have packed the giant convention hall, for the final evening of this annual pageant. It's the climax of the week-long competition featuring 54 of America's favorite daughters, one of whom will be chosen tonight as the fairest of the fair. There will be plenty of excitement as we go along tonight, and from our vantage point high above the great stage we'll be able to bring to you all of that excitement.

Master of Ceremonies Bert Parks introduced the beauties individually, as the traditional Parade of States procession began. Each contestant wore an evening gown and cradled a single long-stemmed rose in her arm. The young ladies' actual names were not used; they were only identified by state designation. Miss Michigan, Ann Marston, wore a strapless white gown with a full tulle skirt. Appliquéd lace flowers outlined by sequins were sewn to the bodice, skirt, and asymmetric sweetheart neckline. A long, gauzy stole, drop earrings, small diamond necklace and full-length white gloves completed her ensemble. When it was Ann's turn to promenade down the runway, she glided by with a wide smile and perky little tilt of her head. Further down the aisle Ann walked past the designated press area and whispered to her friend Ron Tocco: "It's me!" While she was on camera for only a few brief seconds, it was the first and last time that Ann Marston was in a TV close-up that evening. The ten semi-finalists had already been selected before air time, and she was not one of them. She spent the remainder of the telecast either backstage or grouped with the rest of the unfortunate contestants as living scenery on the set.

Correspondent Marilyn Van Derbur abandoned her binoculars in the balcony and went backstage for the finale. The Convention Hall was dead quiet as Pageant Executive Director Lenora Slaughter prepared to officially robe the new queen. The last two girls waited in anticipation as Parks finally proclaimed, "Miss America is Miss Mississippi!"

Queen Lynda Lee Mead was stunned and serene as Slaughter slipped the fur-trimmed robe on her shoulders. Mary Ann Mobley (Miss America 1959), solemnly affixed the crown to Mead's hair. Then Mead slowly walked down the runway, as Parks reverently serenaded her. Miss America paused at the end of the aisle to nod and smile for close-ups. On her return to the stage, she ascended the stairs to her throne. Immediately after she was seated, the curtains closed. Mead had not won the preliminary talent nor the swimsuit award.

As the crowd slowly filtered out of the Convention Hall, the curtains re-opened and there was a final shot of the girls graciously congratulating Mead. The camera cut to the old CBS eye logo, and it was all over. That evening, an astounding 69 percent share of American viewers tuned in to the 1960 Miss America Pageant.

Recently, Mead reflected about the experience. She said: "It was a landmark for all of us. If you can do that when you're 20 years old, you can do anything. I'm sure Ann felt the same way."

The Coronation Ball was held at the Claridge Hotel following the pageant on Saturday night. The beauties were introduced to their escorts, sixty leading members of the senior class from the Air Force Academy in Colorado Springs, Colorado. On Sunday, the girls attended a brunch, the last officially sponsored Miss America event of the year. Then they packed to go back home.

It must have been difficult for Ann to return to her hometown supporters without another victory under her tiara. But she knew life went on, even after the Miss America Pageant, and she looked forward to serving her duties as Miss Michigan in 1960. But across the country there were rumblings about the recent Miss America Pageant. The Tulsa, Oklahoma, *Southside Times* wrote a strongly worded editorial: "Maybe we're getting old or tired, but somehow this year's Miss America pageant left us cold, cold, cold. We're far from prudish, but we sure missed the talent on the show. Reminded us more of something from a not-too-good burlesque where every song is sold with a skimpy costume and not much else. We're told it all depends on the judges. Next year, maybe."

Some members of Ann's fan base were equally unhappy with the final verdict. It was unforgivable to many that Ann did not appear as a semi-finalist, especially since she won the talent preliminary. There was talk that the scoring system was unevenly balanced and in some ways Ann agreed, as did some other participants. Ann responded to a letter from the parent of another one of the Miss America contestants:

Your letter expressed my family's and my opinion to the T. Our phone has not ceased ringing since we've been home. People have waited weeks, months, to watch the Miss America spectacular with the much publicized talent to be presented, as well as the lovely faces and figures, of course … It wasn't complimentary to the Pageant. The newspapers have been running it into the ground and I hate to see this happen. It has always been my opinion that the Miss America Pageant has been the epitome of American womanhood, and one of very high standards …

Despite the fact that the Pageant was extremely well organized, thanks to Miss Slaughter, which certainly is a credit to her, the entire selection of Miss America lies with the judges, and herein lays the responsibility. These judges should know more than anybody what Miss America should personify … Sentiment should be excluded and a girl should be chosen who can best represent America.

Ann had always been a very good sport in competitive archery, and she didn't complain about sour grapes. A multitude of factors affected her when she was shooting, like hot or cold weather, wind, illness, stress, exhaustion, and even biting insects. She accepted her fate when she lost. Thanks to her father's training, she acknowledged the fact that, as an archer and a person, she was totally responsible for her individual performance. She wisely adopted the same philosophy with all facets of her life, and simply prepared herself to face the next challenge.

In spite of the setback regarding the *My Dog Sheppy* film, Ann still harbored show business aspirations. She corresponded with pageant officials in Atlantic City, and received Lenora Slaughter's blessing to use her talent award scholarship funds for singing and music lessons:

Dear Ann,

This is to confirm that you are the recipient of a $1,000 educational scholarship won at the National Finals of the Miss America Pageant, to be used in accordance with the enclosed rules and regulations governing the scholarship awards. Please have all the scholarships bills sent directly to the Miss America Pageant …

We would like to take this opportunity to congratulate you on being a scholarship winner at the National Finals of the Miss America Pageant, and we know that you are going to use this money to excellent advantage in building a splendid career for yourself in the future.

Sincerely yours,

Lenora S. Slaughter, Executive Director

Ann was pleased that her future course of action complied with pageant policy. She was allowed to draw on the scholarship fund for up to four years. She contracted F.R. Arnoldi, director of the Wyandotte Conservatory of Music, to be her guide for musical education. The fee for lessons was $6 an hour for bi-weekly sessions, and books were an additional cost. Arnoldi sent periodic invoices to Slaughter, and she sent him checks for the expenses and statements of Ann's remaining account balance. In a radio interview, Ann talked about her musical ambitions:

> When I won the talent portion of Miss America, I received a $1,000 scholarship, and I also won $500 when I became Miss Michigan. So, rather than go away to school and give up my career, I've been lucky enough that the sponsors of the pageant allowed me to take singing lessons and piano lessons. I love it a great deal and I think it may help me in my career, because I've been sort of typecast as an archer.
>
> I did start out when I was 6. I went to school with Jean Simmons. I went to study drama because that's what I wanted to get into. But people took a liking to the archery ... I tell my agent, "Well, I sing now," and he laughs.

She was about to face a new test while merging her new Miss Michigan persona into the established Ann Marston entity. After the Miss America pageant, Ann immediately adjusted her professional rank to reflect the enhanced status. Her public relations packet was re-designed to reflect the upgrade, with her official Miss Michigan portrait on the cover. The Miss Michigan line had top billing and was set in a large, bold font.

Presenting lovely Miss Michigan
Talent Award Winner of Miss America Pageant 1960
Ann Marston, Holder of Eleven National Archery championships
Sports Illustrated Cover Girl – Life Magazine Feature
Plus Many Leading Magazines

She continued with her busy performance schedule with the additional accolades prominently attached to her celebrity. In an interview she said: "I combined my own shows with the Miss Michigan appearances because I was traveling all over the country, as I had been prior to the pageant doing the show." In the fall of 1959, Ann visited children in hospitals across the country as the official National Cystic Fibrosis representative, and personally sponsored archery events for the charity.

Because of Ann's popularity the previous year, the Niagara Falls Maid of the Mist

Festival committee invited her to return as a guest. She earned $750 for the engagement. She made other appearances at fairs in Indiana and New York and sports shows in Ohio, Michigan, and Illinois. While at the Minnesota State Fair, she headlined with David Nelson (oldest son of Ozzie and Harriet), Brenda Lee, and Neil Sedaka.

In Des Moines, Iowa, she was featured with the stars from the *Wagon Train* television show. She performed at Briggs Stadium in Detroit for the Fireman's Field Day; at Dearborn, Michigan's Greenfield Village for the Muzzleloaders Festival; and opened a shopping center. In November, the ambassador for the Union of Soviet Socialist Republics sent an invitation to Ann, requesting her attendance at the Russian Embassy's annual reception celebrating the 42nd anniversary of the Great October Socialist Revolution. It is unknown if she went to the event which was held in New York City.

In 1959, Ann Marston earned $13,944.96. According to the American Institute of Economic Research cost-of-living calculator, the 2006 equivalent would be $96,608.38. In spite of their prosperity, Ann and her family appreciated living in working-class Wyandotte. They purchased a small house at 1075 17th Street. For Halloween fun that October, she dressed in a white and yellow polka dot ball gown and wore her crown to hand out suckers to the neighborhood children. The candy was taped to an autographed postcard of Ann posing with her signature Ben Pearson archery set. To confirm her sincere gratitude to her supporters, friends, and neighbors, she bought an ad in a local newspaper that ran during the winter holidays. It said: "Thank you Wyandotte. May 1960 be as happy for you as you have made me in 1959. Ann Marston, Miss Michigan of 1960."

She appeared on Paul Winchell's show again that winter. After driving back to Michigan from New York City, a winter storm prohibited the Marstons from continuing to Muskegon for a Miss Michigan sanctioned appearance. A week later the Automobile Association of America posted travel advisory warnings again, and they had to cancel another commitment at a Grand Rapids, Michigan, department store.

Later, the Muskegon Junior Chamber of Commerce took issue when Ann refused to alter her existing performance schedule to accommodate a personal appearance request. The Jaycees arranged for her to hand out flowers at a small-town drug store. According to Ann, the purpose was to "work off a $100 prize in merchandise which the store gave Miss Michigan." Her interpretation was that a gift to Miss Michigan shouldn't have strings attached. She maintained that attitude in a press report. She felt that the situation was "… beneath the dignity of Miss Michigan and not in keeping with the standards of the contest."

The matter hit the Detroit papers on Sunday, December 13, when Leonard Van Bogelen, general manager for the Miss Michigan Pageant, publicly accused Ann of shirking her duties. The *Detroit Times* reported that Van Bogelen "charged her with failing to show on several occasions" and stated that "she had made a grand commercial thing out of her title and did a lot of good for just one person—Ann Marston. Our committee is very unhappy and resolved that this sort of thing will not happen again." Van Bogelen customarily acted as the booking agent for past Miss Michigan queens, and the Junior Chamber of Commerce received a significant percentage of the $100 charged for each of Ann's exclusive Miss Michigan appearances. The dispute was fought in the media. Ann flatly denied a conflict of interest and spoke out on a local television show, as reported in *The Detroit News*:

> *Considering that I am a professional entertainer in archery and in great demand all over the country, I think that I am keeping up the high level of standards of Miss Michigan ... I admit that I have made only four appearances solely as Miss Michigan [from September to December 1959]. But there isn't a week that goes by that I am not somewhere performing as a professional archer. I have been all over the state, the country and even to London. And I have been seen from coast to coast on television. If that's not selling Michigan, I don't know what it is ... But because I am a member of a union [American Guild of Variety Artists and Publishers], I must have a franchised agent. The union agreed to let my mother handle my schedule. Mr. Van Bogelen knew this when I participated in the contest.*

Florence added to the newspaper report: "Ann has done a better job of being Miss Michigan than any other title holder. How could a Miss Michigan, who is an office girl or clerk instead of a professional entertainer, get around as much as Ann has ... I think Michigan has a real queen this year." The whole matter was reminiscent of the professional/amateur status conflicts that Ann had experienced in archery tournaments in past years.

Muskegon's Junior Chamber of Commerce was persistent and presented more demands of Ann well into early 1960. She was falsely accused of turning down other engagements and said in an interview: "Only once have I had to refuse ... because of a conflict of schedule and you can hardly blame me for the fact that I can't be in two places at once. Certainly it would be to everybody's benefit if I could." She strongly denied accusations that she arbitrarily charged more money than the usual Miss Michigan fee for appearances. Ann wrote a letter to Jack Bushong, a board member of the Greater Muskegon Junior Chamber of Commerce, defending her good reputation and integrity:

> *... Since the unfortunate publicity, which was put in all the newspapers, I have received hardly any calls to be just Miss Michigan. People now think*

that it is too expensive to engage Miss Michigan, not realizing the fee is still $100 ... This certainly wasn't our intention, but a retraction was never made, and I feel it has been terribly detrimental to the title Miss Michigan-America—which is unfortunate and unnecessary.

I was invited on several TV shows to "blast" after the bad publicity but I didn't, simply because I'm not that kind of person, and two wrongs have never made a right! I'm still the same person who entered the Miss Michigan pageant because it represented to me an ideal that was fine and upstanding, and all I ever wanted to do was uphold that ideal to the very best of my knowledge and ability. It has been made difficult, but I have no regrets. No matter how distorted people have made things look, in my heart I know my sincerity.

In order to fulfill the engagements that Ann was unable to attend, the Jaycees began using former 1959 Miss Michigan Patience Pierce and Susan Westergaard, who was Miss Michigan in the 1959 Miss Universe contest. In the January 30, 1960, issue of the *Detroit Free Press*, a front-page headline said, "Our fair state's got three Miss Michigans." The article was non-biased and fairly explained both sides of the story. Ann obviously had far-ranging obligations as a nationally famous entertainer, and most of her bookings had been established well in advance. The Muskegon Jaycees had the responsibility to schedule a Miss Michigan to appear at business conventions, to serve as hostess at various proceedings, and to reign over Michigan Week events. Once again, a disgruntled Van Bogelen vented his opinion: "We made a mistake in picking a professional model and entertainer." Ann's quoted response in the article was: "I'm proud of being Miss Michigan and as far as I am concerned there is no other Miss Michigan."

The stress of the controversy caused Ann to be hospitalized in early 1960 for reasons, "which my doctor has stated was partly as a result of the aggravations I have been having." Ann was obviously distressed with the negative media hype, and illness was an unfortunate price to pay for her success. Apparently the debate was finally dropped by the Jaycees, and she continued with her demanding itinerary after she recovered her health.

Ann appeared again at the annual Chicago Sportsmen's and Vacation Show, and at another sports show in Cleveland, Ohio. In Michigan, she was a guest of honor at the Miss Wayne Beauty Contest and rode in their parade. While appearing at Oklahoma City's Springlake Amusement Park, she was on the bill with Gordon Scott, a latter-day movie Tarzan. She was billed as "Miss Michigan Archery Champ, Sweetheart of the Bow and Arrow and Talent Award winner of Miss America Pageant." Scott ran around the stage with spare arrows tucked into the back of his loincloth and took shots at the target with his own bow. When Ann missed a balloon he jumped at it and attacked it with his knife.

The family drove their Oldsmobile station wagon from Oklahoma City to Los Angeles. While in California, they visited the home of their dear friends in Encino. James (Doug) Easton was the founder of the Jas. D. Easton archery equipment company and began manufacturing aluminum arrows in 1939. He and his wife Mary, and two sons, Jim and Bob, had been acquainted for years with the Marstons through business and competitions. Florence and Mary Easton were good friends and kept in close touch. The oldest Easton son, Jim, was considered to be a good match for Ann. Their friendship was encouraged by both sets of parents but a romance between them did not bloom. Jim eventually went into the family business became chairman and CEO of Easton Sports Inc. He served for sixteen years as president of F.I.T.A., the international governing body of archery organizations, and is a past vice-president of the International Olympic Committee. During the Marstons' 1960 visit to California, Ann and her parents and went with the Easton family to Disneyland.

Ann appeared at the Los Angeles Sportsmen's and Vacation Show, sharing the bill with the enormously popular Western star Roy Rogers, his horse Trigger, sidekick Pat Brady, and the Sons of the Pioneers band. Adults paid $1 admission and kids were charged 75 cents each to see the show at the Pan Pacific Auditorium. Ann obviously enjoyed working with Rogers, and the Marstons' home movies document their good-humored interaction. Rogers took the microphone and introduced Ann while she skipped onto the stage, and he continued his spirited commentary during her act. They switched places and Ann emceed for Rogers while he aimed the bow, skewered a few balloons, and shot at an apple. Backstage, Ann chatted with the Sons of the Pioneers when Rogers ran up behind her, grabbed her shoulders, and pretended to leap onto her back instead of Trigger's. Everyone chuckled and Rogers finally mounted his horse. Frank obviously took a liking to Rogers, too, and later wrote to Fred Bear and asked him to send a gift to the archery-enthusiast cowboy. The following is a letter to Rogers from Bob Schulze, Sales Manager of Bear Archery:

> *Dear Mr. Rogers,*
> *After Frank Marston concluded the recent sport show that he and Ann were engaged in Los Angeles, headlined, as Frank put it, by Roy Rogers, he wrote to Fred Bear telling Fred of your interest in his bow. It is, as you know, a Bear bow, one of the most interesting appearing and best performing bows we have ever made.*
> *We would like to make one of these bows available for your personal use, and have entered an order for a Kodiak Special Deluxe, 66", 42 pounds and 28" draw, to be sent to you at the above address, with the*

*compliments of Fred Bear. We hope you will get a great deal of pleasure
from this bow. Please allow us about two weeks after you receive this letter to make delivery.*

According to Roy "Dusty" Rogers Jr. the same bow is currently in the collection of the Roy Rogers-Dale Evans Museum and Happy Trails Theater in Branson,
Missouri.

Ann entered the 1960 National Field Archery Championships in Grayling,
Michigan, in June. The *Detroit Sunday Times* reminded readers that, "Miss Marston did not compete in the 1959 nationals because of her reign as Miss Michigan
and preparations for the Miss America pageant. She won the women's championship in 1954, 1955, 1957, and 1958, finishing second in 1956." It was the last time
Ann entered an archery competition. She lost the Free Style trophy to the talented
Cleo Roberson.

Ann's responsibility as Miss Michigan 1960 was coming to an end, and she
prepared to bestow the honor on another worthy young woman. At least someone
in Muskegon was happy to have Queen Ann return to town when she arrived for
the July 13 Miss Michigan Pageant. Journalist Georgia Hughes warmly welcomed
Ann in her newspaper column "In the Passing Scene:"

> *This is Ann Marston's last week to reign as Miss Michigan, a title she has
> upheld with great charm and dignity. She's in Muskegon this week, where
> tomorrow night she will crown the newly chosen Miss Michigan.*
>
> *While doing this, she will wear a gown, tiara, and handbags com-
> pletely covered with pearls, valued at $17,000! I think I'd be afraid to take
> a deep breath in an outfit with that high a price tag! The gown, belonging
> to Syndicated Pearl Company, is just loaned out on special occasions to
> prominent women, and needless to say, is kept in a jeweler's vault until
> the time for wearing it. Incidentally, Ann will do her archery show both
> Thursday and Friday night in Muskegon, and the Friday night show may
> be televised.*

Ann rode in the parade and attended press events and luncheons. At the coronation ceremony, Ann Penelope Marston graciously relinquished her Miss Michigan
title to her successor, eighteen-year-old lifeguard and dress designer Nancy Anne
Fleming. Just two months later in Atlantic City, Lynda Lee Mead also passed on her
crown to Nancy Fleming. Fleming swept the entire contest, winning both the swimsuit and talent divisions and became Miss America 1961.

5

On the Road

OAL-ORIENTED MARSTON AND COMPANY spent 1961 traveling extensively around the country. Ann loved show business even though her performance schedule that year was exhausting. She signed with the prestigious MCA talent agency, which booked her in fresh venues. The family joined the Thrillcade stunt show, and Ann was a popular new attraction on the rodeo circuit.

Ann spent virtually every day and night with her parents while they were on tour. She was nearly twenty-three years old and beginning to resent her mother's rigid control over her professional and personal life.

Innovative business partners Lew Wasserman and Jules Stein had operated the Music Corporation of America since the 1930s, and the organization quickly became the 20th century's standard for talent management. Wasserman was both respected and feared for his forceful business practices in the entertainment industry. By 1961, MCA's lineup of movie stars, musicians, writers, and singers was unsurpassed. The company represented James Stewart, Frank Sinatra, Marlon Brando, Marilyn Monroe, Bette Davis, Ronald Reagan, and hundreds of other top performers across the country. With all of MCA's show business, political, and Hollywood connections, the company's influence was enormous. Eventually, MCA branched out into motion picture and television production with intimate affiliations with Paramount Studios and NBC. The entity became the dominant entertainment force in America. Signing with the MCA agency was unquestionably the right move to further Ann's career. She was assigned to MCA's Chicago office, under the tutelage of Eldred Stacy of the special events department.

Immediately after signing the twenty-two-year-old Ann, Stacy began to promote her talent aggressively. *The Billboard Cavalcade of Fairs* magazine touted the MCA catalog of elite variety entertainers. Recording artists included the Crew Cuts, Johnny Cash, Bob Crosby, Paul Evans, and the Vagabonds. Cowboy stars Allen Case and Clu Gulager were available for performance bookings. They were very familiar characters to television audiences, and both men appeared in episodes of *Wagon Train, Have Gun-Will Travel, The Deputy,* and other television dramas.

In 1961, Johnny Carson was in his fourth year of hosting the ABC game show, *Who Do You Trust,* and MCA promoted Carson as a stand-up personality for the 1961 Fair Season. He didn't become the host of the *Tonight Show* until 1962. The MCA *Cavalcade of Fairs* publication hyped dozens of other acts, including comedic musicians Homer and Jethro, sexy Jane Morgan, and 1958 Miss America runner-up Anita Bryant. Bryant also was known as the "Coke Girl" for the Coca-Cola Company's "To Be Really Refreshed" campaign in the 1950s. Bryant was a big draw at fair grandstands since she recorded several successful hit singles in 1959 and 1960 including "Till There Was You," "Paper Roses," and "My Little Corner of the World."

Ann Marston was prominently featured in the same *Billboard* brochure of celebrity performers, with an 11" by 14" full-page advertisement presenting her as "Sweetheart of the Bow & Arrow, The World's Foremost Archery Champion. You'll score a perfect hit every time with this rare combination of beauty and outstanding skill-talent."

Under MCA's umbrella and with the expertise of Eldred Stacy, Ann began the bookings for the winter show season in January 1961. Her new agent frequently attended her performances around the country, and in typical MCA style he treated his client like a big star. He took her to dinners and shows, escorted her to press events, and gave her little presents. "He's always so heartening and makes us feel good," Ann wrote. He had big plans for her, and investigated diverse promotions such as attempting to develop a signature merchandise line of archery items. He even tried to obtain a Pall Mall cigarette advertisement for Ann.

The Marstons' schedule began in Miami for a *Sports Illustrated* appearance with Bob Mathias and Don Budge. Four weeks later they were back at the Florida State Fair in Tampa. Ann was accustomed to the diversity in fair talent; she had worked with hypnotists, jugglers, contortionists, acrobats, and ventriloquists. There was huge variety in the animal acts including dogs, chimps, poodles, horses, and high-diving miniature mules. She once said: "The stage show was awful; they *needed* a good archery act." She earned $1,250 for that week-long engagement, not including expenses.

Living on the road was an enormous challenge. Entertainers were generally responsible for paying for all of their own expenses such as gasoline (which averaged 25 cents a gallon in 1961), car maintenance, all meals, and motel rooms. Eggs, candles, balloons, and other props had to be regularly purchased for Ann's act. Her injection kit had to be restocked with needles and insulin. A traffic jam or bad driving conditions could easily throw off their entire itinerary. Beau, their poodle, traveled with them everywhere and required frequent stops for food, water, and exercise. A flat tire required unpacking all of the props from the trunk to access the spare. She wrote: "We had a blowout coming home and changed the tire by candlelight." They had to account for changes in time zones and traffic laws that varied state to state. Ann also embraced a common show business superstition: "Well we got through today without any effects of Friday the 13th."

The Marstons often arrived at their destination in the wee hours of the morning when hotel rooms either were not available or weren't up to minimum standards. Frequently they just slept in the car in a parking lot or roadside rest stop. Room rates varied with the selection of existing accommodations. Sometimes they spent $2 a night per room at Mom and Pop places, and other times they were charged up to $15 for a room at a chain property like Holiday Inn. Ann got her own room if the price was right, but many times the family shared a room with two beds. Occasionally they rented an empty apartment for a favorable weekly fee. Most of the time air conditioning was not available, and heat on cold nights was sporadic at best. On occasion they shared their space with roaches, mice or other unwanted roommates. "We slept at a crummy motel. I thought it best not to use the shower," Ann wrote. "We found a better one the next day down the highway … There's no business like show business." Washing their clothes, including Ann's costumes, was usually accomplished at Laundromats or in bathroom sinks. Both Florence and Ann spent hours at the ironing board. Whatever the conditions, Ann always referred to lodgings as their home. "We got home late after the show."

During January they journeyed to Pittsburgh, Dallas, Nashville, Little Rock, and Springfield, Illinois. While in Arkansas they visited the Ben Pearson family, who took them to visit entertainer Joe E. Brown. While enjoying the warm weather in Dallas she noted: "There is 12 inches of snow in Detroit." Whenever they were close enough to Michigan they drove many extra miles to their Wyandotte base. "We stopped home from Green Bay. It sure is refreshing to sleep in my own bed." Florence usually telephoned their neighbors, Ozzie and Dorothy Hindley, when they were close to arrival. These good friends looked after the house and collected the mail when the family was out of town. The Hindleys welcomed the Marstons home at any time of the day or night. Dorothy put on a pot of coffee and they waited to hear about Frank, Florence, and Ann's latest adventures.

There was always housework and laundry to be done after a tour. The day following that month-long long trip, Ann said, "I got up early and unpacked, dusted, washed the floors and straightened up. It was hard to know where to begin." It took days to go through their correspondence after being away for many weeks at a time. They sometime received untimely bad news, and that winter they learned that Frank's sister Rose had died a month earlier in England.

Ann got heaps of fan mail from all over the country. Most of the letters contained messages of admiration or requests for autographed photos. She always complied promptly, marked her response date on the sender's envelope, and kept the requests in a file box. Sometimes she received suggestive romantic offers that were just plain weird, and she simply ignored them. She was in demand for beauty competitions and received a letter from the organizers of Miss Sun Fun USA to represent Michigan in their pageant held in June at Myrtle Beach, South Carolina. She declined that offer but decided to be a judge in the upcoming Miss Detroit contest. She was invited to attend the Miss Michigan pageant as a special guest, but her schedule wouldn't allow it, and she sent regrets.

The family resumed their normal lives between engagements in the late winter. It wasn't necessary for Frank to work as a plumber while they were traveling with Ann during those years. He wrote an article that winter for *The Archers' Magazine (TAM)* on proper coaching techniques. Frank spent most of his time inventing new props for the act and puttering around the house. The Marstons purchased the home on 17th Street the year before. Photographs of Ann and her numerous plaques and awards adorned the walls of nearly every room.

Frank and Ozzie Hindley installed knotty pine paneling throughout the Marston home. Ann's outfits, props, and gowns were stored in the upper-level room of the bungalow. Frank paneled the room and built long closets under the eaves to hold the collection. In the basement they created a small bar area with shelving to hold trophies and memorabilia. There was a kitchenette, laundry room with a large closet, a bathroom with a shower, and a bedroom for Ann. Wooden shutters provided privacy, and Frank constructed built-in bookshelves and racks to hold her record albums. Ann had the room furnished with her piano, stereo, and a fuzzy poodle throw-rug next to her daybed. Her collection of china poodle figurines resided on shelves that were mounted over a long dresser. It was a charming little apartment that she nicknamed "Ann's Dungeon."

Ann's mother spent her time administering the family business. Florence fielded offers, juggled the appointment calendar, and kept extensive financial records. She spent countless hours creating new costumes and repairing Ann's wardrobe.

Florence collected virtually every press mention of Ann over the years. Wherever they stopped, she purchased multiple copies of newspapers, magazines, programs or advertisements that featured Ann. She had boxes overflowing with clippings and publicity photographs, old and new. Periodically she compiled some articles into packets that were mailed to friends and relatives in the U.S. and abroad, and she included chatty letters that recounted the family's exploits.

Ann continued with music lessons, sewed, organized her closets, and occasionally wrote articles for archery magazines. The Cystic Fibrosis organization was still her favorite charity, and she visited patients in hospitals and performed at exhibitions on the society's behalf. Ann called her school chums and got caught up with friends. She confided in her diary: "Time sure flies. Nearly everybody I went to school with is now married, but I don't envy them. I like my life a lot. I think I'll be a spinster for as long as possible, anyway." She admitted to a friend that she was afraid to have children because of the risk of passing on diabetes.

One show biz acquaintance was Joe Bodrie, known as "the fastest gun alive." Bodrie taught several Hollywood cowboy heroes the secrets of the quick draw, and he was a champion at shooting competitions. Bodrie lived in a neighboring town, and he and Ann often appeared together in parades, sports shows, fairs, and other local events. Occasionally they got together for dinner, movies or a casual evening out. He joked with Ann about getting married and she was amused: "It would be a messed up deal—the fastest gun and the fastest archer or something like that. Anyway he was kidding. I think." She told a reporter once that she had fielded proposals, but "none that appeal to me. And I don't believe in taking a couple of shots at marriage, either."

Ann enjoyed watching television, especially sports and old movies. She was a big fan of Jack Paar and Ed Sullivan. She remarked: "I wish I had a TV show on Saturday night; there's nothing worth watching then." She kept her journal current and frequently commented about world events: "The Russians put the first man into space; I guess it's about the biggest scientific event during my life." She frequently voiced her personal opinion in her diary. "The news is hot these days with the trial of Adolf Eichmann. It seems hard to imagine a man can be that ruthless to kill 6 million Jews. From his picture it doesn't seem possible. He is to be tried in Israel and it doesn't seem right. It should be a United Nations court or something."

Ann was a great sports fan and especially enjoyed watching televised basketball games. During her travels with *Sports Illustrated,* she met St. Louis Hawk Bob Pettit, and they began a long-distance friendship. She watched the Hawks games whenever possible, and he sometimes called her when his team played in Detroit.

It didn't take too long for the gypsy to become bored with her domestic life. By early spring, Ann wrote: "I'll be glad when we get to work again." Some jobs were better than others, though. And after doing three shows a day for three consecutive days at the Saginaw Sport Show she wrote: "We drove home tonight. It's over 100 miles and not worth it." The big money wasn't in Michigan, anyway. "It's funny living in Detroit, we very seldom appear here." She flew to Boston to meet Ted Kennedy when he hosted a benefit for the United Fund in affiliation with President John F. Kennedy's Physical Fitness program. She appeared with other *Sports Illustrated* representatives Bonnie Prudden, Frank Gifford, Wilma Rudolph, Ted Williams, and Johnny Unitas.

That spring Ann and Florence decided to try the popular Metracal diet, consisting of canned milkshake-flavored drinks and special cookies. "Mother and I are *trying* to diet on Metracal; but it's such fun to eat." Her official weight was 118 pounds in the Miss America Pageant. In the eighteen months since then she was up to 140 pounds, according to her doctor's scale. He prescribed diet pills and a new eating regimen. Fortunately, her blood glucose level came down from a previous level of 273 to 178. After a few weeks, she lost a couple of pounds. "The doctor was pleased and said that I should eat more fats." Unfortunately, there were other serious factors affecting her health. She lamented in her journal: "They say the cause of a weight problem is sometimes psychological. Maybe that's my problem. There's always so much tension at home and it gets worse." She said, "We should be the happiest people in the world, but all we do is fight over stupid things. Maybe when we go on the road, it won't be so bad, but then we have the driving problem."

Florence didn't have a driver's license, and she was very nervous when Ann attempted to relieve her father at the wheel during their marathon cross-country jaunts. Her mother was a vocal backseat driver, and there was a skirmish every time Ann drove. However, it didn't seem to endanger Florence's life when Ann drove her to the local stores several times a week to go shopping.

Other diary entries give a glimpse of everyday life at the Marstons. Frank practiced shooting with Ann at the range and in the backyard. A true nature-lover, she spent time outside preparing for spring. "The garden is the one thing I'll miss this summer, but it's good to go again." She washed the laundry and hung the clothes outside on the line. "I don't like using the dryer." Before their summer tour Ann ironed and prepared her travel and show wardrobe and thoroughly cleaned the house. She took Beau to Poodle Paradise to have him clipped. One evening she gave herself a Lilt home permanent and sorted her cosmetic case. Apparently, finances were a bit tight and her parents got a bank loan for $500 to tide them over. "So much money to come and we're still broke."

Finally the news came from Eldred Stacy: The rest of May and all of June, July, August, and September were booked. Ann routed their itinerary and figured the mileage between stops.

Ann Marston hit Fort Smith, Arkansas, like a cyclone. Newspapers touted the Arkansas-Oklahoma Rodeo as if it were the first time anyone out west had ever seen a horse. A parade included vintage horse-drawn stagecoaches and wagons, riders with fancy saddle tackle, and marching bands. Later in the day residents could eat a chuck-wagon dinner and square dance before going to the stadium to see the rodeo. There was a full evening's entertainment with saddle bronc and bareback riding, bull riding, calf roping, rodeo clowns, steer wrestling, and barrel races. Ann was a star attraction and was mentioned in at least ten newspaper articles that week. She did several TV and radio interviews, and practically every civic organization in town invited her to a luncheon or banquet. Headlining the musical entertainment was popular singing cowboy star Clint Walker, star of the hit NBC TV show, *Cheyenne*.

Ann followed Walker with her archery routine, performing to capacity crowds every night. Rodeos were a new venue for her, and provided the perfect setting for her archery skill. She was an expert equestrienne, so a rodeo wrangler selected a spirited steed for her to use for the week. She entered the stadium on horseback, charged around the arena at top speed, stopped, and took the first shot at a target from the saddle. Unfortunately, the equine personality didn't match the performer's style. That first night she wrote in her diary: "Wow! What a ride! That was one of the fastest quarter horses I've had, and with the arrows rattling it was something. I called and arranged for another horse. The new horse was a lot better and it made a nice entrance."

After closing at Fort Smith the Marstons headed to Springfield, Missouri, home base for Austyn Swenson and his Thrillcade spectacular. Originally from Minnesota, Swenson started out in the 1920s as a race car driver. He drove a Model T that he modified for the dirt track circuit and won a championship at the 1921 Minnesota State Fair. His passion for fast cars earned him a job with legendary race promoter J. Alex Sloan in 1924. The following year he developed a new concept and formed Austyn's Greater Flying Circus. With a small fleet of airplanes, some old cars, and a couple of motorcycles, he tried to get a start in show business. Bad weather forced the cancellation of most of his bookings the first year, and he lost everything.

Swenson became a civilian flight instructor when World War II broke out, and later he invested in Florida real estate. Once again he found a business partner and tried to launch the All-American Thrill Drivers show. It, too, was doomed after only one season. By 1949 he finally got it right, and Aut Swenson's Thrillcade hit the Midwest United States fair circuit.

The Thrillcade was a surreal combination of an old-fashioned circus, stunt show, music concert, and NASCAR event. Fans of all ages came to see daredevils risk their lives in "The Ultimate in Sensational 20th Century Entertainment." They watched motorcycles racing through dangerous hoops of fire, demolition derbies, and cars charging up ramps to hurdle over a real elephant. Added to the action was a bevy of scantily clad girls named the Thrillcadettes. These beauties hung on for their lives as they stood on the roofs of speeding race cars. They wore helmets to provide the protection that their swimsuits could not.

A brochure affirmed that during the Texas State Fair in Dallas in 1953, Thrillcade entertained 16,500 fans during its three performances. Later that same day popular comedians Dean Martin and Jerry Lewis attracted only 8,000 for their two shows.

In 1961 there were more than one hundred Thrillcade performances lined up in the country's midsection from Minnesota to Arkansas. The Ford Motor Company provided new 1961 trucks and Falcons, and Phillips 66 was an additional sponsor, promoting fuel and Super Action Tread tires. That year Swenson also formed a "B" unit that was named Austyn's Motor Derby and Thrill Circus. It was scheduled for fifty advance bookings in the U.S. and Canada between June and early October.

Thrillcade continued to offer nonstop action, and Swenson was sometimes compared to P.T. Barnum because of his sensational productions. When fairgoers became bored with livestock and flower exhibits, they looked forward to some entertaining and perilous action. Featured musical recording artist Leroy Van Dyke and his troupe performed, from the roof of a Ford, naturally. Thrillcade stunt drivers included some of the best in the business, such as Jimmie James and Kenny Blaine. The Blitz Ball contest featured go-kart drivers pushing around a large ball to their team's goal post. Motor Polo teams from America and Canada vied for a $10,000 purse. In the Gold Cup Crash Roll Tournament, opponents deliberately tumbled old vehicles end-over-end for points and prize money. The demolition derby was an equally popular attraction with the audiences.

The Thrillcadettes, also known as the Darlings of Daredevilry, were costumed in short skirts and positioned water-ski style on the roofs of Ford Falcons. A unique element was demonstrations of a futuristic X-1 Experimental Air Car, designed by pilot Bob Smith, which was lifted off the ground and propelled with jets of air.

Ann was attached to the "A" unit and immediately named "Miss Thrillcade 1961" for advertising purposes. She complimented Swenson's promotion tactics of using billboards and radio spots, writing: "He's really doing a fine job on publicity. I feel good and I think that everything will work out perfectly." Ann's photo was featured on a handout that was styled like a dollar bill. Under her portrait was the proclamation, "Ann Marston Miss America." A much smaller line said "1960 Talent Winner, Little Miss Sure Shot, and World Archery Champion." The coupons were distributed freely at every performance location to ensure a full house and to generate anticipation for the show. "Admit 1 adult guest. This certificate entitles you to all the excitement you can stand!"

Ann also earned top billing in one of Swenson's four-page advance publicity catalogs. Two large photos of her were displayed on the front page, and her exploits were described in typically dramatic fashion:

... Among the featured performers this season is Ann Marston of Detroit, Mich., the 1960 talent winner in the Miss America pageant at Atlantic City, N.J. A native of England, born in the shadow of Sherwood Forest, in fact, Miss Marston holds 11 women's national archery championships and has established two all-time records.

She does her target shooting from the top of a Thrillcade Ford. Little "Miss Sure Shot" can break balloons at 100 yards, extinguish a candle flame with an arrow at an unbelievable distance and shows a magical touch in flicking arrows through swinging key rings.

Swenson's workshop staff attached a platform to the roof of a car and a handrail for Ann's support when the vehicle was moving. The workmen outfitted another car with a deck for Frank to stand on, and they mounted a target to the base. The two cars made the entrance in tandem, with Frank's car slightly behind Ann's. They looped the entire track and stopped in front of the grandstands about 100 feet apart. When the music started, Ann did her routine and took aim at the target while standing or kneeling. Frank quickly mounted the balloons, eggs, and other props onto the target while emcee Jack O'Dare provided commentary for the crowd. After the performance, the car made another journey around the arena while Ann hung on and waved. She was a big hit and enjoyed ovations at every performance. "The audience was really good to me," she wrote. Ann cheerfully signed hundreds of autographs after each show.

Trapeze and high-wire artists fit into Thrillcade's carnival atmosphere, and there was a talented clown troupe that including zany trampoline aerobatics by Gaylord Maynard. The jesters had a repertoire of go-kart stunts and provided the customary clowny silliness for the crowd. A special guest star was clown extraordinaire Emmett Kelly Jr., who brought his "Weary Willie" hobo-mime character to Thrillcade's lineup. Kelly was a second-generation clown and emulated his father, Emmett Kelly, who was famous worldwide when he appeared with the Ringling Bros. and Barnum & Bailey Circus. Kelly enjoyed working in Thrillcade and respected Swenson. "Aut Swenson was a wonderful man to work for," he said. "You didn't need a contract with him; his handshake was as good as gold and he always paid cash." Kelly described part of his Thrillcade routine:

I opened the show, and then along came four cars, clickety-click, over the ramps at 80 miles an hour. Then we clowns were in the next event in an old car. We'd drive over a low ramp and bust a cherry bomb. Then we'd jump out and run in different directions and the crowd would laugh.

Between shows, Kelly and the other clowns fooled around backstage for Ann's amusement. At one point Florence held the movie camera while Ann tried to teach Kelly how to use the bow and arrow. He did an impromptu comedy routine and pantomimed using the weapon as a bow fiddle. He eventually snapped his big red rubber nose with the bowstring.

Kelly became fast friends with Ann and her parents. When the Thrillcade moved across the Midwest, Kelly often rode in the Marstons' car for overnight treks to the next location. He was fond of "Annie," and sometimes took her to movies or out to eat. She wrote: "I had a wonderful time, and he was a perfect gentleman." Although he was married and twenty years her senior, Kelly became infatuated with Ann. "I respected her and her parents, and never let them know that I loved her." Kelly and the Marstons remained friends, and for more than forty years he kept an autographed photo of Ann hanging in the living room of his home in Tombstone, Arizona.

The Marstons finished the month of June with Thrillcade appearances at Joplin, Missouri; Omaha, Nebraska; Watertown, North Dakota; and Wheaton, Minnesota. Then they headed north in July for a three-week-long tour of Canada booked by MCA. Frank's sister Doris lived in Winnipeg, and they had not seen each other in twenty-one years. Ann became acquainted with her cousins David, Gordon, and Barbara. The family members later attended Ann's performance in Brandon. Also on the bill were Homer and Jethro, the dancing Four Step Brothers, the Amandis family Danish teeterboard experts, and Ann's old friend, gunslinger Joe Bodrie.

In Calgary, Alberta, they performed for enthusiastic crowds estimated to be more than 33,000 people. At Edmonton's Exhibition, Ann made a one-in-a-million shot by splitting an arrow during the act. She had accomplished the feat in practice but never before an audience. They eventually moved on to Saskatoon and Regina. Ann earned $3,500, but at the end of the tour she said: "I've decided I couldn't live in Canada; there's no place like the good old U.S.A."

Ann Marston and company traveled more than 1,500 miles to Altamont, Illinois, and caught up with the Thrillcade for another series of engagements. It was to be a grueling two-week schedule. They were required to drive a few hundred miles each night to perform one-day stands throughout Ohio, Illinois, Minnesota, Iowa, and Indiana. Swenson's publicity machine was efficient as usual, and Ann was prominently featured in billboards, interviews, and media spots along with Emmett Kelly Jr. She had bad luck right away and sprained her ankle the first day. But she was a trouper and carried on, limping slightly through the act.

A week later in Cedar Rapids, Iowa, Ann became ill and vomited all night. Several other members of the cast and crew also became sick. Ann was hospitalized for three days, and doctors attributed the problem to food poisoning, a predictable risk to those who eat restaurant food three meals a day/seven days a week. The newspapers informed her fans, "Ann Marston, archery star of the Aut Swenson Thrillcade, missed the Tuesday afternoon and evening performances when she became ill. Officials at St. Luke's Hospital reported she was hospitalized and listed her condition as fair." After the ordeal they continued with the hectic timetable for the second week, and Swenson paid Ann, withholding wages for the two performances she missed.

They drove all night and most of the following day to reach DuQuoin, Illinois, and Ann took an opportunity to relieve her exhausted father. "I drove a little, but Mother made such a fuss, I quit. I don't know what is the matter with her. It would be so easy for us all if she didn't have this phobia of my driving." After twenty-four hours on the road, they finally found a hotel at their destination. Ann wrote: "The trip seemed interminable. Nothing much to report: just drive and drive and drive. We found a motel. Anything would have looked good, but this was a particularly nice place. Nobody had to rock me to sleep."

Eldred Stacy of MCA booked their appearance at DuQuoin for the Illinois State Fair. There was a superior range of grandstand talent that included The Lennon Sisters from the *Lawrence Welk Show*, the Dukes of Dixieland, and headliners Rosemary Clooney and Nelson Eddy. Ann reported a backstage rumor that Rosemary Clooney was earning $15,000 for her performances. The high point of the week was a 110-mile Indianapolis qualifying race. Legendary champions A.J. Foyt, Parnelli Jones, Rodger Ward, and Eddie Sachs competed for the $23,000 purse. The fair also offered a beauty contest, midway, harness racing, magicians, comedians, and "Ann Marston, the world champion in archery, whose accuracy puts William Tell to shame." It was a busy week. "It seems like all we do is get up, do a show, eat, and then come back to the motel," she wrote. "Today was no exception." At least they had an air-conditioned room to ease the 93-degree heat.

Aut Swenson scheduled Ann for September and most of October with stops in South Dakota, Illinois, Minnesota, Kansas, Iowa, and Arkansas. She was happy to be back with Thrillcade. By now, Swenson and his family of performers were good friends. "I like this unit; we had a packed house." Emmett Kelly Jr. and Leroy Van Dyke and his band were on the show again. Ann's mother, Florence, exuded a very dignified British persona and didn't readily associate with the Thrillcade cast and crew. It must have been a quite an adjustment for her to observe her husband and daughter casually fraternizing with performers, roustabouts, and assorted carnival personnel. At first impression Florence was quite aloof, but as Kelly described: "Later on she'd loosen up, and tell some jokes, too."

Ann made friends quickly, which was an essential skill since they were transient most of the year. Ann enjoyed the camaraderie with the Thrillcade troupe, and often took the opportunity to hang around with the cast and crew after the show. Sometimes they visited the midway attractions, played bingo and the horses, or watched the auto races. Both Frank and Ann enjoyed socializing and organized weekly card games. Ann wasn't much of a drinker, so her parents didn't worry too much about that; however, Frank occasionally over-indulged in the social life on the road. As Ann said, "Daddy came home tonight in his usual condition." He took great pleasure in playing his ukulele, and knew a full range of old standards, along with several bawdy British pub tunes that he readily performed at impromptu gatherings.

Ann became the victim of behind-the-scenes gossip. She was casually dating a young man named Ron Surrett who was the new emcee for Thrillcade. "He's pretty good onstage. He's from Peoria and a real nice-looking fellow. It's nice to see someone on the show who is clean cut." Their friendship was attracting negative attention, which upset Ann. "I guess some people are talking, which makes things bad in the family. This is a nice boy that I enjoy being with, but because of people and their small minds it's wrecking a nice time. It's strange when people are rotten; they think everybody else is, too."

The summer season was at an end and they finished fair engagements in Louisiana, Tennessee, and Alabama in late fall. At the Mid South Fair in Memphis, she shared the billing with Cliff Arquette/Charley Weaver, who had been a judge at the 1960 Miss America pageant. She wrote that, "He's a nice man even though he's not exactly killing the audience." Banjo-playing comedian Jerry Van Dyke also appeared at the fair.

Eventually the show closed for the season, and Ann was sad. "We said goodbye to everybody," she wrote. "These are the greatest people to work for. When I look back in my diary, it hardly seems possible what we've done in the last 3 or 4 months." The car's odometer logged a total of about 35,000 miles. Ann's income peaked at nearly $19,000, the equivalent of $128,000 in 2006 dollars, minus the 10 percent commission given to MCA. The 1962 calendar was completely booked with rodeos, fairs, sports shows and another stint with Thrillcade.

SLEEP, LITTLE MAID

The aromatic vapours of POTTER'S ASTHMA REMEDY soon dispel the bogey of Bronchitis. Marvellous for Asthma, Whooping Cough, Colds, etc. 2/2 all Chemists and Herbalists.

free from the bogey of **BRONCHITIS**

POTTER'S *Asthma Remedy*

1940

Ann at age two

Ann Penelope Marston was born in London, England, in 1938, the only child of Florence and Frank Marston. A wartime gas mask sits on the ground near Ann.

1940-1943

Ad model

While her father served in the British Royal Navy during World War II, Ann appeared in advertisements, catalogs, and needlework instruction books.

NOTE: All photographs courtesy of the Marston family, except where noted.

EARLY SUCCESS

1948

Colonel Bogey *movie set*

Ann's father, Frank, was a world-class archer and was hired as a consultant for the British movie, *Colonel Bogey*, in 1948. Ann was enrolled in a performing arts school and appeared in a small part in the film.

1949

U.S. Girl's Cadet champion

Ann became Britain's Junior Champion at age nine. She was considered a prodigy and earned the U.S. Girl's Cadet title one week after the family immigrated to America in 1949. She was diagnosed with diabetes in 1951, and took daily insulin injections.

1953

Life magazine photo shoot

Joe Clark, the "Hill Billy Snap Shooter," was hired to photograph Ann for a small article in *Life* dated Aug. 31, 1953. He captured her in action with a bow while the arrow pierced an egg.

Fred Bear and Ann

Archery legend Fred Bear was a close friend and business associate of the Marstons. Ann and Fred are pictured at the NFAA Nationals in Two Rivers, Wisconsin, in 1953. Ann broke two world records and won the Junior Girls' Free Style trophy.

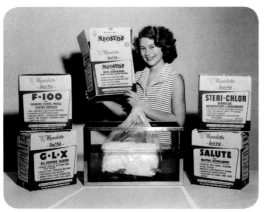

1954

Ann with Ed Sullivan

(top) Ann demonstrated her archery skill to America on Ed Sullivan's *Toast of the Town* in December 1953 when she was fifteen years old.

(above) Ann modeled in the Detroit area for several companies, including the Wyandotte Chemicals Corp. Courtesy BASF Corp.

You Asked for It host, Art Baker

Ann was a nationally recognized sports figure by 1954, and fans of *You Asked For It* requested a demonstration of her skills. She shot an arrow off the head of a mannequin resembling the show's host, Art Baker.

FAMILY & FRIENDS

1955

The family of champions

Ann, Florence, and Frank
Marston all competed nationally.
Despite her young age, Ann
was allowed to participate as an
adult in archery contests. During
personal appearances, she often
shot an arrow through an egg.

1956

Ann and school friends

Ann went to Theodore Roosevelt
High School in Wyandotte,
Michigan. Because she was
on the road much of the time,
teachers allowed her to complete
lessons by correspondence. Ann
played clarinet in the marching
band, acted in drama club and
wrote a sports column for the
school newspaper. She graduated
in June 1956.

1956

Ann and Dick Van Dyke

(above and top right) Dick Van Dyke was host on *The Morning Show* for CBS, and Ann went to New York to be guest weather girl for two weeks. She shot arrows into a map to indicate weather conditions in various locations.

Winchell-Mahoney Time

Florence took this photograph off their TV set when Ann appeared on the *Winchell-Mahoney Time* show. She shot an apple off the head of host Paul Winchell's wise-cracking dummy, Jerry Mahoney. Winchell went on to become the voice of Winnie-the-Pooh's "Tigger."

1957

Publicity photo with Beau

Beau the poodle was adopted by the Marstons and accompanied the family everywhere. Ann often had his fur tinted in pastel colors and his toenails painted for special occasions.

1958

My Dog Sheppy

(top) Kelly the dog got top billing in *My Dog Sheppy,* the pilot of a TV series.

(above) Ann's co-star was Robert Roark. The pilot was filmed in Arkansas in hopes of cashing in on Lassie's popularity.

1958

Ann and her father

Although Frank was a World Champion archer, he took a back seat to Ann as her stage assistant. Florence ran the show behind the scenes, taking care of bookings, finances, travel arrangements, and costumes. Ann's income supported the family for many years while she received a small allowance.

Ann in England

Multi-talented Ann was a hit with international audiences. She performed on television at the London Palladium in 1958, and newspapers across Western Europe picked up the story. It was the last time the family visited their British relatives.

1959

Miss Michigan 1960 and court

Ann displayed her crown and trophy after winning a different type of competition: the Miss Michigan beauty contest. She represented the state in the 1960 Miss America Pageant in Atlantic City, New Jersey.

Souvenir of the pageant

Before the Miss America Pageant, Miss Nevada, Dawn Wells, handed out promotional badges displaying her photo. She later appeared on television in *Gilligan's Island* as "Mary Ann." Ann distributed bow and arrow sets to some fellow Miss America contestants.

The Detroit News
Sunday
Pictorial
Sept. 6, 1959   16 Pages

News Photo by Monroe D. Stroecker

Her Gown Tells a Story

OFF TO THE MISS AMERICA competition in Atlantic City this week goes Ann Marston, Miss Detroit and Miss Michigan. Her gown, a circle of blue and white "spokes," represents the Motor City. **(Story inside.)**

World's Fanciest Fishing—Pg. 14

1959

Miss Michigan float

The Boardwalk parade included the Michigan float styled after the Mackinac Bridge. *Courtesy Ron Tocco.*

(opposite page) Ann was featured in the "Wheel of Detroit" gown in *The Detroit News Sunday Pictorial* magazine. The photo story described her preparations for the Miss America Pageant. *By permission of* The Detroit News.

The pride of Wyandotte

Ann's adopted hometown of Wyandotte hosted a parade to honor their queen. She choked up when the Roosevelt High School marching band played "Oh, You Beautiful Doll." She was later greeted by Mayor Jack McCauley. *Courtesy Ron Tocco.*

1959

Miss America program

The 1960 Miss America Pageant was held in September 1959. The contestants' vital statistics, talents, and hobbies were listed in the program. It reported Ann, at age twenty-one, as 5'7" tall, 118 lbs., with a 35" bust, a 23" waist, and 35" hips. *Courtesy of the Miss America Organization.*

Talent competition

Ann missed the target once in the preliminary talent competition, but she won the contest portion of the pageant — and a $1,000 scholarship. The judges included TV celebrities Mitch Miller and Charlie Weaver. *Courtesy Ron Tocco.*

1960

With Michigan's governor

Governor G. Mennen "Soapy"
Williams welcomed Ann to
the State Capitol. *Photo by
Pat Mitchell Studios. Courtesy
Marston family.*

A busy schedule

Ann traveled coast-to-coast
in 1960 to accommodate her
Miss Michigan commitments
and busy performance career.
The stress caused her to be
hospitalized briefly. She was the
National Cystic Fibrosis Queen
during her reign, and spent
much of her free time visiting
sick children.

1961

The Aut Swenson Thrillcade

(top) Aut Swenson's popular Thrillcade car spectacular annually toured the Midwest. The Marstons logged thousands of miles a year on their car while traveling to numerous engagements in the U.S. and Canada. Ann impressed the audiences with her trick shooting and witty comments.

Thrillcade handbill

Ann was promoted as "Ann Marston Miss America" on this Thrillcade handbill. The show promised to deliver "all the excitement you can stand!"

1961

Wagon Train *cast members*

Ann appeared on the bill at exhibitions, sports shows, fairs, and rodeos with many of America's favorite TV Western stars, including Roy Rogers and some of the actors from *Wagon Train*.

Ann's dungeon

(top right) The Marstons always returned home to Wyandotte during the off-season. Ann earned today's equivalent of nearly $128,000 in 1961, but lived in a small apartment in her parents' basement that she called her "Dungeon." Ann resented her mother's interference and control.

Who Do You Trust?

(above) Johnny Carson was the host of the game show *Who Do You Trust?* before joining *The Tonight Show*. Ann was a contestant on this and several other game shows including *What's My Line?, I've Got a Secret, Truth or Consequences,* and *To Tell the Truth.*

VENING DEMOCRA

Associated Press Leased Wire   Newspaper Enterprise Ass'n Serv
FORT MADISON, IOWA   MONDAY, SEPTEMBER 10, 1962

Archer Is Injured by Brahma Bull

"This just isn't our year," said Frank Marston Sunday evening after he had visited his injured daughter, Archery Expert Ann Marston, at Sacred Heart hospital here.

"Last February," Marston said, "Ann was performing with an ice show in Beckley, W.Va., and she fell and broke her wrist in two places."

"We're grateful here, however," Marston added quickly. "Sunday's accident here could have been a lot worse."

The 21-year-old Miss Marston, one of the nation's most famous archers, was injured during her performance at the 13th annual Tri-State Championship Rodeo Sunday afternoon when attacked by a wild Brahma bull which

1961	1962

Clu Gulager and Emmett Kelly Jr.

Ann, the clown, and the cowboy visited a young fan in a hospital in Fort Madison, Iowa. Kelly remained a life-long friend of the Marstons. *Courtesy of the* Fort Madison Evening Democrat.

(opposite page) Ann often rode a horse named Annie Oakley in rodeos. She could ride almost as well as she could shoot. *Photo by Zintgraff. Courtesy Marston family.*

Injured by a bull

A Brahma bull broke out of its pen during one of Ann's rodeo performances. She dived to the ground of the stadium, and the animal stepped on her, breaking several ribs. It then tossed her father out of his boots and into the air. Both Ann and her father recovered completely in a few weeks. *Courtesy of the* Fort Madison Evening Democrat.

1962

Ann's PR sheet, circa 1962

This promotional flyer highlighted Ann's numerous accomplishments as a skilled competitive athlete and internationally famous performer. She enjoyed instructing and encouraging young athletes.

The Wyandotte Theater

Ann and Frank's movie, *Bow Jests,* played in their hometown in 1962. Ann gave archery exhibitions at the Wyandotte Theater before each showing.

1962

Bow Jests *publicity still*

Paramount Pictures featured the archery talents of both Ann and Frank in *Bow Jests,* a ten-minute color sports short that was shown in movie theaters nationally.

Sunday, September 6, 1964
250th Day—116 days to follow

Beatle Day

Dear Diary,

Today is what diaries are for— Today I met the Beatles. Mother called Whittier to speak to Derek Taylor & by a fluke got to speak to John Lennon, so we spoke about it on the phone— & he was delightful.

At 5 I was invited to the Press Conference & had pictures taken with the Beatles & then saw the show— while it's indescribable they had other acts — but when the Beatles came on stage there was such a roar— like a vacuum & the hundreds of flash bulbs was like World War I & II — and they really worked some of the numbers were: Twist & Shout (which floored), You Can't Do That, All My Loving [...]

1964

Ann's diary

Ann recorded her excitement at meeting The Beatles at Detroit's Olympia Stadium on Sept. 6, 1964. She kept journals of most of her adult life.

The Beatles backstage

(top) This was an original photo taken of The Beatles, Ann and other beauty queens in Detroit. Paul McCartney telephoned Ann occasionally.

(above) Florence altered an image to suggest that The Beatles were alone with Ann.

THE 'KEEENER' CONNECTION

1964

Robin Seymour

The WKNR disc jockeys were very popular and powerful in the Detroit music scene. DJ Frank "Swingin'" Sweeney tried to launch a singing career for Ann. WKNR DJ Robin Seymour and Ann clowned around during a movie promotion.

1966

Target flyer

In her mid-twenties, Ann looked for new challenges away from her archery profession. Miss Michigan's Target Young Adult Nightclub in Dearborn opened in 1966, but Ann closed the club in 1968.

The Motor City Five

(top) Ann was an agent for the MC5 in their early years. They played at countless Detroit-area dances, clubs, and concert venues. The band covered popular songs by The Beatles and The Rolling Stones. *Courtesy Svengirly Music and Michael Davis.*

(above) The MC5 was an opening act for The Dave Clark Five in Detroit, but Ann got the publicity. *Courtesy of the Wyandotte News Herald.*

1969

The band Julia

Several Detroit-area musical groups thrived under Ann's aggressive management in the late 1960s and early 1970s, including Tea, The Ruins, The Satellites, and Julia.

The "enlightened" MC5

After leaving Ann's direction, the MC5 joined John Sinclair's artistic community. In 1969 they hit it big with their first album, "Kick Out the Jams." The group included Dennis Thompson, Michael Davis, Wayne Kramer, Rob Tyner, and Fred "Sonic" Smith. *Photo by Raeanne Rubenstein. Courtesy Svengirly Music and Michael Davis.*

Ann Marston with her poodle, Charlie Brown

Michigan beauty waging battle against blindness

By LOUIS J. SUGO
Detroit News Metropolitan Bureau

Ann Marston, the blue-eyed Wyandotte beauty who 10 years ago parlayed a world archery championship into a Miss Michigan title, today is fighting blindness.

For nearly four months now, the 30-year-old blond beauty contest winner has gone from one medical specialist to another to find some way out of the partial blindness that threatens to end her show business career.

"Six doctors have told me there is no hope, but a local chiropractor has started to help me," said Miss Marston yesterday.

It was nearly a year ago, when Miss Marston returned from a road tour, that she began to feel tired and have nagging headaches.

She consulted a physician who diagnosed the problem as "hemorrhaging behind the eyes," but, according to Miss Marston, the doctor gave her no indication it was a serious condition.

Since that time, however, Miss Marston said doctors have

1969	1970

Sudden blindness

Ann lost her eyesight in February 1969 as a result of long-term damage caused by diabetes. In press releases, her condition was blamed on injuries caused by a rodeo bull in 1962. Even though she was once again dependent on her parents, she kept a positive attitude about her condition. *By permission of* The Detroit News.

Working girl

Ann remained a respected musical agent for the Gail & Rice talent agency in Detroit. She hired drivers and secretaries to help with her music business. This is one of the few photos taken of Ann after she lost her sight in 1969. *By permission of Gail & Rice.*

Death Takes Champion

Massive Stroke Fells Former Miss Michigan

1971

Sudden death

On March 6, 1971, Ann Marston died unexpectedly of a stroke at age thirty-two. Both local and national newspapers reported the sad news and acknowledged that it was related to diabetes. Friends, relatives, and celebrities including Joe DiMaggio and Johnny Carson expressed their sympathies to her parents. *By permission of the* Wyandotte News Herald.

Ann's centograph

Both Florence and Frank were devastated over Ann's death and arranged to be interred next to her at Michigan Memorial Park. A memorial service was held in September 1971, and a brass plaque was installed at her crypt. Congressman John Dingell visited Ann's centograph with her parents.

Memorial Service

MASTER OF CEREMONIES
Paul Williams, Public Affairs Mgr. of the WWJ Stations

INVOCATION
Father Alexander J. Wytwral, Pastor,
St. Stephens Church, New Boston, Mich.

INTRODUCTION OF CONGRESSMAN JOHN DINGELL

PRESENTATION OF CENOTAPH HONORING ANN MARSTON BY
CONGRESSMAN JOHN DINGELL

INTRODUCTION OF DISTINGUISHED GUESTS
HONORING ANN MARSTON

Supreme Court Justice	G. Mennen Williams
State Senator	John E. McCauley
State Representative	William Copeland
Wayne County Commissioner	James DeSana
Allen Park Mayor	John Metelski
Dearborn Mayor	Orville Hubbard
Ecorse Mayor	Richard Manning
Flat Rock Mayor	Lloyd Martin
Lincoln Park Mayor	Robert DeMars
Riverview Mayor	Jay Brown
River Rouge Mayor	John F. McEwen
Southgate Mayor	Bob Reaume
Taylor Mayor	Richard Trolley
Wyandotte Mayor	William Sullivan
Sports Editor Wyandotte News Herald	Bob Graham
TV Producer 'Michigan Outdoors"	Mort Neff
CKLW Channel 9 "All Outdoors"	Jerry Chiappetta
Director WJR	George Phieffer
Sports Announcer	"Bud" Lynch
Board Director Professional Archers Assn.	Karl Palmatlier
President Amer. Fed. Television & Radio Artists	Don Karle
Executive Soc'y. Amer. Fed. Television & Radio Artists	Mary Ann Formaz
President Lions	Richard Hall
District Governor of Lions	Charles Labory
Deputy District Governor of Lions	Edw...
President Patricia Stevens Finishing School	Di...
Miss America 1970	Pam...
Executive Director Miss Michigan Pageant	Ja...
Executive President Miss Michigan Pageant	Lyn V...
Worthy Matron Eastern Star	Ed...
Worshipful Master Masonic Lodge	Emmerso...

MUSICAL TRIBUTE
Gino D'Alessio, accompanied by James Kend...

BENEDICTION
Joseph Czapski

In Memorial
ANN MARSTON

Sunday, September 19, 1971   2:00 p.m.

MICHIGAN MEMORIAL PARK
Main Entrance, Huron River Drive at Willow Road

Dedicated to the Memory of
ANN MARSTON

MISS AMERICA TALENT AWARD
NATIONAL ARCHER CHAMPION
MISS MICHIGAN

AUGUST 7, 1938   MARCH 6, 1971

Ann Marston was a graduate of Roosevelt High School, Wyandotte, Michigan. She was a member of The National Honor Society, Thespians, Quill and Scroll.

Ann won her first target archery title at age nine in her native England. She came to the U.S.A. in 1948 and captured her cadet target archery title one week later. Ann continued winning and breaking all time records to 1953.

1954 at age fifteen, three years ahead of time she elected to shoot in the adult division at the National Field Tournament and won. In winning her first senior title she established three new records, and set the stage for her 1955 and 1957 victories. In all, Ann won eleven national archery titles establishing all time records.

Ann's archery talent in Miss America 1960 was the first time that a sport had ever won this honor. Ann is the youngest to be elected to the Willie Heston Sports Hall of Fame and the second woman. Ann was named the outstanding sportswoman of 1970, for exemplifying the ideals of sportsmanship.

"You can become a champ at anything you want if you try hard enough but you have to lose to prove you're a good sport. A winner never lets this opportunity." ANN MARSTON

And I will cast thee out, and thy mother that bare thee, into another country where ye were not born, and there shall ye die.

1971

Memorial program

The cover of Ann's memorial program incorporated one of her favorite portraits.

Program interior

There was an impressive list of speakers at Ann's memorial service, including Mort Neff, Budd Lynch, Miss America 1970 Pamela Eldred, and Michigan Supreme Court Justice G. Mennen Williams.

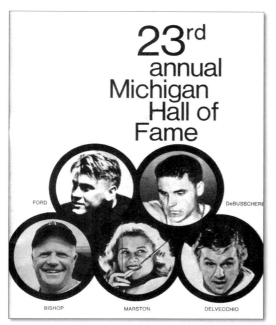

1977

MSHOF program

The Michigan Sports Hall of Fame induction honored Ann along with several other noteworthy athletes, including President Gerald R. Ford. *By permission of the Michigan Sports Hall of Fame.*

Michigan Sports Hall of Fame

Ann's Hall of Fame photo and plaque is displayed at Detroit's Cobo Hall with those of past inductees including Gordie Howe, Ernie Harwell, Earvin "Magic" Johnson, and Joe Louis. *Photo courtesy Jeffery Trudell.*

FILMOGRAPHY

1948. *Junior Toxopholist.* A British Pathe' black and white newsreel that ran for one minute and nine seconds. Charming ten-year-old Ann and her father performed trick archery shots.

1948. *Colonel Bogey.* This full-length movie release was directed by Terence Fisher and starred British actress Jane Barrett. Frank Marston was an archery consultant; Ann appeared as an extra.

December 6, 1951; July 28, 1951. *Paul Whiteman's TV Teen Club.* This ABC talent show hosted by Paul Whiteman was broadcast live from Philadelphia and highlighted talented youngsters. Ann appeared on at least two occasions.

July 23, 1953. *Michigan Outdoors.* A local sports show based in Detroit that was hosted by Mort Neff and Al Nagler.

1953. *Sports Profile/Meet the Sport.* This WWJ-Detroit program featured local sports icons and was hosted by Budd Lynch and Paul Williams. Ann was invited to appear several times.

December 13, 1953. *Talk of the Town.* Ed Sullivan's classic variety show. Ann appeared in Season 7 – Episode 14 with singers Jimmy Boyd and Frankie Laine and possibly on two other episodes.

1953. *Talent Scouts.* Arthur Godfrey hosted this popular family show. Ann's actual appearance date is unknown.

Summer 1954. *You Asked for It.* Viewers requested film documentation of unique places and people. Ann's archery segment featured a replica of host Art Baker as a target.

Summer 1954. *Art Linkletter House Party.* Linkletter's daily TV show.

Summer 1954. *Spade Cooley.* A Los Angeles area TV show hosted by country-western singer Spade Cooley.

April 15, 1954; March 4, 1957; February 28, 1958. *This is Today.* Now known as *The Today Show*, this NBC morning talk show was hosted by Dave Garroway from 1952-1961.

December 5-16, 1955. *The Morning Show.* Early version of the CBS sunrise talk show co-hosted by Dick Van Dyke. Ann appeared for two weeks as a weather girl and shot arrows into a map.

August 3, 1955. *I've Got a Secret.* A CBS game show that was led by humorist Garry Moore.

September 15, 1956. *Captain Kangaroo.* Ann was a frequent guest at the Treasure House with Bob Keeshan on CBS. She gave archery demonstrations, sang and performed in skits.

October 1, 1956. *Ernie Kovacs Show.* This was a short-lived variety show that included Kovacs' wife, Edie Adams. Ann did an abbreviated version of her popular archery act.

October 6, 1956. *Kiddie Spectacular: The Story Princess.* Les Cooley produced this show. Ann read stories and demonstrated feats of archery with her father's assistance.

October 25, 1956. *Winchell-Mahoney Time Show.* Ann shot an apple off the head of dummy Jerry Mahoney while guesting on this weekly kiddie show that was emceed by zany Paul Winchell.

December 1, 1956. *Captain Kangaroo.*

March 9, 1957. *Captain Kangaroo.*

May 18, 1957. *Winchell Circus Time.* The Winchell-Mahoney team invited Ann to return for this special program.

June 22, 1957. *Captain Kangaroo.*

November 23, 1957. *Captain Kangaroo.*

April 1958. *My Dog Sheppy.* Ann co-starred with Robert Roark and Kelly the Dog in this unsuccessful TV pilot filmed in Blanchard Springs, Arkansas.

March 28, 1958. *Captain Kangaroo.*

October 10, 1958. *Jack Paar Tonight Show.* CBS. Jack took the night off and Johnny Carson was the guest host. Carson later became the permanent icon of the renamed *Tonight Show.*

October 22, 1958. *Captain Kangaroo.* The producers asked Ann to consider a regular spot on the show but she was too busy with her career.

January 16, 1959. *Captain Kangaroo.* Ann's eighth and final appearance with the Captain.

February 25, 1959. *Who Do You Trust?* Ed McMahon was Johnny Carson's announcer for this ABC game show. Ann won $100 as a contestant.

September 12, 1959. *The Miss America Pageant 1960,* CBS. The ultimate beauty pageant was hosted by Douglas Edwards and Marilyn Van Derbur. Ann won the preliminary talent contest but was not selected as one of the ten finalists. Lynda Lee Mead earned the crown.

June 19, 1962. *To Tell the Truth,* CBS. A game show with master of ceremonies Budd Collyer. Ann deceived a celebrity panel that included Merv Griffin, Betty White, Kitty Carlisle, and Ralph Bellamy.

June 1962. *Bow Jests.* This color sports short by Paramount Pictures was directed by Richard Winik and narrated by Chris Schenkel. Frank and Ann Marston starred in this ten-minute-long film that was shown in movie houses across the country. Both accomplished amazing trick shots.

August 28, 1963. *What's My Line?* The panel and moderator John Daly didn't guess Ann's occupation as professional archer and former Miss Michigan. She then performed her archery demonstration for the audience.

1962-1969. *Truth or Consequences.* NBC's Bob Barker was the popular host of this long-running game show. Ann appeared several times in road shows for *Truth or Consequences.* Her final archery demonstration was broadcast live from Detroit in February 1969. She lost her sight a few weeks later.

6

ME AND ANNIE OAKLEY

ANN MADE A SHORT FILM FOR PARAMOUNT PICTURES, and she hoped it might lead to more roles. It was possible that a singing or acting career was in her future, so she took voice lessons with the scholarship money that she won in the Miss America pageant.

She was a lonely young woman, and she was becoming weary of life on the road. The Marstons were still traveling as a group with Ann's archery act, which was a big hit on the rodeo circuit, and she rode a horse named "Annie Oakley." A dramatic mishap during a rodeo performance resulted in injury for both Ann and her father. Unfortunately, she also began experiencing vision problems that was mistakenly blamed on the accident, but actually was a dangerous result of her diabetes.

There wasn't much time to relax upon returning to Michigan in November 1961. Eldred Stacy was working hard for Ann and called with very good news. He procured contracts for a ten-minute sport short starring Ann and Frank, and they were to be paid $500 each to appear. The project capitalized on MCA's close connection with Paramount, but the politics didn't matter to Ann. In her diary entry dated November 18, 1961, she wrote: "Well, I think this was *the* day. I don't get excited much anymore, but this looks like IT! We met Mr. Leslie Winik of Paramount Pictures … We ran the TV pilot for him [*My Dog Sheppy*] at the Wyandotte Theater. He wants to shoot a 10-minute sport short for a 50-million audience. It could be the start of something—I hope so. MCA has been in touch with him."

By December 8, they were on their way to the filming location in Georgia. A Sea Island area paper announced the news:

> *A color film on archery is to be made at Sea Island by Paramount Pictures between the dates of December 11 and 16th. Starring in the film will be 20-year-old [sic] Ann Marston, a former Miss Michigan beauty queen known as "the world's foremost woman archer." Her father, Frank Marston, an internationally noted archer, will also appear in the short which will later be shown in movie houses the world over. The Sea Island resort area is to be credited in the film.*

Ann was impressed with the Cloisters Hotel. She was assigned a suite at the magnificent hotel/resort, which boasted a 27-hole golf course, freshwater pool, and beach access to the ocean. She explored while waiting for the film crew to arrive. "This is a beautiful place," she wrote. "The Garden of Eden with improvements."

The film, to be titled *Bow Jests*, was slated to be produced by Leslie Winik, who had a decent reputation in Hollywood. He founded Official Films in 1939, and backed a sizzling jazz short titled *Boogie Woogie Dream* in 1944. One of Official Films' "L'il Musical" series, the picture starred singer Lena Horne, legendary composers Albert Ammons, Pete Johnson, and Teddy Wilson and his band. Winik also produced *A Sport is Born*, a Paramount short feature on freefall skydiving that was one of a *Sports Illustrated* series of newsreels. The program earned an Oscar nomination in 1960 for Short Film-Live Subject. Winik went on to earn another nomination in 1966 for a short movie titled *The Winning Strain*.

The director for *Bow Jests* was Richard Winik, Leslie's son. Ann and Frank met with him to discuss the storyboard and to set up the camera angles for the trick shots. The weather turned cold and overcast but they decided to proceed. The film's concept was similar to the Pathe newsreel that Ann and Frank had made in England thirteen years earlier. The movie opened with a description of the resort and depicted happy vacationers enjoying the facilities. Golfing, of course, was a favorite activity and the camera panned across a rack of golf bags along with … bows and quivers of arrows. The newest sport at The Cloisters resort was "archery golf," and Ann and Frank Marston were introduced as experts in the field.

Clad in white shorts and a bustier, Ann "teed off" on the course with a 200-yard shot using a twenty-eight-pound bow. Frank followed suit and they strolled confidently across the green. The objective was to nail the arrow into the target—through a white four-inch ball mounted on a stake in front of it. The duo presented the value of proper stance, solid anchor point and successful arrow discharge and follow-through. They approached the target together to access their perfect shots.

They then aimed across a water hazard and the narrator described the scene. "Like daughter, like dad. Archery in the battlefield has been passé for centuries but archery on the golf course has a real future. Especially when you keep breaking par like the Marstons. Ann, you've done it again."

After a victorious round of archery golf, Ann sat on the swimming pool's high diving board and shot at floating balloons. She moved back to dry land to accomplish the double-arrow shot. She then demonstrated how she was able to shoot accurately while posed in a kneeling position and modeling a halter top.

Meanwhile Frank was snoozing pool-side, and Ann firmly woke him. He retaliated by remaining in his chair. Then he anchored the bow with his foot and drew back on the bowstring. After hitting the bull's-eye he calmly resumed his nap. In the next scene, Frank aimed the bow over his left shoulder and made a faultless shot while he reclined on his back. He casually stretched and again feigned sleep.

Then it was Ann's turn to show off her skill. She shot over her shoulder and hit all the balloons that were rotating on the pinwheel target. Five long balloons suspended on a pole were shish-kabobbed all at once. Next was the magic balloon stunt: Six balloons of different sizes were blown up inside each other and she broke them one at a time.

Ann proved that she could shoot at candles close enough to snuff out the flames. Next, father and daughter teamed up to shoot double arrows, popping four balloons at the exact same time. Dad then held a balloon up to the target and Ann shot it cleanly out of his hand; he then flashed his two "missing" middle fingers.

For the finale, Ann prepared to shoot an apple off Dear Old Dad's head. After releasing the bowstring, Ann looked surprised: "Whoops, have I missed something?" Frank shrugged his shoulders and turned to walk away, with a phony arrow skewered through his forehead.

They were cursed with bad weather during most of the shoot, mirroring the *My Dog Sheppy* movie experience. Winik decided to use the footage that was already completed, and the rest of the schedule was canceled. In post-production, the film was edited by Irving Oshman, acknowledged as the editor of the 1962 teen angst movie *David and Lisa*. Narration for *Bow Jests* was provided by well-known sportscaster Chris Schenkel. The movie was scheduled to be released in late spring.

In mid-February the Marstons had stops in Kansas City and Little Rock, and finally arrived in San Antonio for the big Stock Show and Rodeo. The advance publicity was great; even the taxicabs had billboards featuring Ann and her co-stars Anita Bryant and Rex Allen. There was a parade with Rex, Anita, and Ann as grand marshals. Ann arrived in a convertible escorted by several Texas motorcycle troopers, and her headdress feathers were blowing in the wind. The celebrities attended press conferences, did a TV show, and were honored guests at several receptions.

Ann was overwhelmed and wrote in her diary: "What a day this was; I had a schedule like the president's."

They abandoned the Robin Hood theme for rodeo appearances, so Florence designed Native American-styled costumes. She fashioned two out of real buckskin. Ann loved them and said they were "great for travel; they just wash and wear." Ann purchased several pairs of moccasins, and both she and her mother hand-beaded headbands and matching jewelry. Ann wore feathers in her hair and fringe on her quiver. Her musical arrangements were altered and the orchestra was given Native American-inspired sheet music to play during her routine.

Rex Allen had a wonderful singing voice, and he was a big draw at rodeos. He appeared in dozens of Westerns that were popular in the '50s, including *Colorado Sundown, Under Mexicali Stars, The Phantom Stallion,* and *The Rodeo King and the Senorita.* His typical movie sidekicks were his horse, KoKo, and buckaroo pal, Slim Pickens. He also starred in the *Frontier Doctor* TV series and narrated several of Walt Disney's animal adventure films. At the end of each rodeo performance Allen flung his ten-gallon Stetson into the crowd. After their run in San Antonio, Allen gave Ann one of his trademark white hats along with a note: "Hi, gal … Watch out for cowboys." Ann enjoyed the entire Wild West experience. "This has been one of the best shows we've done; it could start a whole new career in rodeos."

In contrast to the great response at San Antonio, Marston and company experienced a disappointing week at a fair the following week in Omaha. The weather was snowy, and because of a lack of publicity they had very small crowds. "I wasn't very happy," she reported. "The announcer is awful and the orchestra consisted of an organ and a drum." She didn't care for the show manager and had to call both Stacy and the American Guild of Variety Artists union representative to straighten him out about schedule and salary issues. "He's a little fuehrer and can be nice or nasty. It's been no fun working in Gestapo regime. Thank God I live in America and I only work for this kind of man for his money."

On top of that conflict, she was getting a cold, and was a little disappointed about a scheduled television appearance that was canceled. Instead, she rested in her hotel room, and as a result, witnessed one of mankind's most historic events. "Was supposed to do a TV show but the networks were cleared for John Glenn. He made three orbits around the earth and was returned safely. History—and I saw it." Later she took part in a remarkable trend that was sweeping the country: "I went [with some of the cast] to the Peppermint Cave and we did the Twist, the dance of the day. It's amazing how this thing caught on."

The Marstons moved on to Augusta, Georgia, and Ann experienced a run of very bad luck. She was persuaded to do the archery act on ice, even though she hadn't skated in two years. She practiced a few times and was pleased with the results, and booked a week-long engagement with *Wilma and Ed Leary's Adventures on Ice*. She wrote: "Today I made my debut with an ice show. It was a packed house and I did a pretty good show. I'm no Sonja Henie, but I've got guts. By the time I'm through I'll learn how to use 'em." It was a small production with cheesy snowman characters, ice skaters performing basic stunts, and contained a few musical numbers executed by a precision ice team. Ann did most of her regular archery act on skates and Frank wore shoes to assist her. They were scheduled to travel through Ohio and West Virginia but were sidetracked by an accident:

> *Well, this was the day—I'm writing this six weeks later. It started well; I walked to the show arena to practice ... The matinee was a good crowd, and the night show was very good, until the finale when I fell. I picked up my bow from the ice, and nobody knew I'd fractured my right wrist. I went to the hospital and they put a splint on. I had to go in costume because my wrist was so swollen. I spent an agonizing night. They had given me pain pills that made me delirious almost, and the arm was so painful. I went back to the hospital [the next day] and had more X-rays. A specialist in bone set my arm in a full cast above the elbow.*

Ann's tour with *Adventures on Ice* was aborted and they drove home to cancel the remainder of her engagements for March and April. The injury caused a great deal of pain and she spent the next few weeks recovering. Ann was accustomed to being active and self-sufficient, but now she was feeling a little sorry for herself. She wrote: "In the evening we went shopping. I can't buy anything in the way of clothes because I can't get anything over the cast." She complained, "I feel that I have to get out. I can't write or do much of anything. Mother washed and set my hair—some hassle that! I guess I'm just too darned independent to be sick or disabled."

She missed journaling and scribbled brief notes intended to update her diary entries at a later date. "I'm just counting the hours 'til I get this cast off my arm." Finally it was removed on April 24. "The wrist is still a little swollen. The doctor wrapped it in a bandage and said I could wear a wrist strap." She designed her own regimen of physical therapy by pulling her bowstring until she was strong and finally she attempted to shoot. "I was surprised how well I did ... I shot well despite my wrist, which is still hurting. I think my archery will be better than it was."

Florence was bad-tempered about the decrease of family revenue and she once again tried to interfere with Ann when she dated a local boy. Ann was irritated with her mother's attitude and wrote: "I enjoyed myself despite Mother's dissention. After all, I'm a big girl now and able to make my own decisions. But if it's not this, it's something else." But Ann was responsible enough to be concerned about the summer booking situation and called Eldred Stacy. "I called to find out about June, if we've got anything. I'm sure we'll get a great season, but the wrist has put us behind and Daddy is very depressed."

The Marstons needn't have worried. Eventually Ann was in fine condition and they packed for Steubenville, Ohio's big home show. "We did two shows and I really shot well. Thank heavens my wrist healed the way it did." By June she was 100 percent better but needed a bit of coaching by Frank to stabilize her aim. She went back to her favorite activities—playing tennis, taking piano lessons—and resumed doing the house and yard work. She was mistress of ceremonies for the Miss Detroit pageant and looked forward to a television appearance on *To Tell the Truth* in New York.

She flew alone to New York City a day early and registered at the Victoria Hotel. After checking in at the CBS studio she called her friend, Buddy Basch, and met him for dinner. The following afternoon, rehearsals began for *To Tell the Truth* and they taped later that evening. The show was hosted by Bud Collier, who read an affidavit describing the accomplishments of the mystery guest. There were three women who claimed to be Ann Marston. The panelists asked the challengers questions and attempted to determine who the two impostors were and who was telling the truth. The celebrities on that episode included Merv Griffin, Betty White, Kitty Carlisle, and Ralph Bellamy. After the interrogations Collier demanded: "Will the real Ann Marston please stand up!" Ann and her cohorts stumped the panel and won $1,000 to share among them. She was back home in Detroit by 11 p.m. that same night.

Leslie Winik wrote the Marstons and told them that *Bow Jests* had debuted in New York at the Radio City Music Hall. A month later it opened in Detroit and Ann wrote in her journal: "Today was Memorial Day and it was a memorable day. I saw *Bow Jests* at the Grand Circus Theater. It's the first time I've seen it. It's playing with Bill Holden and Lilli Palmer in *The Counterfeit Traitor.*" She was proud of the film. "I thought it was very good, and the audience seemed to like it too." The family and the Hindley neighbors all went to see it again a week later, and she wrote: "I enjoyed it just as much the second time." Winik mailed them a 16mm print of the film.

Once again, California beckoned, and the Marstons hit the road for Los Angeles. While traveling through Arizona they took time for dinner at a restaurant near the Grand Canyon. "We stopped off and watched me on *To Tell the Truth*. It must have seemed strange to the other customers." It was a long journey of about 2,500 miles that they accomplished in four days. Even Ann almost lost her cool. "This time we really had a rugged trip. I've never experienced such weather—it was 115 degrees in the desert. I'd never do it again without an air conditioner."

In L.A., Ann called Paramount Pictures and learned that *Bow Jests* was to open with *Hatari* the next day at Grauman's Egyptian Theater on Hollywood Boulevard. "We went to see our movie again. *Hatari* was great, and *Bow Jests* got some laughs.

It just keeps getting better and better." She got the opportunity to promote the movie in a guest spot on Mike Stokey's TV show, and appeared with funnymen Sid Gould and Richard Dawson, who was then known as Dickie Dawson. "It was a great show. They all shot and we did about 20 minutes." She also had an interview with sports writer Jack Arthur in San Diego.

The California Exposition was held Fourth of July week in Del Mar, and Ann was booked for four days at a salary of $850. Andy Griffith was the headliner. He told homespun stories and sang songs while he accompanied himself on the guitar. Mark Wilson presented his *Magic Land of Allakazam*, accompanied by his assistant/wife, who was always introduced as the lovely Nani Darnell. The viewing area was filled to capacity with 50,000 spectators. Ann did her act, including the long shot from the top of the grandstand. Backstage after the show, Ann and her parents met Griffith, and Ann took a ride in the Mayberry patrol car.

On the way back east they tried leaving at midnight to beat the desert heat. "Nothing spectacular; we saw the same old things and it was almost as hot. I wouldn't like to live around those parts. Finding a clean bathroom and restaurant is a feat; and it's too hot. We had a detour on a portion of Route 66 where the pavement had raised up two feet from the heat." Those cross-country excursions were extremely hard on automobiles, and later that summer the Marstons bought a new one with air conditioning. Ann wrote: "Well today we bought the symbol of American prestige, success and insane jealousy—our first Cadillac. A Sedan Deville, 6-window in Newport Blue. It's a beauty." Frank loved the car, and they celebrated the first night of ownership by going to the drive-in theater to see a double feature of *Trapeze* and *The Vikings*.

They drove to a job in Roseau, Minnesota, and made it back to Michigan in time to catch the opening of *Bow Jests* at the Wyandotte Theater. It was on a double bill with *Spartacus*. Ann invited the neighbor kids to join her at the show, and her parents took photos and movies of her name in lights on the marquee.

Frank and Ann left Florence at home when they drove 450 miles to the Mesker Amphitheater in Evanston, Illinois, for a performance at a music festival. Popular singer Tony Martin was the lead attraction followed by Ann, the Four Step Brothers, and Jerry Van Dyke. Ann must have been off her mark according to a newspaper report: "… a demonstration of some fancy archery that was off a bit, perhaps due to a refreshing breeze …" The same article also contained a mixed review of Van Dyke:

> … comedian Jerry Van Dyke has also appeared at Mesker and in a local supper club. His act was almost identically the same as that he presented last year, which dimmed much of its sparkle for those who had seen him before. He is still a fresh, promising, and very likeable talent and because

of this can make fairly musty material sound amusing; and new material sound hysterically funny. He plays a mean banjo, too, but rarely completes a number as he interrupts himself with more jollies. He is so personable that I wish he'd drop the joke using the homosexual bit which is unnecessary, particularly in an all-family arena such as Mesker.

Ann met Van Dyke while on tour the previous summer and enjoyed the pleasure of his company one evening in Evanston. "Jerry Van Dyke called my room and we went out dancing. He introduced me to the owners of the McCurdy Hotel." They remained casual friends, and years later she reunited with him for cocktails after his performance at Detroit's swanky Roostertail nightclub.

Ann was alarmed by a newspaper article in early summer reporting that her employer was having difficulty with the government. "I saw in the *Amusement Business* paper that MCA was disbanding its talent division. Stacy was out of the office when I called. I wonder what it's all about." It hadn't hit the media yet, but the MCA organization was in big trouble. Attorney General Robert Kennedy was about to file an antitrust suit with the Justice Department against the entertainment behemoth. Lew Wasserman decided to keep the film and television production end of the business intact to salvage some of his holdings, but he intended to dissolve the talent agency. The industry would soon be in a tailspin as hundreds of the nation's musicians, actors, and specialty performers suddenly were without MCA's protection and promotion. Talent agents scattered like so many lost children, and they lacked the direction to restructure the agency under new leadership.

Eldred Stacy foresaw the disaster and took the initiative to create a company of his own two months before the official demise of the MCA talent division. Ann was satisfied with the new arrangement with Stacy. "I finally got in touch with Stacy. He says MCA is definitely through and he's formed United Talent Management. I'm not really worried about the whole thing; I think it will be for the best."

August kicked off with two weeks on the Thrillcade caravan, and Frank and Ann met up with Swenson's group in Shelbyville, Indiana. "Mother decided not to come on this trip. It's a rough one and she has plenty of sewing to do." Ann celebrated her twenty-fourth birthday on August 7, and after the show, she drove the new Caddy 180 miles on the overnight jaunt to their next location. She and Frank traveled through Iowa and Missouri, appearing with vocalist Candy Candido, movie cowboy star Rex Allen, and Leroy Van Dyke's band.

They made it home for a quick overnighter and to pick up Florence. Ann described the fast turnover: "I didn't unpack; just rearranged. But did the washing and mowed the lawn; pretty good for someone who hasn't slept. I finally got to sleep in my own little beddie." The next day they made the trek north to Toronto for the opening of the Canadian National Exhibition. Publicity was good, and Ann received several favorable newspaper mentions during the week. Their neighbors, Steve and Hazel Heinel, arrived with their children, Bob and Kathy. The Three Stooges also were performing, and after the show, Larry, Moe, and Curly-Joe spent some quality time goofing around with the kids backstage, while Frank recorded the antics on a home movie camera.

The 1962 Thrillcade met the Marstons in September at Mendota, Illinois. Once again they were teamed with Emmett Kelly Jr., the Harmonicats, and Gene Holter's Wild Animal Show, which included an elephant, a juvenile hippopotamus, and the popular ostrich races. Ann's name was lauded in newspapers hyping the fair: "She out-does William Tell! She flicks out candles from impossible distances, breaks balloons at 100 yards, and slips her arrow neatly inside of swinging key rings. The experts scratch their heads in puzzlement. She's not an archer—they say she's a magician!"

In an interview Ann remarked about her new adventures on the rodeo circuit:

> We're doing rodeos along with fairs and theaters. At one time we thought; how are we going to fit in with a rodeo? But it turned out with all those cowboys there has to be a few Indians. So now I ride and shoot, and I really enjoy it because it's a lot of fun.
>
> One never knows quite what is going to happen. With over 600 rodeos in the United States it's really catching on; especially in the West and the South. We travel a great deal with them and I have a little horse whose name is "Annie Oakley."

When they arrived in Fort Madison on Thursday, Ann noticed that all the store windows had rodeo advertisements featuring her picture and Clu Gulager's. They had time to shop, and Ann bought "a lovely squaw dress." They received a wonderful reception from the show committee and city officials, and on Friday they were invited on a special tour. "Daddy and I had a most enlightening experience today. We went through the State Penitentiary here. It was most interesting. I went in a cell and into the dining room. We had a guard take us through. One inmate had a parakeet on his shoulder."

Later Gulager, Emmett Kelly Jr., and Ann visited young patients in the children's ward of Sacred Heart Hospital. The *Fort Madison Evening Democrat* took photos for Saturday's front page story. The newspaper also showed a photo of spectators huddled under umbrellas and raincoats as Kelly the clown mingled with the crowd during the soggy show. The caption read: "Rodeo Sets Record for Wetness."

Ann's diary entry for Saturday night said: "It just poured with rain, but we did the show and all got soaked. I think it was the wettest we've ever worked in. In the evening after we dried everything, it cleared up. But the mud was like walking in cement. We got through the show OK." They checked out of the hotel early on Sunday morning in anticipation of driving to Ohio right after the show, but they never made it to Peoria. Ann described the calamity later in a radio interview:

> Accidents do happen, and this was a very big freak. I was doing my show and in the middle of the act I saw this big black head coming out from under the chute. We are next to closing on the show, and then they have the bulls. While I'm on, the audience can't see that they are preparing these bulls—putting the flank straps around them with a bell on it—which is what makes them buck.
>
> I was shooting and the next thing I knew this Brahma bull was in the arena. I didn't quite know what to do, because I couldn't run. It had been raining; it was an outside arena and it was thick mud. It was sort of like a nightmare where you're trying to run, but you can't move. This was me exactly. I thought that the only thing I could do was lie down in the mud, and maybe he'll bypass me. But he didn't, and he charged.
>
> I've heard that you think of your life and what's happened. But I can remember at all times I was thinking: "Now what's the best thing to do to get out of this situation?" Fortunately, my father rushed back into the arena, and he grabbed some arrows and tried to wave the bull off. They couldn't get the outriders into the arena because the gate was blocked by people watching in a state of panic. They finally got them through, and they drove the bull off. The bull had broken three of my ribs and badly bruised me. And my father—I didn't realize what he'd done at the time. He, too, was hurt and pulled internal muscles.

Ann recorded this condensed version of the episode in her diary:

> Today is one I shan't forget. During the act at the rodeo a Brahma bull escaped from the chute and charged me. Daddy saved my life probably, when he ran up to the bull. The big black beast then charged him. I remember thinking clearly to lie down. It was a freak accident. I managed to ride around the arena, then they took us to the hospital. Daddy was badly bruised and I stayed in the hospital. If it hadn't been so muddy perhaps I could have moved faster.

One spectator out of the crowd of 7,000 captured part of the incident on his movie camera, and he gave it to the Marstons. Only a few seconds were recorded, but it confirmed that the bull deliberately approached Ann, and they momentarily stared at each other, nearly eye-to-eye. She immediately dropped to the ground with her arms up protecting her face. The animal lowered his head and stepped forward onto her body. Frank ran up from behind, frantically brandishing a handful of arrows.

According to Ann's account, she considered shooting the bull, but instinctively knew that the lightweight aluminum arrows would not have stopped the animal. She heard the cowhands on the sidelines hollering for her to lie down. After stepping on Ann, the bull spotted her father. It butted Frank in the side and knocked him down, right out of his boots. Finally, the side riders were able to herd the beast back to the holding pen. Trouper that she was, Ann pulled herself up out of the muck and had a cowhand help her mount "Annie Oakley." She waved to the crowd as she slowly circled the stadium and exited.

An ambulance immediately took both victims and Florence to Sacred Heart Hospital. Frank was treated for severely bruised muscles and Ann was admitted for further observation. X-rays confirmed she had three broken ribs, but it was necessary to rule out internal injury. "I had a pretty bad night. They took tests every hour all night to make sure my spleen wasn't ruptured." She also had a deep cut on her leg.

Ann's room at the hospital was filled with flowers from well-wishers and friends, including a telegram from Wyandotte city officials. The rodeo committee members visited, and a local grocery store sent a large food basket. She was released the next day and the family went back to the hotel to rest. They had their meals sent up to the room. Ann later wrote: "It's still pretty painful to move, but towards the evening I felt a little better. Daddy's pretty sore, too."

A photo of Ann in her hospital bed appeared the next day on the front page of the *Fort Madison Evening Democrat*. Florence took decisive action and pulled some strings to get them home. "I still didn't feel too good today," Ann wrote. "Mother called Gary Hughes and they arranged to have Mother and me flown home in Schaeffer's [ink pens] private jet. Daddy left ahead of us [in the car] and we took off around 3 a.m., making a stop first in Chicago then on to Detroit."

The news of Ann's mishap quickly spread from Fort Madison to Wyandotte. When the plane landed in the early hours of the morning at Detroit Metropolitan Airport, several reporters were there to greet her. The previous day's headline in *The Detroit News* read: "Rodeo Bull Injures Ex-Miss Michigan. Wyandotte Beauty Trampled. Father Butted in Attempt to Distract Beast." When reporters asked her how she felt, she said: "Just like a bull clobbered me. My father stepped up just in time to save my life. I'm happy I'm here to tell about it." In the next day's *News* they ran a photo of Ann waving tenuously as she was transferred into an ambulance to be shuttled home. Frank arrived in Wyandotte unceremoniously around 1 a.m., after driving all the way from Iowa alone.

Once settled at home, Florence called their physician who recommended that Ann's injury be checked by a specialist. The doctor came to the house for the examination. Ann still suffered from a shortness of breath and was wrapped with an elastic bandage, which helped her breathing. She continued taking medicine for the aches and pains, and finally got some much-needed sleep in her own bed.

During the next few days Ann was forced to take it easy. Perhaps it was the result of prescription pain medication, but she was inspired to type a nine-page biography of her life. It included an exceptionally dramatic account of the "bullfight:"

> ... *As we presented the egg shot and snuffed out the candle flames, I was conscious of the audience's roar of approval. As always it sent a thrill shivering down my spine. But then I heard a different kind of roar. This time a roar as 10,000 throats gasped in horror! At the same time I heard a crack and saw the black head of a Brahma bull crashing through the chute. The sight of it will live in my mind forever. With the weight of 2,000 or 3,000 pounds of bull against it, the heavy-wooded chute gate gave way like so much plywood. He was free!*
>
> ... *In fury, he knocked over the target and plunged toward where I was standing, coming to a halt not 10 feet away. My first impulse was to run, but my feet stuck in the mud making it impossible to move. It was just like a terrible nightmare. The bull was so close that I could have reached over with my bow and touched him. As I faced the bull, his eyes glistening, I knew I must make a decision that could mean the difference between life or death. The audience watched frozen; you could have heard a pin drop. The bull seemed fascinated. He'd seen plenty of cowboys and clowns, but this was something different. Here was a young, blonde girl with a bright red feather in her hair and sequins flashing in his eyes. The fascination wore off! He did what he had been born and bred to do—he charged.*
>
> *My decision was made for me. In that instant I knew that if I remained standing, I would be tossed into the air like a rag doll and gored with those lethal horns. I threw myself down in the mud, burying my head in my arms. I forgot my new red costume. "Let him pass," I thought hopefully. Instead I felt a terrific jab as he butted into my left side, then again. I felt so helpless, I couldn't get my breath. I couldn't move in the mud, it was like quicksand. My strength was depleted. I braced myself for the next attack. There was none.*
>
> *My father, who was within easy reach of the gate and safety, had fought his way back, grabbed some arrows, and was rushing toward the bull, waving them in his face. He purposely set himself up as a target for*

the bull. I still wasn't aware of what my father had done. In saving my life, it was one of the most heroic deeds ever performed in a rodeo arena. It has been said that parents will do the most amazing things when the safety of their child is involved. This is one case where this thesis was proved correct. Furthermore, I truly believe that had my mother been able to make her way to me, she would have also taken on El Toro.

A week later Ann went to her doctor for a follow-up exam and received a tetanus shot that caused complications. Her sense of humor was obviously restored and she said: "Last night I developed a rash, and the doctor said it was from the horse serum. No wonder I have no appetite; Mother's been giving me meat instead of oats!" After a recovery period of about two weeks, Ann was feeling fine and ready to go.

She kept her faith in Stacy as her agent, and signed a contract with his new United Talent Management organization. Apparently, he suggested that she lose some weight, and she was a bit depressed about it. "I guess he's right," she wrote. "He wants me to lose 15 pounds and be 118. I'll do it." In the meantime, MCA notified their clients that the company was in the process of purging files. They were microfilming all contracts between their artist/clients and various other parties and would continue collecting commissions on pre-existing bookings. Ann had several weeks to request documents for future reference.

Ann's fall schedule included the star-studded Bloomsburg, Pennsylvania fair with Jimmy Dean, Anita Bryant, Candy Candido, the Harmonicats, and Homer and Jethro. Ann worked on solid ground and didn't attempt to ride a horse.

The Marstons traveled to Waco, Texas, for the first of their October bookings at the Heart O' Texas Fair and Rodeo. Ann's bull incident was still big news out west, and the *Waco News-Tribune* interviewed Ann. She recounted the story and explained that the injuries prevented her from riding into the arena. By the time the Marstons arrived for the Huntsville Prison Rodeo a week later, Ann was fit as a fiddle and ready to ride for her last big show of the year. According to the Huntsville, Texas, Chamber of Commerce, the Prison Rodeo had a long history:

The famous Prison Rodeo attracted thousands of visitors to Huntsville every October from its founding in 1931 until the prison system closed it down after the 1986 performances. The rodeo was billed as "The Wildest Show Behind Bars" as convicts competed for prizes and the mastery of wild animal stock.

Ann shared equal billing with Anita Bryant, who traveled with her own poodle and husband Bob. The *Houston Chronicle* offered a Texas-style compliment and called Ann a "downright dangerous doll." The article went on to affirm that she "can plug a bobcat with an aluminum arrow faster that a frog can lick flies."

The Marstons received a nice comment from the rodeo publicist. " … Ann Marston and her family were the most cooperative people we have had to work with. I spent an entire day with them in Houston making the rounds of newspapers, radio and TV stations. It was the eighth consecutive day of record-breaking heat and they never once complained. Ann demonstrated that she is a real pro and enabled us to get an enormous amount of publicity."

They traveled from the Prison Rodeo to the Firemen's Rodeo in St. Louis, where cowboys and cowgirls competed for prize money worth a total of $11,000. Appearing along with Ann for an audience of about 6,000 people was John "Slim" Smith from the *Laramie* TV series and dog trainer Loral Armstrong. During the week the headliners took members of the cast and the show's clowns to two local hospitals and visited sick children.

Ann didn't have much of a love life those years on the road, and at twenty-four years old she was very lonely at times. Apparently there was no male in existence who was up to Florence's impossibly high standards for her daughter. Her father joked about Ann's single status in an interview: "She is never in one place long enough to get acquainted with a boy," Frank commented. "She meets one she thinks she might like, and by the time she sees him again he is married and has six kids."

When Ann performed that fall in St. Louis, basketball player Bob Pettit called her at the hotel and took her out to dinner. The second night he saw her show and afterward they visited a nightclub. On a subsequent trip to St. Louis, they went on a date after a Hawks basketball game. Ann described how she went to see him, "just in time to catch the last quarter of the game. We Won! Afterwards I met Bob backstage and we went to a place where all the basketball players go. It was a real nice evening."

Pettit's polite attention sparked a romantic interest for Ann, and throughout the late fall and winter she followed the Hawks games religiously on the radio. "I came home and listened to Bob Pettit get 45 points in the San Francisco-Hawks game." Ann started a basketball scrapbook with articles about the Hawks. She recorded Pettit's December birth date in the back of her diary:

> *Tomorrow is Bob Pettit's birthday. I sent his card yesterday. Lately, I've been thinking of him a lot; maybe because I'm not busy and have plenty of time. He'd be quite a man to have, but he's a long way away. He's hard to figure. Being the gentleman that he is makes me feel like I'm the only girl he's ever known; which is one of his remarkable characteristics.*

The Hawks played in Detroit the following week. Pettit apparently snubbed her and she was very disappointed:

> *I take back everything I said about Bob Pettit. He's a cad—he didn't call! That's no doubt what attracts me to him. He's the most elusive man I've ever known. Of course, they play a double header tomorrow and he probably was afraid that he might get involved or something, but he still could have called. It was a miserable day. I guess I'm destined to a life of romance with a career. It's more profitable.*

After Christmas a few weeks later, she listened to a radio broadcast of a Hawks game and lamented to her diary: "I haven't heard anything from Pettit. I wish I could dislike him for it. I think I ought to make a New Year's resolution to forget him—but how?"

Ann wrote to Lenora Slaughter of the Miss America Organization and asked her opinion about continuing with singing lessons. Slaughter replied, "Your nice letter of January 24 was received and I hasten to tell you that you may proceed with plans to take voice lessons as outlined. Lots of good luck. I think it's an excellent idea for you to study voice." Ann had a pleasant, lilting voice with a hint of English accent combined with a slight Midwestern drawl. Singing wasn't her strong suit, but she was adequate and steadily improved with the lessons. She spent much of the winter practicing with her reel-to-reel tape recorder. In her diary Ann noted, "My range is getting higher."

As usual in the off season, she did handiwork and knitted herself a sweater. She went bowling weekly with one of the neighbor women, and the family played cards and Password on winter evenings. Her folks remodeled the kitchen, painted the exterior trim of the house, and installed awnings on the front windows. Frank had not worked in the industrial plumbing trade for years since traveling with Ann's successful archery act.

Ann and Frank attended a basketball playoff game at Cobo Hall, with the Hawks vs. Detroit. "I don't know if Pettit saw me. We'll see if he calls." Later she noted in her journal, "I expected Bob Pettit to call but he didn't. I decided to call him, but he wasn't in his room. I left a message." He telephoned her the following day but a romance never sparked.

It was time to set up business arrangements for upcoming shows. The Michigan Fair Conference was based in Detroit, and Ann's parents did not permit her to navigate the ten-mile journey to Detroit due to a storm. She was annoyed and said, "The roads were snowy, so 'naturally' they didn't feel I was capable to drive, so they took me."

The family went to the Denver Rodeo Convention by rail. "It's quite an experience to travel by train; you sure see some funny things. We had an old lady and she wrapped everything in plastic bags—even herself. The one thing nice about the train is that it is quite social, but you have to be pretty rugged." At the convention she agreed to tour again with Swenson and to make appearances at rodeos at Fort Smith and in Salt Lake City. She was still working with her UTM agent. "I called Stacy. It looks good just when things were looking bleak. That's show biz. I love it!"

She was on the bill at a fair in Lake Charles, Louisiana, with the cast of *Bonanza*. For some reason, "Hoss," Dan Blocker, couldn't make the show and was replaced by Clint Walker. Ann met Lorne Green and said, "He seems to be very nice." They moved on to Baton Rouge and she appeared on the roster with Michael Landon, although she didn't meet him. Ann and her father took a side trip in February: "A momentous day. Daddy and I went to Mardi Gras in New Orleans; an experience I wouldn't have missed. The floats were fantastic and the costumes beautiful. They threw away jewels and souvenirs from the floats and we caught several. The people here are very nice." They took their movie camera and recorded some of the festivities.

Ann flew alone to New York to appear on the *What's My Line?* television game show. When host John Daly invited her to "enter and sign in please," Ann wrote her name on a blackboard. Her profession was then revealed to the audience. According to the *What's My Line?* episode guide on www.tvtome.com, she was "Miss Ann Marston, Professional Archer (from Wyandotte, MI, a suburb of Detroit). In 1960 she was Miss Michigan in the Miss America Pageant and won the preliminary talent award. She works with her father and is the only professional woman in this field. She performs a 240-foot trick shot."

Ann was then introduced to the panelists. The regular panel consisted of Arlene Francis, Robert Q. Lewis, Dorothy Kilgallen, and Bennett Cerf, and was moderated by Daly. The game show's concept was simple; the panelists took turns asking questions and the guest contestant answered either "yes" or "no." Each time the guest answered "no," they earned $5, up to a total of $50. After ten negative responses the panel was stumped and the game was over. Three other sessions were played, and the guests were Marc Bohan, designer for Dior; Yolanda Ostrowski, who tested suntan lotion, and Joey Bishop as the "Mystery Guest." Bob Hope and Lucille Ball were appearing in another episode that evening and Ann was introduced to both celebrities. It is a little-known fact that Ball lived in Wyandotte briefly when she was a small child. Ann commented in her diary about the show: "I taped *What's My Line*. It went real well and nobody guessed." The episode aired later that summer on August 25.

While in New York City in May 1963, Ann visited Buddy Basch, Keith Morris of *Sports Illustrated*, and her UTM agent, Stacy. Comedian Jack Carter was on the

Ed Sullivan Show, and she caught the taping while she was in town. She also introduced herself to Jerry De Fuccio, associate editor of *Mad Magazine*. De Fuccio was a fan of Ann's, and earlier that year he had sent a letter requesting her photo. He included a box of jelly beans and an autographed picture of the *Mad* mascot. "Ann, I'd like to be your 'bow!!' Madly yours, Alfred E. Neuman." Both the envelope and the letter were decorated with comical sketches depicting Ann in various situations. One showed her expressing despair while Alfred was holding a bow and arrow at the fictional "Ann Marston Archery School." In the background was a stretcher, with Alfred's victim skewered with an arrow and an apple lying on the ground. Ann later wrote about her experience with the zany crew at the *Mad Magazine* offices. "Met Jerry De Fuccio and Sergio of *Mad*. I also met the publisher and Feldstein, the editor. I thoroughly enjoyed the visit."

She appeared in Pittsburgh, and on July 4, flew to Philadelphia for a *Sports Illustrated* Spectacular with Buster Crabbe and Don Budge. "There are some old has-beens doing this, but otherwise it was nice." She judged the Miss Detroit beauty contest and rode in a parade in Riverview with sharp shooter Joe Bodrie. The family later drove to Salt Lake City for a week at the rodeo with Charlie McGrath of *Wagon Train*. The Marstons went to Columbus, Ohio, to discuss the possibility of investing in the new Hoyt archery lanes, a similar concept to a bowling alley. The target automatically moved up to the archer for scoring and arrow removal.

Ann commented on current events in her journal and frequently voiced her opinion. "The world is up in arms over the latest astronaut Gordon Cooper. He started on a 22 orbit mission. It's great, however, there are plenty of heroes being unrecognized; the test pilots and submarine missions. The Russians are two years ahead of us, and have a man who went 64 times in orbit. Let's spend more money on medical research."

Perhaps that last comment stems from the fact that she was beginning to have trouble with her eyesight. She visited an optometrist who apparently did not make the connection between her failing sight and her chronic diabetes. "Mother got reading glasses, but I'm a different story. It seems my eyes are very bad and I'm going to have contact lenses. I had one in today but it's going to take some getting used to." After two weeks she reported, "These contacts sure aren't easy to get along with." She tried bowling with them, "which was a handicap." She went back to the eye doctor and "told him of my misery, and he discovered that they didn't fit properly. So now I have to get others, and this time they'll be blue." After the trial period the new lenses were still unacceptable, and the doctor ordered another pair, and then another. "The doctor thinks the contacts are not going to work out, but I'm determined that they will." After several failed attempts she settled for reading glasses. The family was convinced that Ann's injuries from the bull accident were responsible for her deteriorating eyesight, so they consulted a lawyer. "He advised us to sue Fort Madison, so we start now."

In August, Ann joined Thrillcade's annual tour of the Midwest. She appeared that summer with Emmett Kelly Jr., Anita Bryant, magician Mark Wilson, and Gene Holter's Wild Animal Show. The Marstons had shared billing with Holter in previous years. His menagerie included llamas, camels, donkeys, lions, tigers, hippos, elephants, tortoises, and ostriches. He provided trained animals for motion pictures and operated the Movieland Animal Park in California. Holter had a traveling show in the summer that hooked up occasionally with Thrillcade.

Thrillcade, Marston, and Holter appeared in Canfield, Ohio. For publicity photos, Ann lay on the ground and posed with the elephant's foot on her face. It ran in the *Youngstown Vindicator* Sunday roto. The caption read, "This huge mastodon has more than enough delicacy to match his weight, as he proves by resting his foot gently on the face of a pretty Thrillcade trouper." Ann interacted with the big cats, too. "There is a leopard in my dressing room." Her parents took movies of Ann wearing a leopard patterned outfit while petting a cheetah. The animal attempted to chew off her leather wrist guard. She also rode the elephant in the home movie and shot her bow and arrow from its back.

They arrived in Little Rock for the rodeo and the Arkansas Livestock Exposition. In a newspaper story, reporter John Heuston described the Fort Smith incident from the previous year. In that interview Ann noted, "The same bull is appearing in this rodeo, but we've changed my act so that I no longer appear before the bull riding events." She was honored to perform on October 3, 1963, for President John F. Kennedy, who was in the audience in Little Rock.

"I hope next year is good to us, although we can't complain about this one." The year's earnings of $10,956 was well below her peak of nearly $19,000 in 1961. She was still signed with Eldred Stacy and his United Talent Management Company, but she was no longer happy with his services. Along with that discord, Florence was trying to recover overpaid commissions from MCA. She called a lawyer and union representatives from the American Federation of Television and Radio Artists and the American Guild of Variety Artists to help straighten it out. Finally the Marstons made the decision to leave UTM. Ann wrote: "Guess we'll terminate the contract. I'm not terribly disappointed. Stacy will get quite a shock."

That fall Ann addressed and stuffed more than 200 envelopes with her brochures to generate business. The Marstons traveled to the show convention in Chicago and had lunch with the Swenson family. Before she retired for the winter, Ann signed on for an engagement with Thrillcade for the summer of 1964.

7

SHE LOVES YOU

ANN MARSTON was inspired to make major personal changes in her mid-twenties. President John F. Kennedy's death affected her deeply, the controversial Vietnam War was in full swing, and youth culture embraced new, revolutionary types of music and behavior. After being controlled and sheltered all of her life, Ann consciously rebelled against her mother.

A defining moment occurred on the day that Ann met both The Beatles and Frank Sweeney in September of 1964. Her interest gradually shifted away from archery and toward the music industry.

Ann worked hard to build a singing career. At the same time, she became a part of the Detroit area's evolving rock 'n' roll scene by successfully managing several promising groups, including the Motor City Five.

> FRIDAY, NOVEMBER 22, 1963. *President Kennedy was assassinated today. I was having my hair done and didn't believe the tragic news. It occurred during a motorcade through Dallas. A suspect named Oswald is being held. Mrs. Kennedy was with him; also Governor Connolly of Texas was shot, but is still alive. The President was shot from a window by a rifle. All the facts are still not clear. The nation is in a state of shock. He had two children, Caroline and John, who will be three within four days.*
>
> SATURDAY, NOVEMBER 23, 1963. *A dreary day today that began the*

first full day of mourning for President Kennedy. It appears that the as-
sassin is Lee Harvey Oswald, a 24-year-old who has Marxist background
and a Russian wife. The Dallas police seem to have much evidence on him
including the rifle.

SUNDAY, NOVEMBER 24, 1963. This past weekend has been bizarre. I
arose this morning and was combing my hair when I heard on TV that
they had Oswald and were taking him to the county jail from the city
jail. I rushed in and saw him shot on TV by a man identified as Jack Ruby.
It's all unbelievable and very sad. There are tributes to Mr. Kennedy from
around the world. I feel very sad myself. Never did I feel that a man I'd
never met could affect me so by his deeds. But I'm not alone, for millions
feel this way, I know. I suppose justice will never be brought about now.
Oswald died without a trial and so is innocent according to our laws. But
I can't help but feel there is more to come.

MONDAY, NOVEMBER 25, 1963. From early morning to late tonight we
had two television sets showing President Kennedy's funeral and taped
events leading up to it. There were various heads of state in attendance.
The fact that one man can leave such a deep mark on so many people
is a credit to him. It was truly impressive. There were small things that
impressed me—the folding of the flag that had covered the casket, little
John-John saluting during ceremonies, Jackie Kennedy's courage.

The entire thing had no purpose. He was born a rich man. Instead
of enjoying his life lazily he dedicated his life to the hardest work a man
could find—and so was shot for it. Our flag still flies at half staff.

The arrival of The Beatles to the international music scene was just what the
country needed to provide a distraction from the lingering pain and shock from the
assassination of President Kennedy three months earlier. The Beatles completely
took over the airwaves, and any American who was old enough to read or to switch
on the television was aware of them. Their tremendous success is now legendary,
and media hype reached new standards in both serious reporting and ridiculous
publicity stunts.

By January 1964, "I Want to Hold Your Hand" sold 1 million records and was
No. 1 in Detroit according to WKNR's weekly *Keener Music Guide*. The group's appearances on *The Ed Sullivan Show* for three consecutive Sundays in February 1964
fanned the flames of their popularity, with an estimated 73 million viewers the first
night. On February 9, in Manhattan's Studio 50 at CBS-TV, the 730 members of the
audience included many teenagers who screamed their adoration. Even Ed Sullivan
was visibly overwhelmed, telling the audience, "Please, I must remind you that there

are other great stars on this stage." The Beatles held America captive in the time it took to sing five songs. Some sources reported a marked decrease in the national crime rate during the group's performance. History would have been made again if they had been scheduled to perform the week following their final appearance, when *The Ed Sullivan Show* was broadcast for the first time in color. With her interest in show business news, Ann was well aware of The Beatles' phenomenal entrance to popular culture. She carefully analyzed their television debut, saying, "They were good, but the other acts were awful."

The Marstons were on their spring tour schedule. In Nashville, Frank put a moptop wig on their little wooden dummy, previously introduced to audiences as Liberace or Oscar. Ann shot the apple off his head, saying, "thank you veddy mooch" to a huge ovation. A photo of the event ran in the *Nashville Banner*, and the gag was kept in the act. On the way back to Wyandotte from the Nashville show Ann claimed: "We started driving and we were 'Beatled' all the way. What a publicity campaign! Four boys from Liverpool with guitars and drums, and it's all you hear on the radio." Sensitive to the "British Invasion," she commented, "England is a good place for showbiz these days. I wish we could get there." In June she went to The Rolling Stones concert in Detroit with Doris Wood and later related, "They were at Olympia but they only drew about 400 people. I've never seen anything like it. Musically they were very good. However, you couldn't hear them over the screaming girls throwing peanuts at them. Well, it was quite an experience. I felt like a den mother."

The Marstons continued on the summer circuit of Thrillcade and rodeos. As a result of the split with MCA, and because of her withdrawal from Eldred Stacy's UTM organization, she no longer had an agent. It was not a very busy summer, and Ann was toying with the idea of a new venture. She developed a concept for a radio show to be called *The Cavern*. Her idea was to feature the "Liverpool Sound" and provide biographical information on different performers. Most of her free hours for weeks were spent revising and re-recording the show's demo tape. She was proud of "her brainchild," and she asked friends such as Doris Wood to play the tape and invite criticism. When she felt it was ready, Ann called Hugh Dallas of Columbia Records to arrange an audition, which apparently did not occur.

Ann purchased The Beatles' records as soon as they were released, and she had them all in her personal collection. She filled a new scrapbook with Beatle material, and her cousins in England sent articles from the *London Free Press* and *Daily Mirror* newspapers. She pasted her collection of Beatles trading cards in the book and included the front cover of *Life* magazine that featured the group. Her scrapbook contained extensive biographical sections for John, Paul, George, and Ringo that described each man's personal likes and dislikes, family background, and their favorite type of girl. (George liked small, friendly blondes.) Her diary also documented her obsession. "I had a ball doing it. Some people think I'm nuts, for example my mother and father. I wrote a letter to George Harrison of The Beatles … just to prove that I'm completely potty on them. It will probably never be read by him, but one never knows." When advance tickets for *A Hard Day's Night* became available, she went to the Wyandotte Theater box office to purchase hers. "I bought my tickets for The Beatles movie. Yeah, yeah, yeah." She went to the off-beat film on September 2, joining hundreds of local Beatlemaniacs. "*Hard Day's Night* premiered here. I went to the Wyandotte Main, and what a great picture it was. The girls screamed for the first five minutes, and on and off all the way through, but it was definitely an adult movie. I must see it again."

The Beatles' first North American tour consisted of twenty-four cities, starting in San Francisco in June 1964. The "Fab Four" criss-crossed wildly between locations covering 22,500 miles in the U.S. and Canada. They presented thirty-two shows in thirty-four days in a wide variety of venues. They appeared in locations ranging from the Hollywood Bowl in Los Angeles to the Forest Hills Tennis Stadium in New York, performing for crowds numbering up to 30,000.

The group was scheduled to appear at Olympia Stadium in Detroit on Sunday, September 6, for two shows at 2 p.m. and 6 p.m. Ticket prices ranged from $3 to $5 a seat. Olympia was the city's best suited facility for the concert. Home to the Detroit Red Wings hockey team, it had a seating capacity of more than 16,000 people. The newspapers were full of Beatlemania of all kinds for weeks preceding the concerts. Enterprising hotel managers along their route cut up the linens from The Beatles' beds and sold three-inch squares for $10 apiece. The barely controlled media hysteria was firmly in place in the Motor City, as it was in other stops on the tour. One paper ran a story about a minister who wore a floppy wig in an attempt reach his parishioners on a mod new level. One UPI story featured photo-enhanced pictures of the boys sporting hypothetical crew cut hairstyles. There was even a Detroit-based campaign to "stamp out The Beatles," which was just a publicity stunt. A reporter at a New York press conference told John Lennon, "In Detroit, there are people handing out car stickers saying 'Stamp out The Beatles.'" Lennon's response was, "Yeah, well, we're bringing out a 'Stamp out Detroit' campaign."

Local top 40 radio station giant WKNR highlighted The Beatles' blitz of Detroit. Strictly by accident, the station casually known as Keener 13 was the only radio crew present at Detroit Metropolitan Airport's Executive Terminal when the band arrived. The event was broadcast live on the station. WKNR's exclusive access to The Beatles was exploited to the fullest extent; John Lennon even recorded a radio promotion for disc jockey Scott Regan's "Burger Club." Ann was distracted by their presence while she was performing in Windsor, Ontario, on Saturday night.

"Tonight I did a second show. I shot and then sang, too. I was more interested in hearing The Beatles arrive in Detroit."

On the morning of Sunday, September 6, Florence Marston placed a telephone call to the Whittier Hotel in Detroit and spoke to Derek Taylor, a former newspaper reporter with the British *Manchester Daily Express*. In 1963, he quit the newspaper business to become Brian Epstein's personal assistant and The Beatles' press officer. Within a few moments Ann was on the telephone conversing with John Lennon.

> SUNDAY, SEPTEMBER 6, 1964. *Dear Diary, It's Beatles Day. Today is what diaries are for, because today I met The Beatles. Mother called the Whittier to speak to Derek Taylor and by a fluke I got to speak to John Lennon. So we spoke for about half an hour and he was delightful. At 5 p.m. I was invited to the Press Conference and had pictures taken with The Beatles, and then saw the show, which was indescribable. They had other acts, but when The Beatles came on stage there was such a roar, like a vacuum, and there were hundreds of flash bulbs like World War I and II.*
>
> *The band really worked. Some of the numbers were "Twist & Shout," which opened, "You Can't Do That," "All My Loving," "Boys," "If I Fell," "Things We Said Today," "Hard Day's Night," "Roll Over Beethoven," "Can't Buy Me Love," and the last number I didn't know. I sat on the stage and I met a lot of people there. The DJ's and Derek Taylor were all very nice. I was at the press conference when I asked, "We don't want to stamp you out. When are you coming back?" It was really a highlight in my life. Derek took some of my material and brochures etc., and said he'd send it back, but he wanted a "proper look."*

Ann brought her own publicity packet to the show. With her long experience in show business, she recognized that she could not miss that unique opportunity to advance her own career. Nevertheless, the day Ann met The Beatles was an experience she would never forget, and it marked a momentous turning point in her life.

MTV and rock video was a 1980s phenomenon , but in the mid-1960s, radio was king of music media. There were no personal MP3 players or even 8-track or cassette tape players. Kids didn't have many choices for musical variety. There were radios and record players in their bedrooms, and car radios while driving around or making out. Lucky ones had portable transistors to play while hanging around with friends. It was impossible to bring a record player in the car, so teens relied on the local radio stations to give them the hottest and newest sounds. The disc jockey was the master of the airwaves and could easily make or break a band. Often a song's success depended entirely on the blessing of the DJs, who decided when and how often to play the tunes. Their on-air critiques caused record sales to rise or drop on a whim. The DJs would spin vinyl at the sock hops and teen clubs, and between record sets they often featured live bands to give new groups exposure to teen audiences. The system allowed the jocks to judge the kids' response to the bands and songs first-hand. To be introduced at a local hop by a popular DJ was a dream come true for many new groups who hoped to be launched into show business.

The Detroit area was a hot spot for musical entertainment in those days, and was breeding a group of outstanding musical artists in every genre. In 1959 Berry Gordy Jr. started Motown Records, but Motown was not the only game in town. At the tender age of 15, rocker Bob Seger started singing with The Decibels in 1960. Billie Lee and the Rivieras evolved into Mitch Ryder and the Detroit Wheels. The Lourds could barely contain singer/guitar madman Ted Nugent. Del Shannon sold over a million records of his hit "Runaway." Glen Frey of The Subterraneans and The Hideouts later became front man for The Eagles. CKLW jock Terry Knight planned to leave radio in order to pursue a musical career with his group Terry Knight and the Pack. A version of that band reconvened later as Grand Funk Railroad.

Detroit-based station WKMH was morphed into a new Top 40 format at midnight, October 31, 1963. With new call letters of WKNR, the new station adopted the nickname of "Keener 13." The station was totally geared to a teen audience. The "Keener Top 13 Countdown" was a commercial-free block of music that was instantly popular. Playing only the hits kept the kids tuned in, because their new favorites would be heard again real soon on fast-paced Keener. The controversial, mumbled song by the Kingsmen, "Louie, Louie" was No. 1 on the first *Keener Music Guide* on November 7, 1963.

From the beginning, WKNR phone lines were jammed with listeners calling in to make song requests or dedications. The gifted news staff presented reports so concise that it seemed as if the music lineup was barely interrupted. Wacky publicity events were the station's trademark, including cash prizes for on-air contests. The "Think Summer" campaign (which ran in the winter) encouraged listeners to send in newspaper entry forms for the chance to win prizes with a summertime theme. Promotions such as bumper stickers and the weekly *Keener Music Guide* boosted the station's presence in the music departments of local retailers from S.S. Kresge dime stores to the upscale J.L. Hudson's department stores.

The snappy "Keener Sound" was a hyperkinetic blend of sound effects, jingles, gimmicks, and great music, but their zany disc jockeys added the spice to the station's personality. The morning drive guy was Mort Crowley, then radio veteran Robin Seymour carried the late morning from 9 a.m. to noon. Afternoons were filled with the voice of Jim Sanders. In the evening, crazy man Gary Stevens and his imaginary "Woolie Burger" sidekick took over the world from 3 p.m. until 7 p.m. Bob Green's snappy patter finished the night from 7 p.m. until midnight, and Bill Phillips had the graveyard shift.

By early 1964, Keener was No. 1 or No. 2 in all time slots, so when they scooped the news of The Beatles arrival in Detroit on October 6, it wasn't really a surprise. Two new jocks had taken up residence at WKNR by then; Jim Sanders was replaced by Jerry Goodwin from noon to 3 p.m., and the station brought in Frank "Swingin'" Sweeney to replace morning man, Mort Crowley. WKNR hosted The Beatles' first Detroit show at Olympia Stadium, and it was a major event for the Motor City. It was on that same day that Ann Marston met Frank Sweeney.

According to Ann's journals, she was enjoying the publicity generated by her close encounter with The Beatles. The day following the concert, she called CKLW disc jockey Terry Knight to discuss her experiences at the concert. WKNR's Robin Seymour mentioned her on his *Teen Town* afternoon television show and displayed photographs of her and the group. *The Detroit Daily Press* newspaper ran a photo with Ann and The Beatles, as did the local *Wyandotte News Herald*, whose front page headline on September 10 read, "Beatles Flick into Town … and the Gals Go Wild."

> *Wyandotte's Ann Marston got the chance many girls have dreamed of—meeting The Beatles. Because The Beatles and Miss Marston, a world-famous archer and former Miss Michigan, have a mutual friend in England, she was asked to meet them when they came to Detroit Sunday.*

A few days after the concert, Ann visited the WKNR station in Dearborn and re-introduced herself to Sweeney. As one of the station's top DJ's, he was present at The Beatles' press conference. Ann and Sweeney went to Windsor together that night for a record hop and later stopped for dinner. The next day they attended a dance in Taylor, and she recorded in her diary that he was "a very interesting person."

Ann must have mentioned her singing aspirations to Sweeney, because by September 14 he arranged to take her to Motown Records for an audition. She wrote: "I sang 'Bill Bailey,' 'I Got It Bad,' and 'What Kind of Fool am I?' I met Mr. [Irv] Biegel and Mr. [Barney] Ales, both white, who are the VPs. Then I sang for four colored fellows, one of them Dozier and I think Holland. They were very noncommittal." And then later, "[Sweeney] came home here in the evening. Motown said 'no dice.' I was a little surprised because it had gone well, I thought. But their music is colored rhythm and blues mainly, so I'd like to think that's the reason."

Ann was undeterred by the Motown disappointment, and worked hard taking voice lessons. She spent hours singing into the tape recorder. Sweeney continued to try to make a deal for her in the recording industry. He took her to the WKNR studios and she recorded "Paper Roses," "He'll Have to Stay," "Burning Bridges," and

"Everybody's Somebody's Fool." He tinkered with the engineering on the songs and added a minor echo effect. Ann said he was excited about the tape, and he played it for some people he knew. She collected some publicity stills and sent them with the tape to Henry Jerome of Decca Records in New York. A week later Jerome responded that "the voice is good, but he had a girl under contract that was doing the same type of thing." Sweeney left for Nashville to attend a DJ convention. Meanwhile, he was trying to make connections with other recording companies, including Fraternity Records and Golden World.

Sweeney and Ann built their new friendship with long telephone calls that lasted late into the night. She felt they shared many of the same ideas and talked the same language. He was still on the early shift at WKNR, and had to be on the air by 5 a.m. She did occasional archery shows at area clubs in the area such as the Latin Quarter Nightclub in Detroit, and he sometimes drove her home after performances. The only thing that irritated punctual Ann was that he was often late and frequently didn't call her about last-minute changes in plans. She wrote: "When I think of all the times I've waited for him … He knows how it feels, but *he* doesn't like it." Sometimes he fell asleep and did not wake up in time to meet her—which would later turn out to be a recurring problem for Sweeney.

Meanwhile, Florence was not at all pleased with Ann's new friendship with Sweeney. He was not a particularly handsome man. He wore thick-rimmed glasses and his hair was slicked back. Many people felt he emanated a pompous attitude. Sweeney was several years older than Ann, he was married, and Florence was definitely not impressed by his fame and charm. She was openly rude to him when he came to the house. "Mother pounced on him almost before he got through the door." Ann, too, was frequently informed of Florence's strong opinions, as reported in her journals. "I had another blast with Mother. She should mind her own business and not be so domineering. She's still treating me like a 12-year-old, and I ain't. I'm old enough to know what I want and what I can do."

Her father was pushed into having a talk with Ann about the future and her archery career. Show bookings had dropped off in the last two years, and money may have been getting tight. Ann no longer had a car, and Frank planned to go back to his trade through the plumber's union. Ann still performed at a few archery exhibitions and sports shows. She was twenty-six and had spent sixteen of those years as a very active participant in the archery and show business world. She told a friend, "I'd rather be selling hair ribbons at the dime store than continue my life as a performer." Obviously, her heart just wasn't in it to tour aggressively with her parents, and she was more excited about the prospects of a singing career. Her personal thought was that "the archery is a flop and I might as well try this." But she continued to practice shooting to meet her upcoming show commitments for the spring season.

Finally in November, Sweeney scored an opportunity for Ann to record with Prism Records. He drove her to Dayton, Ohio, and they met a management team at the studio. By 8 p.m. that night the producers called for the Acorn Sisters and musicians for backup. They recorded "Cry Baby Cry" and "Living on Love," finishing at 2 a.m. with take No. 18. They continued the next day, as Ann recalled:

> *The studio is like a garage, and it has every instrument. It has a mike which is covered and I stood in a tented affair. Today we started recording and after hearing the [original] tape of Kathy Dee singing "Living on Love," you would never recognize it. They changed it with the Roy Orbinson "Pretty Woman" beat. I really belted it and we used take No. 9 on this one.*

With the help of Sweeney's connections in the music industry, Ann was steering toward her new goal of becoming a singer. But he resisted Ann's intervention when she attempted to be involved with the contract negotiations. She described the incident in her diary:

> *I had a bit of a to-do with him, about something I'd said [about the contract] that he didn't like. I could see no harm in it. Well, we did settle it and it was much better! We had to straighten things out on the way home. We came home with a nice two-year, 3 cents per record deal. We arrived home late, and he came in and we talked about the weekend. Later he came over and we all went over the contracts.*

The contracts were signed and sent to Prism two days later. Ann had photographs taken for the record sleeve and composed a brief biography. She had high hopes, but a few weeks later someone at Prism made the decision to scrap the song. Ann returned to Dayton to record "Dark Moon," which she liked much better. The "A" side would be "Living on Love." Prism later planned to change distributors, but for some reason the release was put off twice and the record was never pressed.

Life in Sweeney's world was exciting. As a top-rated disc jockey, he organized and hosted hops all over the Detroit area, and Ann accompanied him frequently. She was introduced to Tony Orlando, Neil Sedaka, and Jerry Lee Lewis. In December, Ann and Sweeney joined The Beach Boys and Jay and the Americans at a pre-concert cocktail party at the Sheraton Cadillac Hotel in Detroit. Ann took the neighbor kids Sandy and Doug Heinel to the Keener Holiday Show of Stars with tickets that Sweeney acquired, and Ann got an employee pass and took them backstage. When WKNR hosted a big March of Dimes show, it featured two of Motown's biggest acts—The Four Tops and The Marvelettes—presented by disc jockeys Gary Stevens and Robin Seymour. Ann was a night owl because of her many years in show business. When she was out with Sweeney, many nights ran late and into the morning. "The poor guy was really out of it. He says he went 30 hours without sleep."

Fashion-conscious Ann noticed that the hemlines were getting shorter, so she spent her free time altering skirts and dresses to conform to the miniskirt trend. At that time, girls were wearing white knee-high boots, ruffled blouses, and A-line dresses with hems two inches above the knee.

Sweeney and Ann often ate at area restaurants, and she was not very careful about the healthy content of meals. With her solid athletic build and curvy figure, Ann was not the image of the pale, ultra-thin models featured in mod fashion magazines. She averaged about 140 pounds. After visiting a doctor she once again got a prescription for diet pills; "[Sweeney] came over in the afternoon, and drove me to Dr. Christian's. I lost 7 pounds and am now 136. I'd like to lose 10 more, but then I like to eat. I'll never be a skinny Annie."

She continued to experience vision trouble, most likely because of bleeding in the tiny blood vessels behind the retina; a hidden but dangerous complication of high blood glucose levels. She had her eyes examined by another eye specialist, who apparently was not too concerned about her diabetes, and offered no further treatment besides a prescription for new reading glasses.

In an effort to keep up with her traditional social life, she attended Detroit Lions and University of Michigan football games with a family friend, Russ Hill, who owned private boxes at both stadiums. She half-heartedly dated guys her age, but wasn't pleased with the selection of single men that were available, so she spent most of her time with Sweeney.

Apparently Sweeney was unhappy with her decision to go to Chicago for an annual show convention and they quarreled. But she took the Greyhound bus alone and went anyway. She saw her former UTM agent Stacy and his associate Syd Harris, visited with her fellow performers, and attended exhibitions and parties. Friend Lex Luxumburg took her out for an exciting evening at the Playboy Club, The Bistro, and the Whiskey A-Go-Go. On the last day of the convention she went to the banquet, danced and had a good time, and old pal Glen Wade provided her with an automobile ride home to Wyandotte.

When Ann arrived back at home Florence gave her an unrelenting hard time about Sweeney and the archery career situation. Ann bemoaned her troubles to a sympathetic Sweeney, and her journal: "He's the only one I know who really cares how I feel, but why he should be bothered, I'll never know." She wrote, "I don't know what's going to happen. It's bad news because I'm miserable and I should be happy. My life is quite a turmoil of late … one day maybe I'll escape!"

There apparently was trouble in paradise with the new man in her life. Ann's diary entries reflected several disturbing incidents:

> *Got my hair done and therein lies a story. Louise did my hair in a very high fashion twist … which I liked. When he arrived he made fun of it. We had a hash all the way to Fort Street on the way to a hop. At the red light I got out and started for home. He turned around but I ducked down a street, so he missed me. He called me later and we talked until 3:45 a.m. on the phone. Didn't resolve much though; I was pretty mad …*
>
> *[The next day] I spent most of the day on the phone with him, but it's no way to hash over an argument. We later went to WKNR and finally sort of made up. I gave him a letter opener for Valentine's Day and he gave me a lovely record charm.*

A few weeks later Ann danced with one of the students at a hop for Detroit's Wayne State University. "It caused a five-hour argument. I shouldn't record this, but it happened. Anyway, it was straightened out by the time he got on the air at 5 a.m., and we talked until 7:15."

Ann spent time preparing for the 1965 show season by practicing at Gill's Archery range. Sweeney sometimes went with her, and she attempted to teach him to shoot. The family left in mid-February to do a show in Omaha, but first made a stop in Davenport, Iowa, regarding their lawsuit over the 1962 rodeo incident with the rampaging bull. They met with their attorney to file a deposition, and a plastic surgeon examined and photographed the injury to her left leg.

On opening day of the first show in Omaha, Ann was a bit nervous: It had been a while since she had performed. It went well, but she was exhausted. Sweeney called a few times and sent her a letter. She was lonely on the road, even with her parents traveling with her, and she bought wool to knit a sweater for Sweeney. After a few days back at home in Wyandotte the Marstons were off again, this time to Lincoln, Nebraska, where they performed on the bill with singer Ricky Nelson, The Mills Brothers, a group of log rollers, and other minor acts. When they came home, Ann gave Sweeney the sweater, but it was too big and she had to alter it.

They made plans to meet after she got into town, but he was late again. She was becoming increasingly frustrated. "A friend invited me to a party and I thought of going. I guess I should have gone, because it was 10 p.m. before he [Sweeney] arrived here, and I was mad again. But then he needs his rest. However, he should tell me what time he can make it instead of leaving me hanging." They connected the next evening and went to the radio studio. "He was really out of it … it's amazing. He doesn't seem to know how tired he is. I got home at 5 a.m."

The April 1965 show schedule for the Marstons included stops in Winnipeg, Canada, and Green Bay, Wisconsin. Ann was offered a spot on *The Mike Douglas Show*, but had other commitments. They left directly after the last show in Green Bay and drove back to Davenport, Iowa, for the trial regarding the "bullfight." The first day of the proceedings included the selection of the jury, and then the judge invited testimony from the witnesses. Both the Marstons' doctor and the doctor for the defense seemed to be sympathetic to Ann and her father, based on the injuries they received when the bull charged them. The next day Ann testified on the stand for several hours. "Sure was tired; it's quite an ordeal." Her lawyer brought up several points of negligence and read the doctors' depositions. At the noon recess, the judge suggested that Ann and Frank accept the $1,000 settlement that the defense offered, but they decided to proceed with the case.

The jury began deliberations at noon on the third day of the trial. While they were waiting, the family went out to look at damage caused by floods covering the downtown area. Like the rain that drenched the rodeo in Fort Madison three years earlier, Davenport had been hit by a tremendous series of storms and much of the city was under water. When the jury returned to deliver the verdict three hours later, the Marstons received very good news. Frank was awarded $2,000 and Ann received compensation of $12,000. The family members decided to combine the amounts and split it down the middle for $7,000 each. After the lawyer was paid his one-third the Marstons headed down the highway for home.

By the end of June 1965, Ann fulfilled most of her archery commitments, but that summer was full of excitement. While she was exploring possibilities for her future, her old life often overlapped the new.

Her school friends were getting married and expanding their families. Consequently Ann attended several weddings and baby showers. She was an avid movie fan and accompanied her friends to the theater to see current hits that included *Thunderball* and *Beach Blanket Bingo*. The ten-year reunion of Roosevelt High School's class of 1956 was in the planning stage. She enjoyed going to meetings with her old school crowd and dutifully called classmates seeking current addresses for the mailing list. She attended an induction at the Willie Heston Sports Hall of Fame. She was delighted when she occasionally received a telephone call from Paul McCartney or George Harrison.

The country was experiencing disturbing changes. The news media carried reports of the massive civil rights march in Montgomery, Alabama, and the escalation of the war in Vietnam. Ironically, at Detroit's Motown Records, Berry Gordy released Martha and the Vandellas' celebration song, "Dancing in the Streets."

Ann considered alternative employment options that would be entirely different than archery. She consulted with Bob Reaume of River Oaks Realty. "It looks like a good business opportunity, me selling real estate. It's 6% on a house, of which I get 30%; River Oaks 30%; and 40% for listing it." She was eager to learn, but quickly became disappointed about being the rookie. "I spent the afternoon calling old listings. I don't know when the training begins, though." A few days later she said, "I went to River Oaks but just did more calling, which is rather discouraging, and I think a waste of time." She never returned to the office and spent a few weeks coaching Miss Oak Park in preparation for the Miss Michigan Pageant. Ann was the emcee and sang six songs at the Miss Detroit Pageant in June. In the audience were her parents, some of her neighbors, and Frank Sweeney.

With his continuing attempt to have Ann release a record, Sweeney took her to WKNR and she recorded "Cotton Fields" and "Puff the Magic Dragon." They later went to Golden World Records in Detroit. A staff member listened to the tapes, but nothing came of it.

Evenings were full with Sweeney's bookings several times a week. He was one of the most aggressive DJs in the Detroit area and worked all the teen hot spots. He organized high school dances and arranged hops for up to 500 kids at Motor City Roller Rink or the Detroit Dragway. The Detroit area held an endless pool of enthusiastic young garage bands, so Ann and Sweeney hosted a successful Battle of the Bands. Competing groups included The Entradas, The Henchmen, The Mastertones, The Legends, and Ken & the Silvertones. The Mastertones, who featured a ten-year-old drummer, won the contest.

Another big dance featured The Del Roys, The Arcasions, The Four Gems, The Daybreak, The Epics and The XL's. Patricia Stevens' modeling school provided go-go girls for an event in Walled Lake. Sometimes Sweeney worked one hop and Ann took over another on the same night. She even performed an archery exhibition at an all-night prom in Northville. "I did the act for the first time alone. [Sweeney] was my prop boy; it worked out very well." A new disc jockey, Dick Purtan, started working at WKNR and the staff celebrated his birthday. "I was bored stiff," Ann said. "Everybody there threw everybody else in the pool; not my idea of fun."

Ann felt that she and Sweeney could provide top-quality dances in Wyandotte, so they made a formal presentation to the city council, with the support of Councilman Clifford "Skip" Clack. They immediately ran into opposition from a local youth group, the Knights of Columbus Columbian Squires. The Squires already hosted popular Friday night dances that were the club's main source of income, and they strongly opposed any competition. Eventually Ann and Sweeney withdrew their offer. In a newspaper interview Ann seemed disappointed and said: "We could have brought to Wyandotte a well-controlled, well-supervised dance that would have featured all the top names in the recording industry and all the top bands in southern Michigan. There is a need for it in Wyandotte."

While scouting for bands they were impressed with the talented Satellites from Allen Park, and Tom and the Fugitives, who were based in Wyandotte. They booked these groups frequently. As a result of a last-minute cancellation at a local wedding, Ann called in a new band, the Motor City Five. This group from Lincoln Park had recently turned down Sweeney as their manager. Their collective impression of him was that he was too arrogant and controlling. But they agreed to work for Ann, even though the event was a Polish wedding reception located in a church basement in Wyandotte. The guys plugged both guitars and the microphone into a single 15-watt amp. Ann visited the reception that night and later commented: "They were a good band; but smart-alec kids."

The Marston-Sweeney duo looked into the possibility of creating a formal business partnership to organize sports shows and dances, and to manage local rock bands. But, Ann's relationship with Sweeney continued to deteriorate, and they argued frequently. "We've not been getting on the last few days, and this was one of those days. Had another argument … a real one, I'm afraid. I'm not going to record the details. It seems like that's all we do lately," she wrote. "I guess it's my fault, but then why should I take all the blame. I'm a little fed up and he knows it." He was late another evening and she confided her personal turmoil: "I was mad; we had another argument. I sometimes wonder, and these days I do. Diary, even you can't help me on this one." Another entry read, "Frank came over late and we had an argument like we haven't had in a long time. We got it settled; however, it leaves us both weak." After an explosive disagreement she sometimes wrote letters to him, intending to end the relationship. "I gave him 'the' letter. I didn't want him to read it till later, because I knew we'd never break it up once he read it. We spent until 4 a.m. talking things over again. Oh, at [Victor] Lim's restaurant my fortune cookie read, 'In youth we do more for love than later we will ever be able to do for money.'"

Her parents openly disapproved of Sweeney. To explain Ann's relationship with Sweeney, Florence lied to her friends by saying that Ann worked for WKNR. She often tried to stir things up. Ann's diary chronicled another unhappy incident: "We spent a nice evening here in my little dungeon. Father went to a union meeting. Mother went next door, so it was very peaceful. Later, we went to his house and made up a list of bands. I don't care to remember too much about this one. Mother called his house [looking for Ann], and it upset both of us a great deal. In fact, I haven't seen him that upset in a long time."

When Florence was on the rampage, not even her daughter's personal journal was sacred. Ann was obviously distressed when she was caught between Florence's tyrannies and Sweeney's temperament. She lamented, "Had all kinds of trouble today. I discovered Mother has been going through my diary … yes, you! She also has taken the letter he wrote me, plus read all the others. She called Marie

[Sweeney's wife] and said all kinds of things. I spent the day looking for the letter to no avail. We had a hop at Lincoln Jr. High and [Ann and Sweeney] had a big fight after. What a turbulent life I'm leading."

Florence continued her dramatic protests that summer. She smashed some of Ann's china figurines and left home for a week without telling the family where she was going. Ann was neither surprised nor upset. "Mother came home last night ... I certainly wasn't delighted."

Sweeney kept the pace of a hectic nightlife, but he still had to be on the air at WKNR for the early morning shift. "Out with Frank, but he was so tired I had to drive him home." Ann also helped him answer fan mail ("it's quite a job") and assisted him when it was his turn to decide where the hit records ranked on the weekly *Keener Music Guide*. He was on the fast track for a promotion at WKNR, and Ann helped him compose and type the necessary letters to Walter Patterson, the general manager, and to Mrs. Fred Knorr, wife of the station's founder.

Things changed dramatically in early August. "Frank did a hop for Robin [Seymour] in Hazel Park. We did it in the Keener wagon, as he doesn't have his car. He was so tired I took him home and drove myself home in the wagon." The next morning there was big trouble at WKNR. Jerry Goodwin was working overtime on the late night shift and Sweeney didn't arrive on time to relieve him. The result was that Sweeney was out of a job. Ann described the events of August 7, 1965: "Happy Birthday to me. I woke up to Frank [on the radio]. He sounded bad and I knew something was wrong. Then I learned he was late. Marie slept through the alarm and Jerry Goodwin didn't call. So it's a long story, but Frank quit Keener. The day was turmoil."

A version of the incident is described in David Carson's book, *Rockin' Down the Dial; The Detroit Sound of Radio*:

> WKNR's Swingin' Sweeney was plagued by a severe case of insomnia, and more than once on the air had been transformed into "Sleepin' Sweeney." According to Keener's Bob Green, one morning after introducing "I Got You Babe" by Sonny and Cher, the morning disc jockey's head began the slow descent, eventually resting on the console beneath the microphone. As the record finished and the needle continued to circle the empty grooves over and over, Sweeney snoozed. When he awoke, WKNR let him know he was on notice. Management was happy with the response Purtan was getting at night, and they were making plans to move Sweeney to the position of assistant program director and have Dick take over mornings in late August. On a Saturday morning about a week later, Sweeney had finally managed to get to sleep at home. Now the problem was waking up. For

some reason, midday deejay Jerry Goodwin had been doing the all-night
show that morning and was more than ready to go home at 6 o'clock. Af-
ter Sweeney's late arrival at a little past 7, a fight broke out in the Keener
studios. When the records and tape cartridges had stopped flying, Sweeney
was sent swingin' on down the road and Dick Purtan was moved into the
important morning drive hours two weeks ahead of schedule.

Sweeney was forced to look for a new job, and for a period of time he traveled
throughout the country on his quest for new employment. Perhaps Ann was a little
relieved: "Sometimes I think he likes to see me miserable. Well, I won't be seeing
much of him anyway. I drove him to the airport. This time he'll be gone three
weeks. I decided to think things through while he's away."

Ann was becoming a popular celebrity in her own right with the local teens,
and emceed beauty contests and dances. She spent hours on the telephone booking
groups for events and built an impressive stable of bands. Her contact file held business cards for more than seventy groups. With a newfound confidence, she said, "Today I had three bands working. Band business is good." She went to the Hamilton
Motors dealership and bought a car. "I bought a Plymouth Fury III. A lovely black
with red interior, AM-FM reverb radio, 383 engine—everything." Local musician
Don Gutz was chauffeured to auditions by Ann when he was still in high school. He
recalled: "She was so busy. Ann was the first person I met that could eat fast food and
drive at the same time." She continued scouting bands for management and was approached by Wyandotte's Tom and the Fugitives for representation. Front man Tom
Beaudry later formed Frijid Pink using his stage name "Kelly Green."

The Satellites were a group of young boys who had the experience of performing together for two years. The musicians included Dave Fero on lead guitar, Frank
"Floor Show" Schiavulli as drummer, Ken Sipos on rhythm guitar, Carl Sweets on
bass, and lead singer Frank Vargo. Fero had been playing in bands since he was twelve
years old, and he and Vargo backed up Tim Tam and the Turn-Ons for their recording, "Wait a Minute," which was due to be released in early 1966. At an average age
of fifteen, the boys were freshmen at Allen Park High School, and none of them had
a driver's license. Ann had been employing them at local dances, and she liked their
wholesome stage presence. They wore Beatle boots and collarless suits or matching
sweaters to dances. Ann bought matching vests for them and attended rehearsals
to help with technical issues and choreography. Their set list included "Shake a Tail
Feather," "Summertime," and naturally, several Beatles tunes. They signed on with
Ann in October 1965. They worked every week and were booked into most local
venues, from The Chatterbox teen club in Allen Park to the Harbor Theater in Lincoln Park. Ann thought The Satellites had great possibilities and took her protégés to

Pioneer Studios in December to cut a demo record. They recorded "I'll Feel a Whole Lot Better" and "You Really Got a Hold on Me." It never made the charts.

The Satellites continued to build their popularity in the local music scene. On a snowy night in January 1966 they pulled a crowd of 177 kids at the Southgate Teen Center, breaking the winter attendance record for the club. Transportation was a challenge and Ann often picked the kids up after school for rehearsals. Some of the boys' parents donated the necessary funds to buy an equipment trailer so they could drive the kids to gigs. A favorite venue was the Grosse Ile Naval Base, where the fathers could get adult beverages while waiting for the band to finish the show.

The song "Wait a Minute" by Tim Tam and the Turn-Ons was released and climbed the charts to No. 3 on WKNR's *Keener Music Guide* for the week of January 19, 1966. The record sold more than 30,000 copies the first week, and twice as many sold the second week. While The Satellites were hanging out at Ann's house one night, she called WKNR jock Scott Regan. Vargo was interviewed on the air about his role playing drums on the song. He put in a good plug for his band and identified all the members, providing the group with free publicity. Unfortunately, Faro and Vargo never received royalties for their performance on the record. Tim Tam and the Turn-Ons enjoyed success for years, and had several hits on the charts, including "Cheryl Ann" and "Kimberly."

The Motor City Five had a gimmick; there were only four members when the band was started in 1964 by Wayne Kramer and Fred Smith. Kramer played guitar with The Bounty Hunters, and Smith was in the rival Vibratones while both were still in high school in Lincoln Park. Rob (Derminer) Tyner was originally selected to play bass guitar, but he left the band. His replacement was Pat Burrows, who joined the rhythm section partnered with Bob Gaspar on drums. These four guys incorporated the first version of MC5. When Tyner returned in 1965 to take over the lead vocals, the Motor City Five finally had its fifth member. Their early material was mostly instrumental including "Red River Rock," "Ramrod," "Walk Don't Run," "Underwater," and of course, "Wipe Out." The group also had a hard-core R&B foundation, and they pounded out Chuck Berry's "Oh, Carol," "Round and Round," and Little Richard's energetic "Tutti Frutti." The group covered popular Beach Boys songs and learned essential Beatles tunes such as "Twist and Shout." The members of MC5 admired the raw sound of The Rolling Stones, and Mick Jagger was an unruly new role model. The Motor City Five had a business card that announced "On the Move with M.C. Five. Specialists in Rock-Rhythm-Blues."

Besides the last-minute emergency at the Polish wedding reception, Ann began booking the Motor City Five regularly in 1965. They tied with The Satellites at a battle of the bands dance. The members of the two groups joked about their friendly rivalry at the competitions. Sometimes after a gig the band went out to eat, and blew all the money they earned for the performance. One night at a restaurant a waitress asked for the group's name. They jokingly told her they were Booker T and the MGs and the girl believed them.

Ann booked the MC5 into the Deer Hunt Inn, a lodge outside the metropolitan Detroit area. Ann said the manager at the Deer Hunt Inn "wasn't too keen on this group, although I thought they were great." She wasn't concerned, because The Satellites had played there previously and the manager didn't like them, either.

According to Wayne Kramer, the Motor City Five was enthusiastic about being scheduled for the opening lineup for The Rolling Stones in November 1965:

> *We were working with [CKLW] DJ Dave Shafer for about a year, playing record hops all over tarnation. You did these things for $10 and got your name on the radio all week … The rumor was that The Rolling Stones were coming to Detroit, and Dave said that he booked us on the show to pay us back for all the work we had done for him. We were going to open for The Rolling Stones. It couldn't have been better for us. We had to learn all new songs because we did so many Rolling Stones songs. We were so excited, and bragged to all our friends. A couple of days before the concert, somehow we got bumped, and The Mastertones got added to the show. I was crushed, and literally I wept because it was such a blow to me. I was so disappointed and so disillusioned with the people in show business …*

As a consolation, Ann managed to score a great job for "her boys" in December. The MC5 was slated to open for the British rock group The Dave Clark Five at Cobo Hall in Detroit. Kramer was thrilled about the opportunity.

> *We were a solid band in those days. We specialized in hard rock and Chuck Berry stuff. We knew what we were up against and it was our first really big concert. Fred [Smith] and I discussed it a great deal: how to act when you're on stage, how to "put out" for a room that big. After all, this was what all the work was for—to open at Cobo Hall for a band like The Dave Clark Five. Hopefully you could get a picture taken with The Dave Clark Five, which you could then use for publicity purposes. The idea was that if you stand close enough to the flame, some of it will wear off on you.*
>
> *The night of the concert came and we were very excited. We did our show and Fred and I both realized the power of "the wave." If you turned to the side of the stage and waved to the crowd they would all scream. The sense of power was intoxicating. We stayed high on that power the rest of our lives. And we did get our picture with The Dave Clark Five.*

The next evening the MC5 band members came to Ann's house to discuss the show experience. It was Rob Tyner's twenty-first birthday, and they had a few beers while the reel-to-reel tape machine recorded the celebration. The session resulted in a true basement tape, as the members of MC5 had a fab party in "Ann's Dungeon." There was a lot of horsing around and a little music, including Ann singing with the guys. Kramer played an elaborate Spanish guitar number and Rob "Robin" Tyner wailed out a bluesy B.B. King tune.

There were jokes about how much makeup the Dave Clark group wore during the performance, and Ann pointed out that it was a show business fact that the bright stage lights washed out facial features. The members of the band were amused that, in their interpretation, the DC5 emulated the name of MC5. Ann's diary entry said: "We all came over here and tape recorded and generally it was good fun. I finally threw them out at 5 a.m."

A week later, an article in the *Wyandotte News Herald* showed only Ann in a photo with three members of The Dave Clark Five. The caption read, "When The Dave Clark Five from England appeared at Detroit's Cobo Hall last weekend, Wyandotte's Ann Marston, a former Miss Michigan, was among those who personally met them, here shown with three of them. Miss Marston is helping to promote bands, including the Motor City Five, which was the only band to appear with The Dave Clark Five." On December 22, the *News Herald* ran the photo of the MC5 and The Dave Clark Five that was taken backstage.

Ann maintained a casual professional relationship with her bands, and they often stopped by her home in Wyandotte. Michael Davis was hanging out with MC5, and officially joined in the spring of 1966 when bass guitar player Pat Burrows left the group. Davis recalled visiting Ann's home in Wyandotte:

> The guys said, "We're going over to see Ann Marston." So we went over to hang out and listen to records. It was kind of a business meeting/party. She was really excited, and into the band. There was a lot of energy in the air. She wanted to be connected to the young crowd, the whole rock and roll world, and the excitement that accompanied The Beatles, The Stones and the British Invasion.
>
> It was like the wolves going into the queen's boudoir. We were all in the rec room in her basement. Right away I was struck by how pretty she was; she was a really good-looking woman. It was a contest with us, and we were laying bets on who was going to claim this one because she was so fine. Of course, nobody stood a chance. But we were in fierce competition. We were all doing our best to impress her with our British personas; talking in British accents like Paul McCartney or George Harrison. We

tried to be as impressive as possible, plus maintain our business aloofness. She had our number; we weren't really getting over on her. We were "her boys," but we guys continued to try to be as seductive as possible when Ann was around.

Ann kept closely involved as the band's manager and often visited them when they played. "I went to the Pit where the MC5 were working. It's actually the Sportsman Club." They were confident in her management, and the boys often asked her for advice. When drummer Bob Gaspar wanted to leave the group, she counseled him. "I went up to Wayne's with the MC5 and had a talk with the drummer. He wants to quit. I think I straightened them out." Kramer was a very ambitious young man and felt that Ann was the best manager for his group at that time. He said:

She was very confident and assertive; not at all like most women in the early '60s. She didn't live in the shadow of a man. She felt that she could make things happen. She had power, and that's very attractive. Ann had what managers must have, which is vision. She saw how it could develop, how to take an artist from this level to the next level …

I'm better for having known her. She made me feel like what I was doing mattered, that I wasn't being silly or frivolous, that I could actually be an artist and contribute something. She validated my life with her commitment to help me … Ann was an artist's advocate. And, she was really doing a pretty good job juggling the MC5 and The Satellites. She was moving us up, finding us better places to appear, getting higher profile jobs.

In early 1966, the MC5 played a Big Three Dance at Wyandotte's Lincoln School. The Big Three included students from all three high schools in town, and the dances were very popular and crowded. The entry rules were strict and required that the kids show proper school identification and follow a dress code. Guys wearing sweatshirts, football jerseys or having long hair were not admitted.

There was an interesting variety of engagements for the MC5, and on one occasion, Ann was the warm-up act for them at a benefit for the Job Corps. The boys were impressed with her archery skill. Davis later said, "She had her little outfit on and did an archery exhibition. Then the MC5 were our swarthy selves, and came on to rule the scene." Davis also had high hopes of success in show business under Ann's direction and explained the process of hitting it big with a record in those days:

We started playing at teen clubs, The Chatterbox, the Hullabaloos. Those were the kinds of places that were available. We were always trying to impress DJs because that was our connection into the business. Back in those days we figured all that we needed to do was go to a recording studio and record a single 45. If you got it played on the radio, bingo, you could get a hit record and you were as big as The Beatles.

The band experimented with innovative sound techniques like feedback, and eventually MC5 developed its own unique brand of talent, fame, and notoriety that would define their future success. Rob Tyner was pioneering ideas that influenced and inspired Wayne Kramer, who was excited by the artistic changes in the world. Kramer described his impressions of that time:

Tyner was just having a creative burst. He was coming into the band with all kinds of new ideas. Tyner was an amazingly musical guy; he could find a melody on a flute or on a zither or guitar. Whatever he picked up he could find a way to make it sound musical. He was getting into the idea of writing his own songs ...

The hippie movement hadn't exploded yet, but we had a sense that something was happening. It was in fashion, and there was a spirit of rebellion. The young people were breaking away in San Francisco, and also in swinging England. Hopefully for us, it wasn't going to be just nightclubs on Michigan Avenue and four sets a night.

We didn't want to cover other bands' music on the radio; we wanted our music on the radio. This is where we had a break with Gaspar and Burrows because their vision was more limited. So we started to see that the way to really be able to do this for a living was to write your own music.

It was an ongoing conflict, and we were told [by Ann], "I can't get you jobs because you won't learn Top 10-type songs." We would compromise with Ann and learn some Kinks and Beatles songs. But we took a stand, and later became adamant that we had to do our own music.

Sick of the band business and the demands of rock 'n roll, drummer Bob Gaspar left the group in spring of 1966 to get a "real job." Kramer knew of a young drummer, Dennis "Machine Gun" Thompson, who was a senior at Lincoln Park High School. In early March 1966, Ann booked the band into Inkster's Crystal bar. Thompson described the engagement. It was the first time he formally played with the band:

Wayne Kramer came over on his motorcycle one night to my house. He said he had this great gig and this new band called the Motor City Five.

121

"We just fired our drummer. What are you doing? Would you like to play? It's this great bar and we need a drummer. Would you do it? We'll have flyers on cars and everything." This sounded like the big time, so I said sure, I'll do it. Being invited to play with them was very exciting, because I was still playing in a wedding band called Jeff Warady and the Paramounts.

They had already gotten "Bohemian" but I was still in school. I was a National Honor Society student, straight B plusses and As, teacher's pet, that kind of a guy. Wayne and Fred and Rob were already beginning to explore other avenues of thought with the new youth culture and the splinter from conservatism. They were pretty much ahead of me in their thinking.

We went to the Crystal Bar audition, and I was awkward and nervous. I was used to playing in front of people, but there was nobody out there. It was a dive and a dump, and not at all as good as what Wayne said. It was not a great gig. I'd played in better places with my brother's band.

The American way of life in 1966 reflected an immense variety of taste and talent. Popular television shows ranged from *Batman, Star Trek,* and *Bonanza* to *Gomer Pyle, U.S.M.C., The Lucy Show, The Andy Griffith Show,* and *The Red Skelton Show.* Men and boys were wearing their hair long and sporting beards and big sideburns. Miniskirts were rising to four inches above the knee, and 10,000 anti-war demonstrators stormed the White House to protest military actions in Vietnam. While most American teens were playing Twister, the government outlawed LSD and other hallucinogens. Timothy Leary took acid trips, Lenny Bruce died of a heroin overdose, and someone finally invented panty hose.

Popular music was changing direction dramatically, and The Beatles and Stones were no longer the only bands influencing the landscape of the musical world. The Beach Boys still had a strong presence on the charts, and The Monkees, Bob Dylan, and Nancy Sinatra all had hits. A new freedom of expression allowed groups to grow and learn. Thompson sensed the changes and the inspiration it provided for innovative musicians, and he decided to stay with the MC5 and follow the flow of creativity the band was taking:

There was tons of music to love. Music then ranged from Johnny Rivers to Jimi Hendrix, with the Jefferson Airplane squeezed in between with the Beach Boys. There was the English wave and there was folk music and early jazz, soul, R&B, Wilson Pickett, Otis Redding, and the whole Motown book. And it was all good music, and it was deep.

Davis viewed the awful Crystal Bar gig as the first step on the path to new opportunities for the Motor City Five. The young musician was ready to take his chances and try a new challenge:

> The Crystal Bar was a turning point for us. When you play venues like that, doing multi-sets, you play three or four sets a night, so you have to have a lot of material. You do a lot of duplicating, and you're playing for people who aren't really around for a rock and roll band; they are there to drink. The bar owner was always telling us to "tune down." We made fun of him because he meant "turn down." Our brand of rock and roll was a little too raucous for a neighborhood bar. We knew it wasn't where our bread and butter was; we weren't that kind of an act. Ann was more involved in conventional culture, more mainstream."

After playing the Crystal Bar, the MC5 looked for a new type of exposure for their unique sound and material, and appeared frequently at hops, school dances, and teen clubs with Keener disc jockey Jerry Goodwin. Davis realized the group's main objective should be to gain experience by performing at any location, such as the Teen Fair at Bob-Lo Island and on the grandstand at the Michigan State Fair. He described the band's determined evolution from mainstream music:

> We had to keep raising our profile. The MC5 was probably the hardest working band. We played more gigs for free than any other band in Detroit ever. We would play anywhere, just to get out there to the fan base. After the Crystal Bar days, we realized that we needed to do something more radical. So everybody left their parents' houses and moved down to Downtown Detroit, in the Wayne State University area. We started being street guys and lived in one apartment. It was shortly after that we met John Sinclair, and the rest is history. Ann was back in the suburbs.

Ann got the message and continued on without the MC5. She worked the 1966 sports show season accompanied by her high school friend Charlotte Crum as companion, costume manager, and show assistant. They got along well and Ann enjoyed her first tour without her parents. Newspapers in Kansas City advertised a week-long sports show and mentioned that she was appearing with log rollers, retrieving hunting dogs, and Sparky Jr., "The Almost Human Seal." A photo article in the *Kansas City Star* reported that, "In Detroit, where she lives when not touring, she manages rock and roll music groups." She didn't have many archery bookings in 1966, but she reported earnings of $6,000 that year.

Ann took The Satellites to United Sound Systems on June 13, 1966, to cut "Midnight Hour" and "I Believe." Studio sound man Les Cooley mixed the recording. Later that year, Cooley engineered the song "Persecution Smith" for Bob Seger and the Last Heard on the Hideout label. In Ann's opinion, The Satellite's record sounded very good, but it wasn't released. The group later won a competition on the WXYZ-TV show called *Talent Town*. Host Rita Bell awarded the grand prize, a Sears console stereo system with AM/FM radio. The guys decided to keep it in Frank Vargo's basement because that was where the group practiced and hung out, and Vargo's parents were "band friendly."

In October 1966, The Satellites hosted a fundraising dance in Southgate for AL-SAC, an organization devoted to assisting leukemia-stricken children. The proceeds for the show brought in more than $500. The guys were honored to personally meet Danny Thomas, the national spokesman for the charity. He presented the musicians a recognition plaque for "long and faithful service." The event rated a photo in the local newspaper, and it was terrific publicity for the band.

In California, Governor Ronald Reagan observed that, "A hippie is someone who dresses like Tarzan, has hair like Jane and smells like Cheetah." Hippies were in the news, on TV, in San Francisco and, of course, in Detroit. The Plum Street community district was Detroit's counterculture response to Haight Ashbury. Three dozen shops located on Plum between 4th and 5th Streets housed antiques, jewelry, posters, and fashion. The hippies loved it, the residents were skeptical, and Ann was curious about the new culture. She visited the area with next-door neighbor Bob Heinel. "Bob and I went down to Plum Street to see the Hippies; and I was with one! Bob has been in 22 countries and is now a hippie himself. Plum Street is a giggle; early dime store brings big money."

Meanwhile, rock music history was made when the Motor City Five was the featured band at Detroit's Grande Ballroom on its opening night, October 7, 1966. Founded by DJ "Uncle" Russ Gibb, the Grande hosted the biggest rock groups in the world, including The Who and Janis Joplin. The MC5 was the designated house band, and was billed as having an "avant-rock" style. A now-classic poster designed by artist Gary Grimshaw announced MC5's debut at the Grande's grand opening.

Ann understood that MC5 was "on the move" in a new direction without her. She proudly followed the band's career and tape recorded several of their radio show interviews. The band members occasionally mentioned her on the air, and referred to her as one of the group's first friends from their early days. Ann Marston moved on, too.

8

"Keep Your Face to the Sunshine"

Detroit's music scene in the late 1960s was drifting away from chaperoned dances, and the new popularity of teen clubs inspired Ann to open one of her own. She refitted a room behind an archery range on Michigan Avenue off Greenfield Road in Dearborn and opened "Miss Michigan's Target Young Adult Night Club." The club had chairs, a stage, pool tables, and a refreshment area. A promotional flyer stated, "You must be under 21 and prove it. Minimum age 16." Ann hoped this would be a perfect way to showcase local bands, particularly the ones she managed.

In December 1966, she hosted a dance featuring The Youthful Offenders, The Innsmen and The Satellites. Keener DJ Dick Purtan fronted a successful hop at the Target Club using groups Terry Knight and the Pack and The Endless Chain, and on another night they used The Daybreaks, The Cavaliers, and Southbound Freeway. For the most part Ann was not pleased with the attendance and the clientele at the Target Nightclub. She wrote, "There was a big crowd of guys in black leather coats and almost a fight." On another occasion she said, "We had a very small crowd tonight. I don't ... yes I do, know what's wrong with the place. It's too small and crummy. I hauled in more chairs, but it's just not happening."

She represented a couple of new bands, including The Renegades, who had recently recorded "Mary Had a Little" and "Just for You" at Fortune Records. The Lower Deck was another clean-cut band, and Ann coordinated their stage wardrobe and took them shopping for new equipment. Rick "Tim Tam" Wiesend asked Ann for backup players to help him practice for a recording session. She sent two of the Renegade guitar players. She was excited about the prospect, and wrote: "This was The Satellites a year ago with "Wait a Minute.""

Ann was becoming increasingly concerned with the attitude of the members of The Satellites, and tried to give them direction. "After the performance I had a knock-down argument with The Satellites. They play too loud and they don't do what they're told. I'm very concerned about them, but they couldn't care less about me. I'm really fed up with them. It was a delight to see The Lower Deck doing what I asked." She wrote a letter to each member of The Satellites asking for their coop-eration. The next night they showed up at the Target Night Club while The Lower Deck was rehearsing and apologized to her, and she said: "They are spoiled brats ... and Frank Vargo admitted it."

The Satellites were growing their hair and trying to change the focus of their band. They saw the huge success that MC5 was enjoying and wanted a piece of the action. One night the guys didn't show up for a gig and attended a bachelor party instead. Ann knew all their friends and tracked them down. Dave Fero recalled:

> She was madder than a hornet, but forgave us. We knew what we were doing, though. We had enough years of being the pretty boys in match-ing suits, and wanted to pursue the Rolling Stone-type adventurous path. Out there was the San Francisco psychedelic wave with Jefferson Air-plane, Grateful Dead and Big Brother. We had a successful program that had worked for many years and probably would have worked for many more. But it was a new path that we chose to take, and we eventually made an amicable split with Ann.

Fero contacted her occasionally afterwards as a friend, but The Satellites moved into new musical territory, changing band members and names over the next several years.

Ann was in Louisville doing her act at a sport show in spring of 1967. The *Louisville Courier-Journal* said that she benefited by "... the archery career that has enabled her to become the owner of a young adult night club in Detroit and the manager of two rock and roll bands." Ann commented in the interview about per-forming: "I truly love it. It's like I told my bands; if you're enjoying yourself on the stage, the people in the audience will be enjoying it, too." She traveled to New York City with her father to perform in another *Sports Illustrated* tour. Ann made the front of the sports section in an article by Maury White while appearing in March in Des Moines, Iowa. "Ann appeared around here about 6 years ago with a rodeo that encountered bad weather. She never did get paid. 'The boss promised to sell a bull and send my money,' she recalls. 'I'm still waiting.'"

The infamous summer of love in the United States was in 1967. For California, it meant San Francisco's tie-dyed hippies populating Haight Ashbury, and swarms of music lovers at the Monterey Pop Festival that featured Jimi Hendrix, The Who, and the Grateful Dead. For the United States Armed Forces in Vietnam, it meant the loss of an estimated 17,000 troops since 1961. In Detroit, there was a love-in gone wild.

Poet, political activist, and head hippie John Sinclair sponsored the event at the city's Belle Isle park in April. Hoping to bring copious amounts of love and peace to dreary Detroit, Sinclair's TransLove Energies community planned an enlightened cultural gathering. Several bands were scheduled to appear, including MC5, who were now a part of Sinclair's anti-establishment commune. The public was invited to attend this peaceful celebration of hippies and artists. When more than 6,000 people showed up, the serene love fest evolved into a raucous brawl. Flower children and members of the Outlaws motorcycle gang clashed with police, and the throng was forced to leave the island via the MacArthur Bridge. The MC5 barely escaped with their equipment. Businesses on East Jefferson were looted in the melee, and a legion of more than 150 police officers finally dispersed the crowds. Several injuries and ten arrests were reported in the newspapers the next day.

There was very little love left in Detroit later that summer as the city suffered the most horrendous race riot in United States history in late July. When police tried to break up an after-hours party at a blind pig drinking and gambling club, it triggered an urban uprising. Blocks of the city erupted in flames, looters terrorized both white and black businesses, and gunshots peppered the haze for five days. It took a force of nearly 75,000 soldiers from the National Guard and several thousand paratroopers from Fort Bragg, North Carolina, to disperse the mob. The tragic confrontation between police and Detroit residents resulted in the death of forty-three people and caused more than $200 million in damages. More than 7,000 people were arrested and nearly 1,200 were wounded.

The city of Wyandotte, where the Marstons lived, was located only 12 miles south of the carnage in Detroit, and the terrorism was too close for comfort in the peaceful and predominately white community. Citizens were watchful in case the violence encroached into the quiet suburbs down the river, but it was contained within the big city. In all, the United States suffered race riots in more than 100 different cities in the summer of 1967. Ironically that summer, Detroit powerhouse singer Aretha Franklin scored a national hit with her song, "Respect."

Ann's relationship with her mother, Florence, began to improve slightly after their very long personal siege. They went shopping, visited friends, and saw movies together. Part of the reason for the truce was that Ann finally inched away from her mother's dominance now that the family was not touring as an archery act together. Florence was gradually getting used to her forced retirement, and was no longer vicariously in the limelight provided by Ann's former fame. Ann's father went back to work as a plumber, so the household finances were more stable, and they bought a new Cadillac. Frank Sweeney was working at a radio station in Toledo and was no longer a significant part of Ann's personal life. This spared Florence the immense embarrassment of her daughter's connection with a married man. Ann was out of the house most days on band business, and could more often than not ignore her mother's theatrical outbursts. At age twenty-nine, Ann Marston had earned her most valuable trophy—her independence.

One of the younger neighbor girls, Nannette Spaulding, styled Ann's hair. She knew about Ann's confined past and was sympathetic to her. "If you could sum up Annie's [character] in three words, they would be kindness, generosity, and wholesomeness," Spaulding said. "She rarely had a chance to show those qualities. She was told what to eat, what to say and what to do. Unfortunately, most of her life she was a china doll set up on a shelf."

Spaulding allowed Ann to borrow her own hippie-style clothes, and from time to time they went to local nightclubs such as the Painted Pony. Ann was delighted to go out incognito. "People there did not know that they were sitting with a very famous woman, and she never would have told them," Spaulding recalled. "They had fun with her, and she sang songs and told jokes. She'd leave happy and singing like crazy."

While the country was turning on, tuning in, and dropping out in 1968, Ann was enjoying her new-found freedom. She got a black poodle puppy named Charlie Brown, to replace Beau after his death, and took him everywhere she went. The Lower Deck was playing regularly at dances and teen clubs, and she closed the failing Target Nightclub. She was still considered a local celebrity, and occasionally performed her archery act at sports shows. She sang in nightclubs and judged local beauty pageants. She represented Van Heusen as a men's grooming consultant for a while, and did radio interviews and personal appearances at the better department stores in the Detroit area. She was asked to record a demo commercial for a local Cadillac dealership.

Ann counseled local teenagers who were mixed up with the wrong crowd or experimenting with drugs, and she tried to teach them responsibility by helping them open accounts at Wyandotte Savings Bank. In an interview she commented: "Kids just don't realize what drugs can do to them, it's terrible!"

Ann was confident that the rock band business was a good investment. She went to Gail & Rice Talent Agency in Detroit and convinced them to hire her. Owner Al Rice was initially skeptical about representing young bands, but he was fond of Ann and put her on the payroll. It was a good business decision for the agency, because at that time there were several hundred working bands in Michigan. "We had booked Ann in shows beginning when she was thirteen or fourteen as a variety act, and she was outstanding at an early age," Rice recalled. "She came to us later for a job. She had lots of vitality, and was the first person in the office to want to represent bands. We were mutually happy to have her there."

Working for Gail & Rice was a great opportunity for Ann, and she enjoyed the professional stability. She scouted for bands all over southern Michigan and signed several for her personal supervision, under Gail & Rice's well-known reputation. A company brochure described her as a valuable asset: "Ann Marston is a former World's Champion Archer, former Miss Michigan and now a recognized specialist in the pop music field. Ann has rapidly become one of our most successful rock and pop music agents."

In late February 1969, Ann performed her archery act at the *Truth or Consequences Show* that was televised from Cobo Hall in Detroit. A short time later she mentioned to her parents that her left eye felt like it was full of specks of dust. The following day, she went to her office at Gail & Rice in Detroit and experienced a sudden loss of vision. "I had driven to work that morning, but as I sat in the office, I could make out only vague shapes ... I had to ask my father to come and take me home."

Diabetics have the potential of suffering from a large number of health risks, including blindness, amputation, kidney disease, and stroke. They must constantly be on guard to prevent these devastating complications. Ann was fortunate to have been diagnosed early in life, when she was eleven or twelve years old. As a Type 1 or juvenile diabetic, Ann was dependent on insulin injections for the rest of her life to manage her glucose levels. Ann rarely let anyone besides her parents see her use the hypodermic needle, and most of the family's closest friends and business associates were not aware of her disease.

The fact that Ann was a powerful athlete all of her life convinced the Marstons that the diabetes was under control. She visited the doctor periodically to have her glucose level tested and gave herself an insulin shot every morning. Her mother encouraged her to eat good food, but Ann was not vigilant about maintaining a healthy diet. Throughout her life she suffered from frequent, severe colds, and was always concerned about weight gain. She experienced fatigue and exhaustion that sometimes required hospitalization. Her parents always felt that these weaknesses were caused by the stress of performing and the result of following a demanding tour schedule.

The prevailing medical theory at the time was that diabetics did not need to be overly concerned about the potentially horrible impacts of the disease. The disease was considered to be easily controlled with the prescribed use of insulin, a proper diet, and exercise. Florence took great care not to mention to news media that Ann was diabetic. It was a stigma that didn't fit Ann's image of a successful, athletic, healthy female. Her chronic eye problems were publicly attributed to the injuries incurred from the bull incident in 1962.

Her parents took her to a half-dozen different doctors and eye specialists in the next few months. The consensus was that Ann suffered from "light perception blindness." The condition was considered irreversible, and corrective eye surgery was not an option at that time. The doctors' collective prognosis was that she would be blind for the rest of her life.

Diabetic medical specialists identify the eye condition as retinopathy. It involves tiny blood vessels in the eye that supply blood to the retina, the part of the eye that senses light and delivers images to the brain. When a diabetic's blood is thickened because of high glucose levels, the vessels become blocked. The resulting pressure causes the body to create minuscule new vessels for the eye, but they are very weak and periodically rupture and leak blood. As scar tissue is formed at the site of the broken blood vessels, the retina is pulled out of place, causing vision distortion and blindness. After Ann's diagnosis, Florence shared the sad news with friends and relatives. A letter dated April 28, 1969, to her niece and nephew, described her despair:

> *Dear Carole and David,*
> *So nice to hear from you, and I am sorry I haven't been able to answer sooner. We've been so unhappy for this past 10 weeks and don't know how to face the sad future. Ann became blind 10 weeks ago, and we have had to revamp our entire lives. She has what is termed a "light blindness" and cannot see anything other than perhaps dark shadows approaching; no details at all.*
>
> *We have seen seven top specialists so far and she has to see a doctor every day for treatments, sometimes twice a day. I don't drive, so we take cabs or buses, otherwise it would be too costly for Frank to take time off. We have cried so much, unbeknownst to Ann. She is being wonderful and adjusting to life so well. She amazes us.*

The news of Ann's sight loss was publicly announced to the media on July 1. The story was quickly picked up by newspapers all over the country via the Associated Press. Ann was quoted as saying, "I won't get ready to be blind … I won't accept the fact that I'm blind." There was no mention of Ann's diabetes in the Associated Press release. Her condition was once again blamed on injuries inflicted during the dramatic bull incident in 1962. "Seven years ago Ann was performing at a rodeo in Fort Madison, Iowa, when a bull broke loose and trampled her, breaking three of her ribs. She thinks this might be when her spine was injured."

Ann described her sight limitation to Associated Press reporter Evelyn August, and optimistically joked about what would happen when she regained her sight.

> ... It's like a screen over my eyes. I can make out figures, sometimes I can see colors—red or turquoise—but that's about it. It's better when there's a lot of light. But it's just terrifying falling down curbs. People think I'm snubbing them when I don't say hello after they've nodded at me. Most people don't know about my eyes, that is. If you lose hope or the desire to get better, you never will get better. If you believe, it will happen.
>
> It's going to be hilarious, because all this time I've been getting just impressions of what people should look like, and so far everyone looks like Paul Newman to me.

After the public announcement of her affliction, friends and strangers rallied to her side. The telephone rang for three solid days after the news broke, and Ann almost lost her voice taking the calls. Mrs. Artelle Reed, Ann's Miss Michigan chaperone, sent a telegram. Her former New York agent, Max "Mickey" Nathan, sent a letter teasing her about her spending so many hours in doctors' offices just to get attention. Strangers left flower bouquets at the house. She heard from many people who recommended various vegetarian, vitamin, and herbal treatments. One person made the prophetic observation that lasers were being tested in the military, and he speculated that sometime in the future they might be useful for medical operations. A story in the *Wyandotte News Herald* quoted Ann's response to the outpouring of concern: "There are real good people around here."

She received a touching letter on official penitentiary stationery from an inmate at Michigan's state prison in Jackson:

> Dearest Ann,
>
> I have just read about your misfortune. It has really touched my heart very deeply, and I want to say this. Ann, I will gladly give you one of my eyes if there is not hope or another way for you to regain your sight back. Although I am a convict I want to do something good in my life for someone. I have never been bad or hurt anyone. I got in this trouble by helping someone, but not in the right way. Doing this for a lovely person as you—I know I would be happy about it ... I pray that if you do need someone, to please consider my offer that is from the bottom of my heart to you.

Once again Ann was in the news, and Florence Marston was on the job to promote her in the media, just like in the old days. She arranged for the *Detroit Free*

Press to do a story about Ann's hardship. The headline on July 8, 1969, stated, "Ex-beauty Queen's Sight Fails, but Her Hope Thrives." Ann described her condition in the story, saying she saw "the movement of objects and forms of people, but not their features. It's like having a screen of little grains of dust in front of my eyes." But with full faith in her doctor, she made the optimistic statement that, "Seven is lucky and the seventh doctor, a chiropractor, told me he can help. He's given me hope, mainly." She continued with a prediction: "I'm only on a vacation, though. I feel that everything is going to be all right. I'm just telling everyone to wait a minute, and I'll be right back."

Ann's misfortune made the front page of the *National Enquirer* in September 1969, with the headline, "Beauty Queen Refuses to Give Up Hope After 6 Doctors Say She's Going Blind:"

> Six eye specialists have told beauty queen Ann Marston she is going blind—but she isn't learning to read Braille or walk with a white cane. She is fighting the verdict, determined to retain her sight. "I am not going to become blind … If you have a faith, a belief, and a religion then a crisis, even one like this, shouldn't make so much difference. But it's groovy to get all the prayers that you can. And you've got to have faith in yourself, in God and in your doctor."

Dr. Clair W. O'Dell graduated in 1936 from Palmer College of Chiropractic and established his practice with the personal conviction "to get as many sick people well as soon as possible, at the least possible cost." Ann turned to O'Dell in the hopes that he could help restore a portion of her sight. He X-rayed her spine and found evidence of an injury, and attributed it to the accident at the rodeo in 1962. He was positive that he could improve her condition with intensive chiropractic treatment. He said, "I wanted to save her if it was the last thing I did on earth." Ann was convinced he could help her. She and her mother took a bus several times a week to O'Dell's office. Florence called O'Dell frequently for private consultations, almost to the point of being a pest, according to the doctor. After a few adjustments O'Dell claimed that Ann informed him, "I can tell you the color of your tie."

Ann said she was discouraged and depressed by most medical doctors when she was interviewed for an issue of the chiropractic trade journal titled, *Life and Health*. She was a convert to the benefits of chiropractic treatment and shared her new philosophy:

> The very fact that my chiropractor is very confident that his adjustments will improve everything and in time, heal the scar tissue, truly relieves

much of the tension, and certainly helps keep up my spirits. Depression is the worst ailment in the world. Many MDs are blunt; I know I have to face the truth, but it's the way they put it. On the other hand, the chiropractor puts my mind at ease. Not only am I in a better frame of mind, but I feel more relaxed, and am much better physically since going to the chiropractor. I had terrible headaches and great pain in my neck, but the pain is all gone now.

I would like to see doctors of every type—MDs, chiropractors, osteopaths, even witch doctors—to get together, share their knowledge and compare notes. All doctors should be more interested in helping suffering humanity rather than promoting private theories, professional jealousies, or seeking headlines for themselves. If an approach is not harmful, why not try it? Chiropractors and doctors should leave their private cliques and get together. Why, if all doctors would get together, they could cure all of man's physical diseases.

Florence was meticulous in her search for a cure and had acquired newspaper clippings and a brochure regarding a faith healer near London, England. This man claimed to possess the ability to cure seeing-impaired diabetics. Florence asked Victor Marston, her brother-in-law who lived in the area, to investigate. Victor said:

Florrie had heard that there was a séance man in this country who was a bus driver in Golder's Green, a suburb of London. She had pamphlets regarding this man's claim to heal people. He claimed that he could [cure] people who were suffering from extreme forms of diabetes and who were going blind. She asked if I would see if he existed. I did go to his house; his séances were held there in an outbuilding, but I didn't see him. Florrie would have brought Ann over if there was a chance it would work. I told her about him, but she never did any more about it.

Ann had overwhelming personal challenges to conquer. In spite of her optimism, she was once again dependent on her parents. She required assistance in menial daily tasks such as picking out clothes to wear. She couldn't drive or see well enough to dial the telephone, pour a cup of coffee, or watch TV. Reading music was impossible, so she learned to play the piano by ear. Basic mobility required intense concentration, and she had to be cautious when walking around the house to avoid running into the door jambs and furniture. Her apartment in the basement was dark, and the stairs were steep. She was forced to move slowly, and it took patience to make her way around the surroundings that she used to know so well. She told a *Free Press* reporter that, "I miss driving my car, but even more than that I miss putting on my false eyelashes. Try as hard as I could, there was just no way I could get them on."

Since Ann's continued health depended on proper nutrition, Florence prepared her meals based on the strict recommended diabetic guidelines. Unfortunately, Ann was quickly gaining weight because of the forced inactivity, and her high blood pressure was becoming a very serious concern. She occasionally suffered severe headaches that were most likely caused by eye strain.

At home on 17th Street, some of the neighbors helped Ann by transcribing written messages into large print that she could distinguish. A Roosevelt High School student named Karen Stewart came over frequently to help Ann with correspondence, to read to her, and take her to doctor appointments. Florence said Karen was "sent from heaven."

Even though she was forced to hang up her bow, Ann found ways to continue a somewhat normal life. She missed working on her flower garden and the yard, so she pulled out the lawnmower and cut the grass, sensing the difference in the level of the turf that needed to be cut. She and Charlie Brown took walks, even though her concerned mother felt he was definitely not a qualified Leader Dog. Ann listened to her large collection of reel-to-reel tapes in her spare time, and labeled them according to their content. She kept as busy as possible and imitated Helen Keller's point of view when Keller said, "Keep your face to the sunshine and you cannot see the shadow."

Ann was determined to maintain a fundamental level of independence and continued working at Gail & Rice, managing and booking her bands. She was driven to the office an average of once a week and had a second telephone line installed at home. She wrote notes on contrasting white sheets of paper by using a very bright desk light and a big marker, making the characters three-fourths of an inch high so she could read them. Unfortunately, she could no longer write in her journals. She wore thick but stylish glasses and stuck tape to the keys of her typewriter to help direct her fingers onto the correct rows while typing. She folded currency in specific ways to distinguish the bill denominations. She still responded to requests for public appearances and rode in the River Rouge Heritage Days parade. She described some of the changes in her life in a typed letter to a friend:

> *Dear Fran,*
> *It was so nice to receive a letter from you … It's been really a wonderful feeling to know that so many old and new friends are praying and pulling for me. I hope you'll forgive my delay in writing, but I wanted to write personally and I have to wait for the sunny days so I can do it in the sunlight.*

At the present I am still working with a talent agent booking rock and roll bands for schools and colleges. I love it. It's hard to get around because I can't drive, but I have a lot of people watching out for me, especially my folks.

Drivers were hired to take Ann to doctor appointments and to the dances and clubs to monitor her bands. Wyandotte native Jim Skolasinski was one of her chauffeurs. He was referred by a mutual musician friend, and earned about $15 a night driving her around in the Plymouth Fury. Florence often packed a light snack for Ann and Jim to take with them. After making the rounds for the evening, they returned to Ann's house and her father would drive Jim home. After a while they trusted Jim to take the car overnight if he was going to be escorting Ann the next day. "When I took the car home, I was supposed to park it and leave it there. One time her dad called me and said that he had driven by my parents' house and the car wasn't there. I had taken it to get it washed." Jim liked working with Ann, and was very impressed with her professionalism:

When I picked her up she had a big pile of contracts and paperwork. I was surprised at how many stops we would make in a night. It was amazing how often she booked groups.

I was young, only 17, and didn't know where I was going. I was impressed that she could give me driving directions to everywhere we went. I thought, "This woman can't even see and she knows her way around." She must have gotten around a lot when she had her eyesight. We would go places, and she knew a lot of people, and they would come up to her to talk.

She often got frustrated about not being able to see. She held my arm when walking up stairs, and I'd have to tell her "Ann, there's two steps." Sometimes she would get bitchy with the frustration of not being able to do the things she wanted to do, or if something didn't go the way she thought it should have been with the bands. Overall, she had a pretty good outlook.

According to a newspaper report, Ann faced unique challenges with the boys in the bands. The article stated, "One problem she encountered was getting a long-haired band member to cut his shaggy locks. 'I asked him if he cut his hair, and he said yes, but I found out later he hadn't. I just couldn't see him.'"

Ann fiercely protected the reputation of her groups. There was an unpleasant incident after a high school dance featuring one of her bands named Julia. The principal was told that someone affiliated with the band [Ann] was intoxicated. Ann got on the telephone and spoke authoritatively to him. She tape recorded part of the conversation.

> *This is Ann Marston, and I would like to speak to you in regards to what happened Friday night. I'm very distressed about the whole situation. I don't know if you know who I am, but I have a rather a good reputation. I was nominated as outstanding Sportswomen of the Year by the United Foundation in view of my accomplishments in the past. I was 11 times archery champion and am a former Miss Michigan. About two years ago, I lost my eyesight, and am now legally blind.*
>
> *These two groups that I manage and represent also have good reputations. Some gossip went on amongst teachers [at the dance] that has jeopardized our reputations, and I think it definitely should be straightened out.*
>
> *On Friday night I went up to the teacher's lounge and spoke to three teachers in the room. Apparently someone assumed that I had been drinking. I know that eventually someone was bound to say that "she looks a little drunk," because I'm sure I do at times. I don't carry a white cane, because people sympathize with you when you carry a white cane. So I have a friend that goes with me, a driver. I do stumble and I am terrified of stairs.*
>
> *… It's too bad that it should reflect on the group. These boys have done so much. They raised $600 last year for the mentally retarded home in Plymouth. None of them even smoke cigarettes, let alone take dope, and they come from very fine families. I'm very disturbed; because the first thing people say these days with long-haired musicians is that they drink or are on dope.*
>
> *I can't afford it with my reputation, and it only takes one school to get bad information all over the city. I deal with these young people, and I am a very strong disciplinarian when it comes to my groups. They are always on time and they do respect me, and I don't stand for any nonsense.*

According to the tape recording, the principal was nearly begging for forgiveness by the time Ann finished talking to him. He apologized for the teachers' ignorance, promised to stop the gossip, and assured her that all of her musical groups were welcome to play at his school.

She nurtured several bands when she was with Gail & Rice, including The Daybreak and a girl group called Penelope, but she placed her special attention on two groups, Tea and Julia. Based in Rochester, Michigan, Tea featured Phil Nye on guitar, Egg Ralbovski on bass, Bill Doral played drums, Jerry Zubal played lead guitar, Don Lucking was on keyboards, and Rick James was lead vocalist. Zubal taught at Music City. Nye joined the group after leaving the Army and had a background in folk singing. Lucking's background included fourteen years of classical piano training.

Tea was versatile and claimed that 75 percent of the songs in their set list were original, including "Wesley," with a religious message, boogie-woogie inspired "Toronto," and a power rock tune called "Rock Band." Along with these originals, they played "Rock and Roll Woman," "New York City Blues," and "Light My Fire." Ann booked them into the most prestigious venues in the area including the Eastown Theater, the Grande Ballroom, and the Roostertail, as well as on Mackinac Island, and at the Kentucky State Fair.

The *Detroit Free Press* did a story on Ann's management of Tea and Julia, but didn't even mention the band members by name. The focus of the article was her past history as archer and beauty queen, her career as a talent agent, and what she had been doing since stricken with blindness. *News Herald* reporter Meg Bremer predicted a miracle for Ann in an article dated October 14, 1970:

> *This is a week of tremendous hope for Ann Marston, Wyandotte's famed world archery champion and former Miss Michigan. Tomorrow or the next day, she may return from New York City wearing glasses ... and seeing for the first time in 21 months. That was the hope not admitted, yet was secretly held in her heart when she and her mother boarded a plane for the nation's largest city.*
>
> *For many months, Ann and her parents have searched worldwide for some eye specialist who might be able to give her vision—even a little bit. Her gradually worsening vision has brought letters, phone calls, cards and tips from around the globe ... for Ann gained worldwide recognition in her late Roosevelt High School and post-graduation days for her prowess with the bow and arrow.*
>
> *... Just as she overcame many trials to gain the world archery title, Ann has had the same dogged determination to carry her successfully through this blindness stage. She's still active ... booking rock groups and helping them to plan their shows and to arrange their music.*
> *It took learning to play the piano again and learning to play by ear instead of sight to do what she's doing today. It took adhesive tape on certain typewriter keys to gradually learn to type. It can be done. Ann did it.*
>
> *She has seen many eye specialists and found little hope to see again. Yet hope springs eternal ... is that what was said? So Ann went to New*

York to a specialist recommend by many people. If help is there for Ann, she'll be home tomorrow or Friday with glasses.

Optometrists William Feinbloom and Arthur Jankolovits had an office on East 36th Street in New York City. After an intense eye examination, Ann was fitted with two pairs of special "goggle" glasses equipped with miniature binoculars. The theory was that she could wear them for various periods of time to exercise her strongest eye.

Ann wore her "bottle-bottom glasses" when she wrote a message in black ink on stationery from New York's Hotel Wellington. "Would you believe I can see what I am writing. Now I wish I could use the telephone. Yours truly, Ann Penelope Marston." Another note in Ann's handwriting announced: "Dear People, I am now able to write a letter with my new glasses. Unfortunately in the time that has elapsed since I could last see what I was writing, my penmanship has not improved in the slightest. However, what a wonderful experience it is to be able to see this much. Miss Ann Penelope Marston."

A week later, Meg Bremer proclaimed the good news to the citizens of Wyandotte in the *News Herald* on October 21, 1970. Once again, Ann's vision loss was attributed to the injury inflicted by the bull eight years earlier. There was no mention of her diabetic condition:

There ought to be a rock group named "On Cloud 9." It should be a group that Ann Marston organized and books around the area, the state and the nation. Why? Because "On Cloud 9" is just the way blonde, attractive Ann Marston of Wyandotte is today. She CAN see!

It's not the complete vision as she had before Feb. 21, 1969, but for the first time in 21 months she has hope that in 3 months she'll see more than now; in 6 months maybe her vision will be even more improved. "And maybe in a year," said the New York eye specialist last week, "maybe we'll have you driving a car again." That's the optimism the New York doctors gave Ann last Thursday. At the moment, she didn't really have the confidence that it was true. But when Ann returned to her New York hotel room, switched on the TV screen [and could see the picture] ... then [her mother and Ann] were so excited they wanted to tell the whole world.

In 1969, the Starlight Archery North club hosted the first Ann Marston Benefit Shoot, and continued the tournament in 1970, with all proceeds going to the Ann Marston Trust Fund. Starlight representative Marilyn Nicholas wrote "... she was almost completely blind. However, she sat from the first line until the last—for two days—'watching' the archers shoot in her honor. Tiring as it was, she looked every bit the queen and personally handed out the awards."

Ann appreciated the tribute, but archery was a part of her past. She was now very successful in the band business, and continued to manage Tea and Julia. Gail & Rice booked one of her bands for the company holiday party. Her parents were invited, too, and she brought along her recorder and taped some of the songs the group played. A comment was picked up by the microphone when Ann asked her mother, "Are there a lot of people dancing?"

The Detroit music scene was evolving again. The Goose Lake International Music Festival of August 1970 starring Jethro Tull, Chicago, and Rod Stewart was so over-attended that it turned into a disaster. Detroit groups such as The Bob Seger System, SRC, the Stooges, and MC5 also rocked in Jackson, Michigan, in front of 200,000 mostly doped-up fans.

The MC5 recorded their third album, "High Time," and toured Europe, but the band members were slowly self-destructing because of drug addiction, arrests, and stresses between the guys in the group. Ann's friend from Wyandotte, Tom Beaudry-Kelly Green, hit it big with his band Frijid Pink. Their rendition of "House of the Rising Sun" made it to the Top 10 in the national charts, and was a big hit in Europe. Meanwhile, Vincent Furnier moved back to Detroit, and as Alice Cooper, he taught the Motor City about shock rock. Ann's personal record collection included albums from Jimi Hendrix, Vanilla Fudge, Cream, and "Magical Mystery Tour" by The Beatles.

Ann worked as an occasional radio correspondent, and interviewed Bob Seger on WABX's *Rock and Roll News* show that was hosted by Harvey Ovshinsky in early 1971. On the air, Seger told Ann why he broke up his group, the Bob Seger System, and planned to record a solo album. "I kinda gave up on the group, and now I want to do it as a single," he said. "We've been performing as group for eight years. I'm going to continue to do exactly as I'm doing, but I'm not going to per-form until I'm ready. I just feel it's time that I sat down to read, write, create, and take my time doing it." Later that year he recorded an album called "Brand New Morning," a collection of acoustic songs for Capitol Records.

Ann found the Pagens at a dance in Southgate. The group was headed by song-writer/guitarist Bill Mueller. Ann approached them for representation and they ul-timately changed their name to Julia. The band included Mike Klein, Cal Hughes, Randy Meyers, and Tim McCoy. Mueller is still actively recording in Nashville under the name Blue Miller. He fondly remembers his friendship with Ann:

> ... We didn't have a manager at the time and didn't really know what that all meant. But she was very persuasive with way she carried herself

and the way she talked. It sounded that she could take us to another level. She knew how to handle us. It was the first time I had ever met someone who was as serious about my career as I was. She made a lot of sense in her ideas of management; taking pictures, projecting our image, and telling us what she would and wouldn't let us do. She was great. We spoke on the phone every day; she was big part of my life back then.

... She didn't talk much about her archery career; it was just in her past. Music was her second love, and she was smart enough to realize that she wasn't a great singer. But she did have business talent from her many years of show business.

We got many bookings for jobs around Detroit through her and the other Gail & Rice agents. The only time we got fired was when someone [other than Ann] booked us for a ball at the Church of the Latter Day Saints. We were a rock and roll band, and it was just a wrong call. In the first set we played "Season of the Witch." After the set an old guy came up politely and gave us our money, and he said that they just wanted us to pack up and go away.

Under Ann's direction, Julia began playing most of the hot spots in the area including the Factorie Ballroom, appearing with Tea in August. They played the Chicago Underground with a new band called Detroit, fronted by Mitch Ryder, and a gig with Plain Brown Wrapper at Wampler's Lake Pavilion. She booked them into the Birmingham Palladium, opening for Humble Pie on December 18, 1970. It appeared that Ann was backing another promising musical group. Ann's impaired vision seemed to be a minor inconvenience, and the boys respected her judgment. But Miller and the members of Julia were protective of Ann once they recognized her more serious health limitations:

Ann could see shadows but was considered legally blind. She sometimes came along on our gigs. She had a driver, but other than that she was pretty independent. When we were around her longer we realized that she was diabetic. She would always have to eat an apple or some food to keep her blood sugar regulated. We also knew that she couldn't get her blood pressure up.

9

THE ARROW IS BROKEN

ANN WAS WITH JULIA IN EARLY MARCH 1971, as the band auditioned for club owner Punch Andrews, who also managed Bob Seger. He was considering producing Julia through his recording company. Julia's guitarist, Bill Mueller, who now goes by the name Blue Miller, remembered the events of that evening:

> … She had arranged with Punch to produce us, and he wanted us to come down to the Birmingham Palladium on a night that it was closed. So we went there and set up and played the songs that I had written, so he could decide which ones we might record. Ann was there, and she and Punch listened to what we played. They discussed the material between the two of them; picking out songs that Punch thought may be the hits that he might want to invest in us recording.
>
> That night, after we left, she apparently got in a very heated argument with one of the other bands, and she wasn't supposed to get her blood pressure up. I'm just piecing it together from things I heard, because I wasn't there. But the next day, she had a stroke.

Tuesday morning, March 3, Ann said goodbye to her father as he went to work. Later that day Florence heard the dog, Charlie Brown, whining in the basement.

When she investigated the noise, she found Ann collapsed on the floor. Florence ran out for one of the neighbors and frantically contacted Frank at work. Ann was rushed by ambulance to the intensive care unit of Henry Ford Hospital in Detroit. She arrived in a coma, and the doctors soon determined that Ann had suffered a massive stroke. The next day *The Detroit News* quoted Frank as saying, "The doctors don't give her much of a chance. She suffered from a massive hemorrhage, a stroke, which has left her unconscious … My wife and I have been spending most of the hours in a nearby room at the hospital, but the doctors said they've done everything possible; that it's just a matter of time."

Florence later said: "I was holding her hand and praying that God would grant another miracle for Ann." But there were no more miracles for Ann Marston. She died three days later, at 9:05 a.m. on Saturday, March 6, 1971, at the age of thirty-two. Her parents were at her side when doctors removed life support.

In the days following Ann's death, Florence made many heartbreaking telephone calls to their friends across the country, including Emmett Kelly Jr., the Pearsons, the Eastons, and Fred and Henrietta Bear. They had difficulty notifying relatives in England about the tragedy because of a six-week-long British postal strike. At the same time, there was a labor dispute and walkout by overseas telephone operators. It was more than a week before the sad news was passed on abroad.

The day after the members of Julia heard about Ann's death, they visited the Marston home. Guitarist Blue Miller always liked and respected her parents. All of the boys were shocked about the bad news and were genuinely concerned for Frank and Florence. Miller said:

> *I remember that day; it was crazy. We heard about her death and went to the house. Mr. and Mrs. Marston were so distraught they didn't want us to come into the house. In fact, [her father] was very abrupt, and I started walking away. He then followed me into the driveway and apologized. You could just see that it was tearing them up. They were beside themselves. And our world just came to a stop.*

Wyandotte's R.J. Nixon Funeral Home director, Donald R. Burd, met with the Marstons and personally handled the visitation and burial arrangements. Nixon's was one of the largest facilities in the Downriver area. Even so, the logistics of hosting such a large event were definitely a challenge to Burd and his staff. "She was such a popular young woman. The amount of visitors was fantastic; you could have had Cobo Hall and it would have been filled with friends."

Ann wore a lace gown and lay in a white casket with the lid open. She was surrounded by dozens of floral arrangements. Florence managed to graciously welcome the mourners and make sure that all details went according to her very specific standards. Frank stood by with his usual stoic demeanor and listened to friends who shared stories of Ann's life.

Condolences arrived from many celebrities, including Ted Williams. Joe DiMaggio sent a single orchid in an elegant green glass vase. A newspaper later reported that the family received a sympathy call from Johnny Carson. At some point during the three-day visitation period the film, *Bow Jests* was played at the funeral home. Some of Ann's friends thought it was too theatrical and did not approve. Others were quite moved by the homage, and felt it was totally appropriate. She was laid to rest at Michigan Memorial Park. One of Wyandotte's lifelong residents observed, "Ann was more famous than we realized."

Local headlines pronounced the bad news. "Massive Stroke Fells Former Miss Michigan. Downriver's symbol of beauty and courage died Saturday following a stroke. Ann Marston, former Miss Michigan and perennial archery champion, succumbed in Henry Ford Hospital after suffering a massive stroke Tuesday." After the United Press International service picked up the item, Ann's obituary ran in many papers including the *St. Petersburg Times* and the *Orlando Sentinel* in Florida, and in the show business trade journals *Variety* and *Billboard*. The fact that Ann suffered from diabetes most of her life was finally mentioned prominently.

Dr. Fred W. Whitehouse, doctor of metabolic diseases at Detroit's Henry Ford Hospital, sent a letter dated March 10, 1971, to Frank and Florence Marston.

> *Dear Friends,*
>
> *Your steadfastness and loyalty during Ann's last illness was marvelous to behold, even though much of the time Ann was not physically aware of your presence. It made a great deal of difference to everyone that your feelings for Ann were so deep and so true.*
>
> *All of us, of course, sincerely regret that there was nothing that we could do to help Ann survive this terrible onslaught. We do appreciate the support that you gave all of us during Ann's last four days, and especially since it required a considerable amount of understanding on your part in order to help Ann the best way we knew how. We appreciate the permission for the post-mortem examination.*
>
> *The preliminary findings include a massive cerebral hemorrhage involving the right side of the brain, with destruction of that area and pressure destruction of the other parts of the brain. In addition, there was severe scarring in the back of the eyes, related to diabetic retinopathy. There was no evidence of heart attacks. Some congestion in the bases of the lungs. Some scarring of the kidneys tied in with the diabetes.*

*When I receive more complete reports on Ann's post-mortem exami-
nations, I will be in touch with you again. This may be weeks away. If
there is anything I can do to help you, or any questions that either of you
have, please let me know. I do sincerely regret that we could do so little for
her. She was a wonderful girl, and you will be richer than most because of
the memories you have of her.*

That summer Florence arranged a memorial service for Ann, although she was
still distraught over her daughter's sudden death. She invited friends, relatives, and
dignitaries. Senator Ted Kennedy personally sent his regrets on being unable to attend. On a beautiful day in September, more than 100 people came together again at
Michigan Memorial Park to pay homage to Ann Marston. Family friend, Congressman John Dingell, dedicated a cenotaph, or commemorative plaque, and said, "When
we honor her today, we honor an example of courage in the face of adversity."

The large brass plaque was placed on the outside wall of the facility's mausoleum building near Ann's crypt and has the following inscription:

Dedicated to the Memory of
Ann Marston
Miss America Talent Award, National Archery Champion, Miss Michigan
August 7, 1938   *March 6, 1971*

*Ann Marston was a graduate of Roosevelt High School, Wyandotte,
Michigan. She was a member of the National Honor Society, Thespians,
Quill and Scroll.*

*Ann won her first target archery title at age 9 in her native England.
She came to the U.S.A. in 1949, and captured her cadet target archery
title one week later. Ann continued winning and breaking all time records
to 1953.*

*In 1954 at age fifteen, three years ahead of time, she elected to shoot
in the adult division at the National field tournament and won. In winning
her first senior title she established three new records, and set the stage for
her 1955 and 1957 victories. In all, Ann won eleven national archery titles
establishing all time records.*

*Ann's archery talent in Miss America 1960 was the first time that
a sport had ever won this honor. Ann is the youngest to be elected to
the Willie Heston Sports Hall of Fame, and the second woman. Ann was
named the Outstanding Sportswoman of 1970, for exemplifying the
ideals of sportsmanship.*

"You can become a champ at anything you want if you try hard enough, but you have to lose to prove you're a good sport." A winner never has this opportunity."
Ann Marston
And I will cast thee out, and thy mother that bare thee, into another country where ye were not born; and there shall ye die.

The crowd of distinguished guests was comprised of the area's politicians and community leaders, together with former Michigan Governor and Supreme Court Justice G. Mennen Williams. Also in attendance were Michigan Senator John E. McCauley and State Representative William Copeland, county commissioners and mayors representing ten local communities. The State of Michigan issued House Resolution No. 56, a memorial tribute to Ann and expression of deep sympathy for her parents.

The master of ceremonies for the service was WWJ-AM's Public Affairs Manager Paul Williams. Musical homage was provided by acclaimed classical violinist Gennaro D'Alessio, who studied in Italy and had recently moved to the Detroit area. Speakers at the eulogy included Michigan sports media figures Mort Neff, Jerry Chiappetta, and Budd Lynch. Karl Palmatier spoke on behalf of the Professional Archer's Association. Representatives from the Miss Michigan Organization, Eastern Star, the Masonic Lodge, and the Lions Club paid their respects. Michigan's own Miss America 1970, Pamela Eldred, attended. "She was a great person," Eldred said in an interview. "She taught me to be satisfied with the job I had. That's the most important advice you can give anybody."

Letters and phone calls were directed to Ann's parents for months after the funeral. The local public library accepted books donated in her name. Archery associates from the old days reminisced and sent photographs of young Ann at tournaments. World archery champion, professional archer, and Archery Hall of Fame member Ann Clark said, "She was a beautiful young lady who did much to expose the sport. It was her example that I followed in my early years in archery. I was about to go onstage in Cleveland, Ohio, when I was informed of her death. It was a very traumatic experience for me as I climbed to the top of the coliseum to make my long shot. She was on my mind as I accomplished this feat."

Writer and talent agent Buddy Basch had been affiliated with Ann and her family since the mid-1950s. He made a contribution to a research foundation in Ann's name and wrote Frank and Florence to convey his sentiments:

... I don't have to tell you how much I thought of Ann; I loved her the moment I met her, just as everyone else did. The world was a better place

145

for her having been here, and a lot worse for her leaving. She was the kind of person it was a privilege to know.

I was saddened when I saw her recently, not because of the blindness, but because she seemed to be <u>trying</u> to be cheerful. Somehow, a bit of that spark we all knew had been snuffed out. I hope she didn't sense that I realized it. She will always be loved and remembered by all who knew her. Isn't that the true test of a person's worth? I think so.

Without Ann's strong leadership, Julia was adrift. It was fortunate that Ann had introduced them to Punch Andrews. He assisted them with their bookings and ultimately helped Blue Miller launch his own career by employing him to play guitar and sing backup on two of Bob Seger's albums. Miller was profoundly affected by the loss of Ann's management and friendship:

After she passed away, Punch inherited us and took over management. He picked up where she left off. She had got him to where he was pretty committed to the band, and she had us working steady and making our own money; making our way.

… I know that she was our manager, but somehow she seemed much more than that. She had taken an interest in everything we did. She was my personal mentor, as well. The band was my entire world, and she was at the head of it for a long time.

Florence seemed to be lost, because she lived her life for Ann. I don't think she ever got over it. Frank was the quiet one and didn't say much about it. After I moved away, I would come visit my family in Detroit and pop over there to surprise them. For years they didn't touch a thing downstairs. It was exactly the way Ann left it.

When friends and family came to the Marston home after Ann died, Florence customarily asked if they would like to visit the shrine that was Ann's room. The clothes were still in the dresser and her personal possessions were undisturbed, as if she might come back at any time. Visitors were reverently cautioned not to touch anything without permission. Florence was frequently in complete denial about her daughter's death, and sometimes spoke as if Ann was merely in another room of the house. If she misplaced her glasses, she might say, "Oh, Ann will find them for me later."

Although Frank typically didn't speak often about Ann, Florence occasionally demonstrated her bitterness and personal heartache. Neighbor Mae Davidson was chatting over the fence with Florence one day. Davidson was describing a church event that her children recently attended. Florence responded, "Don't talk to me about your children. I had only one child and God took her away from me. You have five children—why didn't He take one of yours?"

Florence and Frank grieved more than ever at holidays and special occasions. They often visited the mausoleum at Michigan Memorial Cemetery and made arrangements with Nixon's Funeral Home to be laid to rest with Ann. In the years following Ann's death, the Marstons became increasingly reclusive and isolated. Windows in the house were covered over with plastic panels resembling stained glass to provide more privacy. Florence never received her driving license, so Frank took care of the grocery shopping and the household details that Ann used to look after.

In 1973, the Lincoln Bowman archery club partnered with the city of Wyandotte to host the first annual Ann Marston Memorial Archery Tournament. The steering committee was chaired by Wyandotte City Councilman Clifford (Skip) Clack and consisted of city official Sam Palamara, Recreation Director Harold Popp, and archers Marvin Long, Gaye Kaufman and his son, Gerry. Honorary members of the board were Frank and Florence Marston. The contest was sanctioned by the Professional Archer's Association (PAA) and consisted of several professional and amateur divisions, including the Junior Olympic National Championships.

Wyandotte's impressive Yack Arena was reserved for the contest, and invitation letters and entry forms were sent to archery clubs across the nation. Arrangements were made for *Bow Jests* and *My Dog Sheppy* to be shown the week of the tournament at the Wyandotte Theater. There was an extensive display of Ann's awards, trophies, and photographs in the showcases on the mezzanine of City Hall, honoring Ann's memory.

Prize money of $3,500 was allotted to the PAA contest, and more than 150 archers responded. Printed commemorative programs included an extensive biography and photographs of Ann. A single perfect rose was placed on the judge's table to symbolize her presence.

An estimated 2,000 spectators witnessed the contest and browsed through the vendor and demonstration areas. The two-day event was deemed a success, and plans were put in motion to expand the following year.

By 1975, the Ann Marston Memorial Archery Tournament was a premier event for archers, with prize money totaling $5,000 for the PAA events. Registrations poured in, with more than 300 archery participants from across the United States slated to compete. Fred Bear Archery and other companies put up money for corporate sponsorships, placed ads in the program, and hosted vendor booths to boost revenues. That year the competition took in $7,805.00 while expenses were $7,367.52, so at least the venture was in the black. The economy in the Downriver area benefited by the high volume of visitors patronizing restaurants, theaters, and hotels.

To commemorate the nation's bicentennial in 1976, the tournament committee authorized the production of bronze medallions embossed with Ann's likeness that were awarded to each participant. Gay and Gerry Kaufman of Wyandotte Leather underwrote the expense of the dies required for the casting. Darrell Pace competed that year in the Marston shoot, and he went on to win the gold medal for archery in the 1976 Olympics.

On August 7, 1977, the date that would have been Ann's thirty-ninth birthday, the city of Wyandotte proclaimed an Ann Marston Day. "The City of Wyandotte will continue to host the annual Ann Marston Memorial Archery Tournament in her memory as a tribute to her outstanding level of excellence in pursuit of her goals; that all young Americans should strive to duplicate."

Frank and Florence made sure that they were available to present the awards in Ann's name at every tournament. Eventually an auction was incorporated into the event, and posters advertised that the proceeds benefited the Juvenile Diabetes Foundation.

On May 25, 1977, the 23rd Annual Michigan Sports Hall of Fame induction was held at Detroit's Cobo Hall. Ann was the third woman and the youngest member to be inducted. Included in the class were Detroit Pistons player Dave DeBusschere, Red Wing hockey player and manager Alex Delvecchio, and former United States President Gerald A. Ford, who was a University of Michigan football player during his college days. Detroit public school coach Sam Bishop was posthumously inducted. After Detroit Mayor Coleman A. Young welcomed the guests, Ann's old friend from the WKNR days, WXYZ's Dick Purtan, made the presentation on her behalf. Purtan listed her lifetime achievements and mentioned the Memorial Archery Tournament, while projectors flashed photographs of Ann on three screens situated around the Riverview Ballroom at Cobo. Purtan introduced her parents, and Florence graciously thanked the committee and the news media for continuing to be friends to Ann. The Marstons were presented with a copy of the plaque and had a photograph taken with Ann's official portrait. After the ceremony, President Ford signed Frank's program as a souvenir. Bronze plaques and portraits of Ann and the other honorees are on display at Cobo Hall.

These occasional social events kept Frank and Florence going in their later years. After Ann's induction, they were eligible to vote on her behalf for candidates for the Michigan Sports Hall of Fame and usually were present at the annual banquet.

In August 1978, Ann was inducted into the Archery Hall of Fame at Miami University in Oxford, Ohio, during the PAA national championships. At that time, the Hall of Fame was housed at the Fred Bear Museum in Grayling, Michigan. With Frank and Florence in attendance, Ann posthumously joined the ranks of twenty-five past inductees including Fred Bear, Karl Palmatier, Ben Pearson, Saxon Pope, and Earl

Hoyt. The criteria for eligibility was that an honoree must have competed as a shooter for at least ten years on a world or national level, been a contributor to the sport, and had an outstanding influence on the sport, with a minimum involvement of at least twenty years. The Archery Hall of Fame has since moved to Angola, Indiana.

Florence was very willing to talk about Ann wherever she went. Sometimes friends and acquaintances avoided her in public if there wasn't the time to have an extended discussion. *Wyandotte News Herald* reporter Karl Ziomek inherited a thick media file on Ann when he took over as sports writer for the paper in 1980. After reading about her, Ziomek took a chance and made a telephone call to the Marston home. Florence was delighted to be interviewed, and he prepared a retrospective homage to Ann that was published in the *News Herald* on March 25, 1981. Florence revived the dramatic old PR myths and shared them with Ziomek for the extensive article. As was the case with other journalists who interviewed Florence in the past thirty-plus years, he had no idea how much she embellished Ann's life story. She re-wove the old myth of being bombed out of several homes in London during World War II. She beamed with pride telling him how Ann was on the covers of both *Sports Illustrated* and *Life* magazines, when she was never a cover girl for *Life*. Florence was quoted in the article as saying: "Due to a reason that was never clear, she [Ann] lost her eyesight in 1969."

Ann's legend continued to grow, and there were many tributes to her in the years following her death. In December 1986, Ann was one of the first seven members inducted into the new Wyandotte Sports Hall of Fame, housed in the city's Yack Arena.

Florence donated many of Ann's archery costumes and ball gowns for a temporary display at the facility. The Michigan Historical Museum in Lansing hosted a "Michigan Dresses Up" exhibit in 1989 that included outfits from musicians Stevie Wonder and Aretha Franklin, and featured one of Ann Marston's special occasion dresses.

Ann was posthumously inducted into Wyandotte Theodore Roosevelt High School's legion of Distinguished Graduates in March 2003. Ann's cover photo from *Sports Illustrated* magazine is now displayed on the school's Wall of Fame. She continues to inspire people to achieve the best of their ability, and to find strength beyond adversity.

Epilogue

LTHOUGH THEY WERE BOTH INTO THEIR EIGHTIES, Frank took care of Florence himself as she became increasingly ill and used a walker. Family members offered to help out, but he refused. The couple lived on Frank's modest plumber's pension and their Social Security allotments. Florence kept several thousand dollars hidden in her sewing box that she referred to as "Ann's money." The house gradually fell into decline, and they did not have the funds or the physical ability to repair it. All of Ann's possessions were still in the home. Frank sometimes told his relatives privately, "I wish we could donate some of this stuff to a museum." They occasionally gave a bow or a quiver to a close friend, but for the most part, Florence would not part with anything that belonged to Ann.

Frank suffered from digestive trouble and began to experience small strokes. He was placed in a local health care facility in late 2001. A few months later, Florence was reluctantly admitted as well. She had severe arthritis and the beginning signs of Alzheimer's disease. Frank fell out of bed at the nursing home, broke a hip, and never recovered. He died of a stroke on March 2, 2002, at age ninety. Florence was too ill to attend the funeral. Only a handful of friends and relatives came to the service.

Because of dementia, Florence virtually lived in the past, though Ann had been gone for thirty-two years. On January 17, 2003, ten months after Frank's death, Florence Marston died of heart failure. She was ninety-three. Florence joined Frank and Ann in the crypt at the mausoleum, and the Marston family was together again.

After Florence's funeral, her closest relative, Pamela Wood of Fort Wayne, Indiana, was charged with the responsibility of disposing of the Marston estate. The little house on 17th Street was overflowing, and it was a daunting task. Besides Frank's and Florence's personal effects, she had to sort through all of Ann's old things. The upper storage room and Ann's basement bedroom were filled with dozens of archery outfits, dresses, and nearly one hundred pairs of shoes. Boxes were crammed full of costume jewelry, souvenirs, and yards of sewing material and notions.

Ann's prop chest was intact with the equipment used in the act. Several folding cardboard displays plastered with photos were tucked under the eaves of the room. Florence had made these exhibits of Ann's life and career for the memorial archery tournaments. One of these 40" by 60" panels was covered with articles and pictures from the Miss America Pageant. Another was loaded with medals that Ann earned in archery tournaments over the years. There were several boards that had photos of Ann posing with celebrities, and one was dedicated to her career as a child model.

A few photo albums were neatly organized and labeled. There were many boxes filled with literally hundreds of publicity pictures, posters, and newspapers clippings detailing Ann's accomplishments. The most important treasures that remained were films and home movies, reel-to-reel audio tapes, and Ann's personal diaries.

Many items were removed from the home during Frank and Florence's extended illnesses. They include Ann's Miss Michigan crown and scepter, trophies, gowns, and the Ogalala Native American headdress. The baseballs signed by Joe DiMaggio and four books filled with cards, telegrams, and signatures of the mourners at Ann's funeral were missing. It is unlikely the Marstons would have given away those precious objects, but most of the valuables have not yet been returned to the family.

After spending weeks sorting through the property, Wood bequeathed most of Ann's gowns, jewelry, costumes, and related memorabilia to the Wyandotte Historical Society, which cataloged the collection and arranged an exhibit in spring 2003. Selected archery equipment was sent to the Archery Hall of Fame, and school items were donated to Roosevelt High School's Historical Archive Project. Photographs and other family artifacts were sent to relatives in England, Scotland, and Canada.

Karl Ziomek, the *Wyandotte News Herald*'s managing editor, wrote an article after Florence's death that accurately described her devotion:

> *… She was a wonderful woman who lit up like a Christmas tree when speaking about her daughter. I expected her to have trouble talking about the tragic story of her daughter's life, but it was just the opposite. Florence could never say enough about Ann. It was almost as if Ann Marston never really died. In fact, she didn't, as long as Florence was alive.*

Index